100 YEARS
OF
LI & FUNG

100 YEARS
OF
LI & FUNG

Rise from family business to multinational

FENG Bang-yan

THOMSON

Australia • Canada • Mexico • Singapore • Spain • United Kingdom • United States

100 Years of Li & Fung: Rise from family business to multinational
by FENG Bang-yan

For more information, please contact:
Thomson Learning
(a division of Thomson Asia Pte Ltd)
5 Shenton Way
#01-01 UIC Building
Singapore 068808

Or visit our Internet site at http://www.thomsonlearningasia.com

Thomson Learning offices in Asia: Bangkok, Beijing, Hong Kong, Kuala Lumpur, Manila, Seoul, Singapore, Taipei, Tokyo.

Printed in Singapore by Seng Lee Press.
1 2 3 4 5 6 7 8 9 10 — 10 09 08 07 06

ISBN-13: 978-981-265-966-8
ISBN-10: 981-265-966-8

Contents

List of Exhibits

Foreword

Professor Feng Bangyan is a veteran scholar renowned for his studies on the economies of Guangdong and Hong Kong and major publications on the Hong Kong economy, and the development of leading companies. When I learnt that he was interested in doing a study on the Li & Fung Group, I was ecstatic. Professor Feng explained to me that he had picked Li & Fung as a research topic because to him the development of Li & Fung mirrored that of Hong Kong and the whole of Southern China. I found his observation intellectually stimulating and suggested that he should read *Strategy and Structure: Chapters in the History of the American Industrial Enterprise*, a book written by Professor Alfred D. Chandler of Harvard Business School. This book, which I was fond of reading as a postgraduate at Harvard over thirty years ago, attempts to look at the American economic history from the perspective of an enterprise.

On reading *One Hundred Years of Li & Fung—From Traditional Trading Firm to Modern Multinational Group*, I cannot help admiring Professor Feng's erudition, thoroughness, and exquisite writing skills. The multifarious historical, geographical, and personal details that have set the scene for Li & Fung's development in the past hundred years are presented with clarity, liveliness, and vividness without making it seem antiquated. I am moved especially by his description of events—be it historical or familial—that took place to illustrate the rise of Li & Fung through generations of entrepreneurship, perseverance, and ingenuity. I would like to acknowledge my heartfelt respect for and indebtedness to my predecessors, particularly my parents and grandparents, who have always been my role models.

Aside from recounting Li & Fung's development as an enterprise, this book also highlights the rapid changes that Hong Kong and the Chinese mainland have undergone in the past century. It reminds us that historical milestones such as the ending of foreign monopoly on China's external trade, the Sino-Japanese War, Hong Kong's postwar rehabilitation, the industrialization of Hong Kong in the 1960s and 1970s, the inception of China's modernization and economic reforms, the economic integration of Guangdong and Hong Kong, and the growth of the Greater Pearl River Delta region as an economic powerhouse of the world, among many others, have had far-reaching implications for Li & Fung and its counterparts in Hong Kong. Internally, Li & Fung has kept injecting new thinking into its business philosophy and operating model in order to adjust to political and economic changes. I, therefore, believe that this book can be a good reference material to not only those who are interested in individual cases of corporate development, but also those who want to understand more deeply the economic history of Hong Kong and Southern China as a whole.

In the last chapter, Professor Feng succinctly points out what Li & Fung may have to face in its future development. Needless to say, this too will top our agenda in the 21st century as we continue to build not just for the short term, but for the next hundred years.

Victor K. Fung
Group Chairman
The Li & Fung Group

Preface

Ten days after the terrorist attacks on the World Trade Center in New York City on September 11, 2001, I took a trip to Hong Kong to assess the attack's impact on the economies of Hong Kong and Guangdong. During this visit, I met an old friend of mine, Chang Ka-mun, who is the executive director of Li & Fung Research Center. He told me that Mr. William Fung, the managing director of Li & Fung, had just returned from the United States and should have some insight into the subject matter. He then kindly arranged for me to meet with Mr. Fung.

During the interview, Mr. Fung recalled that on the morning of September 11, he was in Boston and was scheduled to fly on Flight 11 of American Airlines to Los Angeles. As it turned out, the plane assigned for that flight crashed into the World Trade Center in New York City at 8.50 a.m. that day. By a stroke of luck, he was seized by an inexplicably strong desire to fly to Seattle that fateful morning to have an early dim sum meal with his elder sister there. He asked his secretary to cancel the flight to Los Angeles and caught another plane to Seattle instead. In Mr. Fung's own words, he owed this narrow escape probably to the good karma of his ancestors. Deep down inside he believes that his family and Li & Fung have always been very lucky, as if blessed by some deities.

The people present to hear Mr. Fung recount the episode in an almost nonchalant manner were naturally dumbfounded and amazed at how lucky he was. He then went on to analyze how the terrorist attack would affect the Hong Kong economy and Li & Fung. I am no stranger to his company. Back in 1997 when I was writing *Chinese Conglomerates in Hong Kong 1941–1997*, Li & Fung had given me generous support by furnishing me with a lot of firsthand information. At one interview, I suggested to Mr. Fung that as an established multinational enterprise, Li & Fung was certainly an excellent subject for an in-depth study. He replied that having read my works like *British Conglomerates in Hong Kong* and *Chinese Conglomerates in Hong Kong*, he saw me as the right person for the job. Thus it was by pure chance that the interview led to me researching and writing this book for four years.

I would like to extend my gratitude to Dr. Victor Fung and Mr. William Fung for their continuous support. During these four years, I made no less than 10 visits to the Li & Fung Group's office for research. I also participated as an observer in their triennial regional management conference. I was allowed not only to look at their published materials, documents, photos, and files, but also talk to them in person amidst their busy schedules. More importantly, the answers they gave were very detailed. During this period, I also interviewed the Fung brothers' aunt, Mrs. Li-Fung Lai-wah, who had once been a board director of Li & Fung, their cousin Mr. Fung Kwok-chor, and their families. In addition, I interviewed the managers and senior employees of Li & Fung's trading, distribution and retailing businesses, including Danny Lau, Henry Chan, Annabella Leung, Jeremy Hobbins, Sunny Wong, Lau Butt-farn, Frank Leong, Richard Yeung, Lam Chuen-lai, Chung Hok-mei, Philip Yau, Louisa Kwan, Fred Ip, Tim Wu, Jimmy Ho, Stewart Kwok, Raphael Kan, and Sam Lau. I thank them all sincerely for their time and support.

My thanks also go to Mr. Chang Ka-mun and his colleagues at Li & Fung Research Center, including Helen Chin, Ada Liu, and Brian Leung. This project would not be completed without their devotion and hard work.

Li & Fung's history has been a due reflection of Hong Kong's economic development in the past century. Li & Fung was founded in 1906 by Mr. Fung Pak-liu who, after graduating from Queen's College in Hong Kong, returned to Guangzhou with the passion to serve his country by becoming a businessman. He did not like the fact that the foreigners monopolized China's external trade and so decided to become their competitor by setting up the first Chinese export firm in China together with Mr. Li To-ming. Back then, Hong Kong was already China's most important entrepôt. With Guangzhou as its head-quarters and a sourcing network in the mainland, Li & Fung was reexporting Chinese goods through Hong Kong. The growth of business prompted them to set up an office in Hong Kong in 1917. In 1937 Japan launched a full-scale invasion of China. Li & Fung (1937) Limited was established in Hong Kong and Li & Fung subsequently relocated its headquarters to the British colony.

The outbreak of the Korean War in the early 1950s and the United Nations' trade embargo on China led to a sharp decline in Hong Kong's reexport trade and also caused the colony to become industrialized quickly. In view of this transformation of the Hong Kong economy, Li & Fung repositioned itself as an exporter of locally manufactured goods and soon became Hong Kong's leading garment exporter. By the early 1970s, Hong Kong had become an industrialized economy that was thriving under a stable political environment. Li & Fung became a listed company amidst a buoyant stock market with the main objective of turning itself from a traditional family firm into a professionally managed modern enterprise. Following the pulse of the Hong Kong economy, Li & Fung was privatized and then relisted. Through mergers and acquisitions and by expanding into distribution and retailing, it successfully evolved into a Chinese multinational trading group based in Hong Kong before the end of the 20th century. A close look at Li & Fung's history should give us a deeper understanding of the transformation and growth of the Hong Kong economy in the last 100 years.

In fact, Li & Fung is a classic example of modern business management. The brothers, Victor and William Fung, the company's third-generation helmsmen, were both trained in business management in the U.S. and have received numerous accolades for their success in that regard. In 1999, they appeared on the cover of the *Far Eastern Economic Review* that described them as the "Brainiest Businessmen in Asia." They were also named "Businessmen of the Year 2005" by *Forbes Asia*. These recognitions speak volumes about the two brothers' ingenuity and the strenuous efforts they have made in turning a traditional trading firm into a leading global supply chain manager. Not surprisingly, Li & Fung's supply chain management has been the subject of four *Harvard Business Case Studies*. I hope that the Li & Fung experience as depicted in this book will in one way or another inspire businessmen, particularly domestic and overseas Chinese entrepreneurs, as well as business management students.

Lastly, I wish to thank Paul Tan and Pauline Lim of Thomson Learning Asia for all their support and assistance. I would also like to thank Carson Chan for the good translation. Much of the project coordination and the reviewing of facts and figures were also carried out by Helen Chin, Oscar Yiu, and Chang Ka-mun from the Li & Fung Research Center, as well as Anne Li from Joint Publishing (Hong Kong) Co. Ltd. I am particularly grateful to Dr. Victor Fung for writing the foreword to this book and to Sir. John Bond, Chairman of HSBC, and Professor Liu Junyi, Vice Chancellor of Chinese University of Hong Kong, for their words of encouragement.

FENG Bang-yan

Chapter 1

The Founding of Li & Fung
—The Canton Years

Fung Pak-liu thought that in terms of social connections, knowledge of local products and so on, Chinese companies were at a relatively advantageous position over their Western counterparts. In addition, it was thought that Chinese export firms run by Chinese businessmen should fare better than foreign counterparts, provided communication was not a problem. With Fung Pak-liu's mastery of the English language, he knew he would have no difficulty in running an export firm. He, therefore, made up his mind to quit working for foreign hongs and start competing with them.

Canton—The Ancient Chinese Trading Port

Li & Fung Company was founded in Canton (now Guangzhou) in 1906. It was the first company set up by Chinese merchants and engaged directly in foreign trade in China, and hence, is regarded as the forerunner of all Chinese trading firms today.

Guangzhou was called Panyu in ancient China. The most ancient trading port in China, it has maintained its importance for over twenty centuries. In the 5th and 6th centuries, frequent wars occurred along the Yellow River and in the middle and lower courses of the Yangzi River which caused local inhabitants to migrate *en masse* to the south, and Guangzhou gradually became a business metropolis and major trading post. In the 8th and 9th centuries, the Chinese government adopted a liberal trade policy by opening five land and two sea routes that reached over seventy countries and thus gave birth to an extensive international trading network. Among these trade routes, the Guangdong Sea Route, also known as the "Maritime Silk Road," was the most prominent. It started from Guangzhou and, via the South China Sea and Malacca Straits, passed through some ninety countries or regions *en route* to the Indian Ocean, Persian Gulf, and the east coast of Africa. It was then the longest sea route in the world, traversing a distance of some 14,000 kilometers.[1] In those days, there were four trading ports along the Chinese coast—Yangzhou in Jiangsu, Ningpo in Zhejiang, Chuanzhou in Fujian, and Guangzhou in Guangdong. Only Guangzhou had a customs office with an embryonic customs and administration system. Tens of thousands of foreign merchants arrived at Guangzhou each year, helping to build up the city's reputation worldwide.

In 1522, only Guangzhou remained as a port. In 1553, Portuguese merchants gained the right to reside in Macau by bribing corrupt Chinese officials. Thereafter, merchant ships sailed to Macau, which gradually developed into a major port in the Far East with the opening of the Macau-Goa-Lisbon, Macau-Nagasaki, and Macau-Manila-Mexico routes, respectively. During this period, Macau also contributed to the prosperity of the provincial capital as Guangzhou's outpost. The rise of Macau also marked the end of China's

---

[1] Huang (ed.) (2003), p. 128.

proactive attempt in reaching out to the world and the beginning of Western colonial powers' aggressive demand for trading rights in China.

From 1757 to the signing of the Treaty of Nanking (now Nanjing) in 1842 between China and Britain, foreign merchants traded with only China through the so-called "Thirteen Hongs"[2] in Guangzhou, thus turning it once again into China's major trading post. As it emerged as a trading hub between China and the West, goods such as tea, silk, porcelains, cotton fabrics, and herbs started pouring in from all over the country and also from all over the world, including Europe, the Americas, India, the East Indian Archipelago, the Malayan Peninsula, and even Indochina and Tokyo. A British merchant once compared the hustle and bustle along the Pearl River to that of the River Thames under London Bridge. To him, the only difference was the look of the sailboats—there was nothing more spectacular than the sight of sailboats lined up for miles along the river.

In the beginning of the 19th century, led by the British East India Company, a large group of British and American merchants engaged in the trading and smuggling of opium in China using Guangzhou as their base. In 1834, the China trade monopoly enjoyed by the East India Company was revoked by the British government. With the withdrawal of the Company from Guangzhou, a large number of British and American hongs quickly took its place. Of these, the "Big Three" were British hongs Jardine Matheson and Dent & Co., and U.S. firm Russell & Co. Jardine Matheson was founded in Guangzhou in 1832 by William Jardine and James Matheson, both notorious opium traders. Thomas Dent, the founder of Dent & Co., was also an opium trader of the same repute in Guangzhou. Rampant opium trade eventually led to the enforcement by Commissioner Lin Zexu in 1839 of an imperial demand for banning the trade, which directly resulted in the outbreak of the Opium War between China and Britain.[3]

After the signing of the Treaty of Nanking in 1942 that ceded Hong Kong to Britain and opened five Chinese ports, including Shanghai, to external trade, Hong Kong replaced Guangzhou and Macau as the leading entrepôt

---

[2] Trading firms or agents that were officially allowed to conduct foreign trade in China.

[3] Feng (1996), pp. 2–14.

for China and the "Thirteen Hongs" system was also abolished. In 1856, Britain and France joined forces in the Second Opium War against China. Guangzhou was attacked and occupied by the British army. Infuriated Guangdong residents burnt down the offices of the Thirteen Hongs. The destruction caused by the war wiped out the prosperous façade of the city where foreign merchants used to meet.

In the early 20th century, despite its declining status as a trading center, Guangzhou was still a robust commercial city because of its proximity to Hong Kong and Macau, the affluence of the Pearl River Delta, as well as the investment made by overseas Chinese. Statistics indicated that in 1911, there were up to 27,000 business firms and more than hundred merchant cliques in Guangzhou. At this point, Guangzhou remained the leading business center in Southern China.

Fung Pak-liu—The Founder of Li & Fung

The founder of Li & Fung was Fung Pak-liu, a young native of Heshan, Guangdong. He was then twenty-six years old and had just returned to Guangzhou after graduating from Queen's College in Hong Kong, eager to use the business knowledge he had learned from the West to contribute to his country.

Pak-liu was born in the small town of Gulao in Heshan, which was less than a hundred kilometers from Guangzhou. Established as a municipality in 1732, Heshan, literally meaning "crane hill," was so named because of the existence of a hill that looked just like a crane. Gulao is in the northeast of Heshan. It is crisscrossed by waterways fed by the Pearl River Delta and is reputed as "the Venice of China." It is famous for its scenic beauty and talented residents. Overseas Chinese living in Heshan are mostly concentrated in Gulao. Today, there are some 38,000 overseas Chinese and Hong Kong, or Macau citizens living in Gulao. It has been said there is a Gulao both inside and outside China. Aside from the Fung family of the Li & Fung Group, the Li family of the Bank of East Asia in Hong Kong also came from Gulao, Heshan.

The Fungs are a large clan in Heshan with an ancient history. Fung Pak-liu came from a peasant family at the end of the Qing Dynasty. His father, Fung Kit-zee, was the son of a farmer in Heshan, though he did not actually farm himself. He was employed by rich landlords to collect land rent and manage their properties. Unlike the rich at that time who normally had several wives and concubines to show off their wealth, Kit-zee had only one wife. This inevitably deprived him of the respect from his fellow villagers but he was not bothered.

Fung Kit-zee had six children—three sons and three daughters. The family was relatively well-off compared to the rest. Perhaps owing to the influence of his father, Pak-liu's marriage was a sensation in those days. He chose his own wife, instead of leaving his parents or a matchmaker to do it for him. His wife, Lam Wai-jing, was also liberal-minded, well-read, and virtuous. While still young, she gave up binding her feet before they were crippled or deformed. Both Pak-liu and Wai-jing were devout Catholics, an unusual choice in the eyes of most Chinese. Pak-liu's religious belief was obviously a direct result of his schooling in Hong Kong.

Pak-liu was Kit-zee's youngest child. He had two elder brothers and three elder sisters. His oldest brother left the family when still quite young to work in the British colony of Hong Kong for a British international telegraph company. By means of an undersea cable system, this company connected Hong Kong with the rest of the world by providing speedy telegraph service. Pak-liu's second brother, who was ten years his senior, was in the civil service in Guangzhou, which enabled the Fung family to have access to the latest information on the political situation. Politically, China was in a state of flux in those days. First, there was the Sino-Japanese War; and then, there was the Hundred Days' Reform which was followed by the Boxer Uprising, culminating in the revolution led by Dr. Sun Yat-sen to overthrow the Qing regime.

Pak-liu yearned to leave his hometown to develop a career in the world outside. He therefore, begged his father to send him to school in Hong Kong so that he could acquire Western knowledge and see the world for himself. His father gave his consent. Pak-liu was sent to study at Queen's College in Hong Kong at the end of the 19th century. While there, he stayed with his big brother. Queen's College was the first government-run English secondary school and is also the oldest school still in existence in Hong Kong. Entering the college was a turning point for both Pak-liu and the future development of the Fung family business.

Founded in 1862, Queen's College was previously known as Central School. In 1889, its campus was moved to Aberdeen Street in Central District and it changed its name to Victoria College. It was officially named Queen's College in 1894. In the 1860s, the colony of Hong Kong was expanded to include Kowloon Peninsula and its total population increased to 100,000. Its social and economic situation gradually stabilized. Some of Hong Kong's oldest business empires such as Hong Kong and Shanghai Banking Corporation, Kowloon Wharf, and Whampoa Dockyards, etc., were founded at that time. In 1860, the Hong Kong Governor no longer doubled as Trade Commissioner and Plenipotentiary to China, as a civil service system was being put in place. Economic and political developments boosted the demand for English-speaking talents.

In the early days, schools in Hong Kong were mainly run by the Church with the single object of fostering Chinese missionaries. The Bible and religious doctrines made up about half of the curriculum. The other subjects included English, geography, arithmetic, and texts on the enlightenment of China. The main purpose of the students, who were mostly from poor families in China, was to learn English.

In 1861, at the advice of Englishman James Legge, the Hong Kong government embarked on reforming the educational system to meet the needs of society. Central School was established against this backdrop. At first, the school was located at Gough Street in Central District and modeled on a English grammar school. Its system also followed that of English grammar schools with eight grades—Grade 8 to Grade 1. Grades 8 and 7 were preparatory classes; Grades 6 to 2 were secondary school classes; and Grade 1 was matriculation class. Central School was officially opened in February 1862. In accordance with James Legge's plan, it was a bilingual school meant for Chinese students and based on the English system. The English curriculum, which was mainly elementary, emphasized aspects of language, such as reading, pronunciation, grammar, and sentence construction. In addition, the Chinese curriculum covered letter-writing and ancient Chinese classics.[4]

Ever since its debut, Central School has been highly popular among the people of Hong Kong and the neighboring Chinese provinces. Applications

---

[4] Wang (ed.) (1997), p. 435.

for admission far exceeded its capacity. Most of its students came from middle-class families in Hong Kong and neighboring regions. They were quite different from their less well-off counterparts studying at missionary schools in that they not only could afford to pay tuition fees, but also knew what they were after and were diligent. Central School was highly popular mainly because of the "business value" of English in the Hong Kong society, which could also have motivated Fung Kit-zee to send Pak-liu to this school. The exact entrance date of Pak-liu could not be ascertained but based on the school's system, it was presumably in 1895 when he was fifteen. Queen's College had already moved to the larger campus at Aberdeen Street and the number of students on its register was over 1,000, in contrast to only 200 in the early days. It emphasized the teaching of English.

This emphasis in fact dated back to the 1880s when the college started shortening the school hours devoted to the Chinese curriculum. The Hong Kong government gradually tried to align the use of English with commerce, practical purposes, and the interests of the British Empire. The Governor of Hong Kong, Sir John P. Hennessy, officially made it a basic policy to step up the teaching of English.

Fung Pak-liu graduated with flying colors in 1902. He was described as "an outstanding student who is intelligent and diligent." He was also awarded the Morrison Scholarship that paid for all his tuition fees. After six to seven years at the College, he was able to master the English language. He of course did not forget his mother tongue. His parents demanded that he should be proficient in Chinese as well, and he readily fulfilled their wish. After graduation, Pak-liu took up a teaching post at his *alma mater* from 1903 to 1904. However, because teaching was not his vocation, after teaching for about a year, he resigned and returned to Guangzhou. He would rather become a businessman and in this capacity contribute to his country. Meanwhile, the revolution led by Dr. Sun Yat-sen to overthrow the ailing Qing Dynasty was gathering momentum.

The Founding of Li & Fung—Early Development in Guangzhou

During the last decade of its rule, the Qing Dynasty initiated some major reforms of a capitalistic nature. The background to this was quite complex.

In the latter half of the 19th century, the disparity or polarization between the urban and rural regions, as well as between the coastal region and the extensive interior of China became increasingly serious. Under the influence of Western civilization, coastal cities like Guangzhou and Shanghai headed toward commercialization and industrialization while culturally, they also began to accept the values of the commercial and industrial economy.

Traditionally, the Chinese social hierarchy consisted of four main classes, namely, government officials, peasants, craftsmen, and merchants—in that order. After the Opium War, particularly after the movement to westernize, the social status of merchants improved substantially with the rise of the business class in the cities, and the establishment of a number of charities sponsored by merchant cliques. With this change in social structure, reformist ideas championed by Liang Qichao pervaded the coastal regions, especially the maritime cities. Led by Dr. Sun Yat-sen, the revolutionary body Tong-menghui also became politically active.

Against this backdrop, the Qing government introduced a series of new policies for self-preservation, including various measures to encourage industrial and trade development. For instance, in 1903, the Commerce Department (later expanded to become Agriculture, Crafts, and Commerce Department) was set up together with the promulgation of company laws and regulations. The provinces also set up departments to take charge of industry and trade. Through legislation and recognition, businessmen's interests and status were protected to some extent. It was under this climate that Li & Fung was founded.

In 1904, Pak-liu met Li To-ming upon his return to Guangzhou and soon they became business partners. Li was a traditional Chinese merchant from a middle-class family that owned a porcelain shop in Guangzhou called Po Hing selling mainly fine porcelain products from Jingdezhen, Jiangxi Province, and the southern and other parts of China. Its business volume was considerable. Pak-liu joined this shop as an export manager soon after returning to Guangzhou. Because he was committed, responsible, and fluent in English, he was trusted by Li To-ming.

In those days, China's imports and exports were largely monopolized by British firms. Fung Pak-liu thought that in terms of social connections, knowledge of local products and so on, Chinese companies were at a relatively advantageous position over their Western counterparts, and Chinese export firms run by Chinese businessmen should fare better than foreign firms, provided communication was not a problem. With his mastery of the English language, he knew he would have absolutely no difficulty in running an export firm. He, therefore, made up his mind to quit working for the foreign hongs and start competing with them on his own. Li To-ming concurred with him. The two decided to enter into partnership to set up a Chinese trading firm. Li was responsible for investments, while Pak-liu took charge of the day-to-day operations.

In 1906, Li & Fung Company was opened on the riverbank opposite Shamian, which later became the Anglo-French Concession, in Guangzhou. Fung Pak-liu held 51% of the share and Li To-ming, the remaining 49%. The company's name Li & Fung was made up of two words in Cantonese that sounded very like the two partners' surnames, with "Li" meaning profit and "Fung" meaning plentiful.[5] The company was unprecedented in that it was 100%-owned by Chinese merchants and it sourced and exported goods directly from China. Li & Fung was in fact the very first firm wholly-owned by the Chinese to export directly from China.

At first, Li & Fung's export business involved mainly what they knew best—porcelain wares—and, to a lesser extent, antiques, and handicrafts. Renowned for their craftsmanship, finish and quality, ceramics had since early times been among China's most important exports. The most famous production base in Guangdong was Shiwan, Foshan, the "capital of Chinese ceramics" that was famous for its colorful *caiyao* products. In the early period of the Qing Dynasty, Guangzhou's ceramics industry used white porcelain stone from Jingdezhen and enamel materials from Europe, and exported the products under the name of *Guangcai* (*caiyao* products from Guangzhou). Li & Fung had been doing well since its establishment by exporting porcelains from Jingdezhen, Shiwan, and Guangzhou, respectively.

As soon as it had established itself in the export business, Li & Fung expanded its product range to include bamboo wares, rattan wares, fireworks, and firecrackers, as well as jadestones and ivory handicrafts. Business flour-

---

[5] Hutcheon (1991), p. 26.

ished. Fireworks and firecrackers were Li & Fung's most important exports. Gunpowder was invented by the Chinese, and the making of fireworks and firecrackers was a major handicraft industry in China, dating back many centuries. These products were commonly used during festivals and celebrations as they were believed to be effective in bringing good luck and scaring off evil spirits. Traditionally, they were made chiefly in the provinces of Guangdong, Hunan, and Zhejiang. After the Opium War, Guangdong became the leading exporter, followed by Hunan, whereas the other provinces had all declined considerably in importance.

In those days, Guangdong, Hong Kong, and Macau exported large quantities of fireworks and firecrackers. Hong Kong had even produced a "King of Firecrackers" by the name of Chan Lan-fong. Chan was a native of Dongguan, Guangdong. He started making firecrackers for exports in the early 1900s. Later he opened a factory in Kowloon City, Hong Kong, with 1,000 workers. In the 1920s, he expanded his business to Macau and Foshan by opening a number of shops. By the late 1930s, Chan Lan-fong was the leader of China's firecrackers export industry.[6]

While it could not compare with the "King of Firecrackers" in export volume, Li & Fung was superior in product design. Inspired perhaps by Western ideas, Fung Pak-liu considered product innovation to be important. Li & Fung gradually gained reputation as an innovative supplier in terms of product design and concept. Traditionally, firecrackers exported from China had mud wrappings. In 1907, Li & Fung replaced it with a paper wrapping that not only gave a louder popping sound, but also produced less smoke and dust as compared to the old days. Furthermore, it was lighter in weight, which saved import tariffs when entering the American market. Considered a major breakthrough for the industry, this innovation was well received by customers. From then on, the Li & Fung formula was commonly followed as a norm.[7]

In those years, it was almost a social custom for Guangzhou merchants to talk business in a brothel. When conducting a deal, they would hide their

---

[6] Z.H. Chen (ed.) (2002), p. 55.
[7] Li & Fung Limited (1981), pp. 16–17.

hands underneath the cuffs and tap on the table with their fingers as though they were using an abacus. The two sides to the table would never sign any document or contract. With the exception of the buyer and seller, nobody would know the contents of the deal thus concluded. The paperless agreement, nevertheless, would be binding on both sides. Fung Pak-liu rarely conducted business that way. He preferred to do it formally in the office and put everything down in black and white. This uncommon business style in a way reflected his educational background.

In a trade deal, it would be relatively easy to agree on the price. The real difficulty was in packing and transportation. The goods would have to be sent from their place of origin to Guangzhou, and then to Hong Kong for consignment to the U.S. and Europe. In the early days of the Nationalist government, the political situation was unstable. The movement of goods was often subject to the threat of bandits or heavy inland transportation tax imposed by the local authorities. This tax was originally fixed at 0.1% of all sales as a source of tax for the local governments. In practice, however, it increased to 5% on goods passing through one province and 20% or more when passing through a number of provinces. In addition, the tax authorities would often raise disputes which would cause delay. Merchants had no choice but to bribe their way out. Whether the tax collected ended up in the government's coffers was another story. Like all the other companies, Li & Fung had to accept this tax system as a fact of life by trying its best to minimize the impact and shorten the transportation routes to within Guangdong province. By 1910, Li & Fung had grown into a sizeable and highly creditworthy export firm in Guangzhou.

In 1915, extensive areas of Guangdong were devastated by heavy floods and riverboat traffic was almost cut off. During this year, Fung Pak-liu was invited by the Chinese government to join its delegation to the Panama-Pacific International Exposition in the U.S. The exposition lasted ten months from February 4 to December 4, 1915. It had two objectives. The first one was to celebrate the official inauguration of the Suez Canal on August 15, 1914, and to commemorate the discovery of the Pacific Ocean by Vasco Nunez de Balboa in 1513. The second one was to showcase the new look of San Francisco after a full-scale rehabilitation program, following the disastrous earthquake and fire that happened on April 18, 1906. Notwithstanding the outbreak of World War I, a total of thirty-one countries sent delegations, of which twenty-five were officials, to the exposition which had attracted up to thirteen million visits. The exposition generated an income of more than two million U.S. dollars and was the first one staged in the U.S. that did not focus on industrial and scientific achievements. Instead, its biggest contribution was to culture and art.[8]

While taking a close look at the American economy and society as a Chinese delegate, Fung Pak-liu did not fail to explore business opportunities. More importantly, *en route* back to China, he met Joseph N. Sipser of Ignaz Strauss & Co. Inc., a New York company. Ignaz Strauss was well known as an importer of goods from the Orient. It was the sourcing agent for several high-class chain stores, department stores, and mail-order companies in the U.S. Pak-liu and Joseph became good friends and Ignaz Strauss one of Li & Fung's largest customers for half a century. Joining the Chinese delegation to the Panama exposition had therefore been a turning point for Li & Fung and the pride of its management for a long time. Thereafter, Pak-liu would go the U.S. at least once a year for the purpose of forging closer relationship with his U.S. counterparts. During that period, many U.S. merchants, including those who had come to China personally, were reluctant to trade with China through British firms and, therefore, jumped at the chance of cooperating with Pak-liu. As a result, since the early days, Li & Fung's business had been very U.S.-oriented.

Li & Fung and Foreign Hongs in Shamian

Li & Fung began diversifying its business in the 1920s by setting up a light handicrafts factory with a warehouse. It also erected a five-story Li & Fung building on the riverbank of Shamian. Headquartering at Shamian was by no means unintentional. Shamian is a sandbank in Guangzhou. In September 1861, British and French officials forced the concession of Shamian, with Britain taking forty-four acres in the west and France eleven acres in the east. The two powers were attracted by Shamian because of its terrain that

---

[8] *Capital*, Hong Kong, February 1992, p. 61.

made docking possible with only minor construction work. Furthermore, it was near Xiguan, home to a group of rich Chinese merchants and would, therefore, facilitate trade. Besides, its natural scenery was also dazzling.[9]

Following the signing of the concession agreement, the British immediately divided up the land under its control into eighty-two lots and sold them at a price of 3,500–9,000 silver dollars each to foreign merchants in Guangzhou. Fifty-two were sold, yielding a total of 248,000 silver dollars; the unsold lots were bought out by the British government for building consulates and churches. Those who had acquired land were each awarded a "Royal Deed" in the name of the Queen of England by the British consulate-general in Guangzhou. The British consulate was the first foreign consulate to enter Shamian, followed by the U.S., Portuguese, German, and Japanese. Subsequently, foreign firms originally set up at the Thirteen Hongs also moved in and business flourished in Shamian.

The establishment of the French Concession commenced a little later. At that time, the French government was engrossed in a construction project in Guangzhou formerly occupied by the office of the Governor of Guangdong and Guangxi. The construction took twenty-five years and 400,000 francs. In 1888, Sacred Heart Cathedral, the largest Catholic church in Asia, was completed. It was a colossal structure built with granite and was later nicknamed "stone closet." It was another French territory outside Shamian. After the completion of the cathedral, France turned its attention to the Shamian concession, first by auctioning off the land it occupied in November 1889, and then by moving its consulate there in 1890. As a result, the French territory also prospered. By the end of the 19th century, there were eight streets in Shamian which was demarcated into several small districts.

Since then Shamian had become a place where foreign banks, hongs, and consulates clustered. In its heyday there were nine banks, including Hong Kong and Shanghai Banking Corporation, Chartered Bank, Bank of England, Bank of France, Bank of Taiwan, etc. opened by Britain, the U.S., Germany, France, Holland, Belgium, and Japan. There were as many as forty foreign

---

[9] People's Political Consultative Committee (ed.) (1992), p. 31.

firms set up by merchants from Britain, the U.S., France, Japan, Germany, Holland, Portugal, Denmark, Sweden, Iran, and Afghanistan. British firms numbered more than ten of all the foreign firms in Shamian; thirteen were more prominent than the others and were, therefore, also called "Thirteen Hongs," but they were of course different from their Chinese namesake during the Opium War.

Among the thirteen foreign hongs in Shamian, the most famous was Jardine Matheson set up at 50–52 South Street. It imported into China cotton yarns, thread yarns, cotton wool, machinery and ammunitions, and exported tea, raw silk, grass mats, and bananas, as well as military supplies like uranium, China wood oil, flax bags and pig hair. Situated adjacent to Shamian, Li & Fung was well-positioned to do business with the foreign hongs. Unlike their foreign counterparts, Li & Fung never had to hire a comprador because Fung Pak-liu was fluent in English and able to deal directly with the trade managers of foreign hongs, which included John Manners, Dodwell, Shewan Tomes, Jardine Matheson, and Deacon. As Fung Lai-wah recalled later, Jardine Matheson, then the largest foreign firm in Hong Kong, bought large quantities of bamboo and rattan wares, as well as redwood furniture from Li & Fung for exporting to Europe and America.

China entered a state of political turmoil in the 1920s. On May 30, 1925, a major anti-imperialist campaign, the well-known "May 30 Movement," began in Shanghai. On June 19, workers in Hong Kong went on strike in support of the massive labor strike in Shanghai. The number of workers who joined the strike surged to 200,000 within half a month. To suppress the strikers, Hong Kong's colonial government urgently declared a curfew and sent military troops into the urban areas, while banning the import of food and imposing an embargo against the revolutionary government in Guangdong. These high-handed measures aggravated the situation. Large numbers of workers left for Guangzhou. On June 21, workers in Shamian also joined the strike, adding fuel to the legendary "Guangdong-Hong Kong Strike."

On June 23, when around 100,000 demonstrators were marching through the street facing the Shamian foreign concessions toward Guangzhou, the British and French military police suddenly fired shots at the demonstrators, killing fifty-two people, seriously wounding 170, and resulting in a larger-scale anti-imperialist campaign. The ports of Shanghai, Guangzhou,

Foreign-owned factories at the Pearl River Delta, Canton (Guangzhou) in 1785.

Clockwise from top:
Mr. and Mrs. Fung Kit-zee, and Mr. and Mrs. Fung Pak-liu.

A blue and white porcelain plate with fine patterns
—the most popular item among Li & Fung's exports in the early 20th century.

Fung Pak-liu as a delegate at the Panama-Pacific International Exposition in 1915.

Fung Pak-liu (right) in the garden of his house in Guangzhou
with business partner, Li To-ming.

Fung Pak-liu (right) and his sons, Mo-ying (center) and Hon-chu (right), at the entrance to Li & Fung's headquarters in Guangzhou.

and Hong Kong were paralyzed for nearly half a year. Many foreign firms had to close or scale down their operations.

However, Li & Fung's business was unaffected. Interestingly, the situation presented it with a new channel for trade and enabled it to enter the agency business. In those days, foreigners were not allowed to build piers in Guangzhou. Making use of his good relations with the municipal government, Fung Pak-liu was given permission to build a pier in Guangzhou exclusively for O.S.K. Line and N.K.K. Line of Japan. Li & Fung also became the sole agent in Guangzhou for the two Japanese shipping lines and Osaka Marine & Fire Insurance Company, thus beginning its shipping and insurance agency businesses. During this period, Li & Fung was also appointed by the British firm, Harry Wicking & Co. Ltd., as the sole agent to handle most of its exports from China. This agency relationship lasted until the end of World War II.

The Second Generation and Fung Yau-yen's "Mutiny"

By the late 1920's and early 1930's, Fung Pak-liu's three children—second son Mo-ying, third son Hon-chu, and fourth daugther Lai-wah—had joined Li & Fung and were gradually becoming the second-generation management team. Fung Pak-liu had eleven children, including Mo-ying (alias Hon-wai), Hon-chu, Lai-wah, fifth son Hon-hing, seventh son Hon-bong, eighth daughter Lai-sheung, nineth son Hon-yin, and eleventh daughter Lai-oi.

Mo-ying, Lai-wah, and Hon-chu were the only ones who had joined Li & Fung. Because Pak-liu's first son died young, Mo-ying was in reality the oldest of the siblings. Mo-ying studied at Diocesan Boys' School, an English school in Hong Kong. He returned to Guangzhou upon graduation in 1927 and joined Li & Fung as a trainee. Later, he was promoted to manager. After the Fung Yau-yen incident, Mo-ying became his father's main assistant because of his flexible business skills. As his son Kwok-chor later recalled, "Father always said that flexibility was the key to doing business."

Lai-wah graduated from Sacred Heart Canossian College and joined Li & Fung in 1930. She was just fourteen. She remembered that every day she would first take a walk with her father in the park and then they would go for *dim sum* at a tea-house called Yung Kee. She would often accompany her father to buy goods. To her, Li & Fung was just like a department store, dealing in a wide variety of products. Fung Pak-liu was on very good terms with his partner Li To-ming. "Uncle Li trusted Father and left everything to him," she said. "Father also loved Uncle like a brother. He would always bring back some precious antiques after closing a deal overseas and he made it a rule to ask Uncle to pick his favorites first. Uncle was also fond of us and we would often take part in each other's family celebrations." Lai-wah also joined as a trainee and later became part of the management team by taking up clerical and accounting responsibilities. She later married a colleague Mr. Li but was widowed after only three years. She had a daughter and a son, whom she brought up all on her own.

Hon-chu joined Li & Fung about half a year after his younger sister and this move was prompted by a crisis in 1931—the "mutiny" by his nephew Yau-yen. Fung Yau-yen, son of Pak-liu's elder brother, was adopted and treated like his own by Pak-liu. As Lai-wah recalled, "For a long time Yau-yen was looked after by our mother as if he was her own kid. In her deathbed, Mother did not forget to ask Father to take good care of Yau-yen. In a way, Father treated Yau-yen even better than his own sons, teaching him everything personally." Pak-liu had even brought in a family tutor from the U.S. to teach Yau-yen English and other science subjects. Upon joining Li & Fung, Yau-yen naturally became Pak-liu's assistant. His title was Executive Assistant that carried with it much executive power. Pak-liu trusted him and allowed him to handle a lot of business-related matters.

However, Yau-yen did not stop at that. He had greater ambitions and his ultimate goal was to control the whole company. In 1931, he initiated a "coup" by walking out with almost all the senior staff and setting up a new firm called Luen Fung & Co. Fung Lai-wah recollected that some of the major clients defected to Luen Fung and broke up with Li & Fung. The "mutiny" caused Fung Pak-liu much pain both mentally and physically. He developed high blood pressure during this time. Li & Fung suffered severely from the loss of some major clients and most of its senior managers. Fung Hon-chu later clearly recalled, "We had to hire new staff and start many things from scratch. At any rate, Luen Fung went broke after just a few years."

Confronted with this difficult situation, Fung Pak-liu asked Hon-chu to join and help Li & Fung. Hon-chu, however, was not exactly thrilled by this request. He had just graduated from Queen's College in Hong Kong and was preparing for the entrance examination to Hong Kong University to study mining engineering. Being an obedient son, he yielded to his father's request and returned to Guangzhou. Deep down inside, he regretted the loss of the opportunity to enter the university, which to some extent, affected his devotion to the new job.

"At the beginning, I did not take what I was doing seriously," he recollected. "And I refused to take any salary. I wasted a few years at the office without getting anything done or any reward in return. My father introduced me to his friend, Joseph Sipser, who tried to get me interested in the trading business but it did not work. I had absolutely no intention of becoming a trader."

Later, however, a watershed incident changed all that. One day Pak-liu had taken Mo-ying to a meeting of the International Rotary Club at the Anglo-French Concession in Shamian. Something happened at the office that required the top management's urgent decision, but none of the senior staff dared to take the responsibility to do that. So they turned to the boss's son, Hon-chu, for instruction. Hon-chu suddenly found that he was interested in tackling the problem. After weighing the pros and cons, he came up with a solution that was put into practice immediately.

"I told Father what happened as soon as he came back in the afternoon," Hon-chu recalled. "After looking at all the details, he said, 'Well done.' Although I knew that he was trying to encourage me with these words, I was proud of myself. More importantly, I had really experienced the challenge of my job and was developing an interest in it. After that incident, Father gave me the assignment as a messenger for a few months and then as a clerk in various departments. I was fully aware that I had to start from scratch. I have since made it a rule to try my best in understanding the crux of any problem raised by my colleagues, which to me is an excellent way of learning from experience."

Hon-chu's siblings, Mo-ying and Lai-wah, had also undergone very much the same kind of training. As a result, the three members of the second generation of the Fung family became highly conversant with Li & Fung's business. They were given increasingly heavier responsibilities, such as the formulation of important policies together with the department heads, and so on. Mo-ying and Hon-chu were appointed as managers to assist Fung senior. Lai-wah was responsible for internal administration, helping her father with reading documents, preparing checks, etc. Whenever Pak-liu was overseas, the three were able to take charge of everything and ensure that business was as usual. Li & Fung could, therefore, recuperate gradually from the damage caused by Fung Yau-yen and move forward.

Crisis in the 1930s

From 1929 to 1933, the U.S. and other Western countries suffered from the severest economic slump in history—the Great Depression. Industrial production fell sharply by 45% to the 1908–1909 level. External trade also decreased by two-thirds to the 1913 level. The economy in the Far East was also adversely impacted. Exports from Hong Kong and the Chinese mainland declined substantially.

Fortunately for Li & Fung, owing to its close association with Ignaz Strauss, it somehow maintained its major lines of export. During this time, Li & Fung exported mainly handicrafts, such as porcelain products, bamboo trays, rattan baskets, fireworks and firecrackers, brass products and enamel wares, as well as Chinese indigenous products, such as China wood oil, cinnamon, bamboo canes, and rattan goods. For quality assurance, Li & Fung was very meticulous about packaging. From the start, experts were hired to ensure the protection of breakable items like porcelains and the safety of combustible pyrotechnics so as to minimize damage. For this reason, Li & Fung had an excellent reputation within the industry and very good relations with its insurance companies.

By the 1930s, Li & Fung was well established in Guangzhou. According to a business almanac published in 1931, Li & Fung was classified as one of the twenty-eight leading import/export firms in Guangzhou. There was only one other firm on the list that resembled Li & Fung in terms of the nature of business. In the mid-1930s, Li & Fung was at the peak of its development in Guangzhou. In addition to its headquarters in Guangzhou, it had twenty-two branches and subsidiaries in various parts of China, sourcing goods from different provinces for export.[10] As Fung Lai-wah recollected, the size of Li & Fung's sourcing business was quite large and each order would amount to

---

[10] *Asiainc*, May 2001, p. 34.

tens of thousands of Hong Kong dollars. In addition, Li & Fung also had a rattan factory in Guangzhou, several firecracker factories in Zhanjiang, Canton Bay, and a porcelain kiln in Jingdezhen, Jiangxu Province. It sold some of its products to the foreign hongs in Shamian and exported the rest to the U.S.

In those days, the Pearl River Delta in Guangzhou was quite shallow and large freighters could not go near the provincial capital. Li & Fung, therefore, had to send its goods to Hong Kong to be reexported overseas. In the mid-1930s, because of the Chinese civil war and the Japanese invasion, the situation in Guangzhou became increasingly tense, causing serious chaos and obstruction to commerce and trade. The Nationalist government was virtually non-existent. The Nationalists and the Communists were engaged in the Second Chinese Civil War. To exercise some control over the restless warlords, the government had to curry favor with them and win their loyalty through bribes and other benefits. The government's increasingly heavy financial burden meant heavier tax burden for the people.

On September 18, 1931, Japanese troops bombarded the railway in Northwest Shenyang and attacked the Northeast Army under Zhang Xueliang, trying to use Manchuria as a springboard to enter the interior of China. On July 7, 1937, the Japanese army staged an illegal military training at Lugou Bridge and, under the pretext of searching for an allegedly missing soldier, tried to force its way into town. At the refusal of the Chinese government, the Japanese attacked and started its full-scale invasion of China. Guangzhou was bombed, resulting in heavy casualties and the destruction of buildings and telecommunication facilities. In September 1938, the Japanese launched an air raid on the Yuehan Railway and Kowloon-Canton Railway which caused the suspension of train service between Guangzhou and Hong Kong. Confronted with the fast-changing and deteriorating situation, Fung Pak-liu realized that the days were counted for Li & Fung's business in Guangzhou. The Japanese invasion and the barriers imposed on trade and river transport had already forced businessmen into a cul-de-sac. It was foreseen that before long, all business enterprises would be subject to the whims and caprices of the Japanese military government. At that time, Hong Kong was the only place that was still relatively stable and immune to Chinese politics and Japanese invasion. Like other firms based in Guangzhou, Fung Pak-liu decided to relocate Li & Fung to Hong Kong, while retaining its headquarters in Guangzhou to carry on with the trading business until the outbreak of the war.

Chapter 2

Taking Root in Hong Kong
After the War

"The days were counted for Li & Fung's business in Guangzhou. The Japanese invasion and the barriers imposed on trade and river transport had already forced businessmen into a cul-de-sac. It could be foreseen that before long, all business enterprises would be subject to the whims and dictates of the Japanese military government. At that time, Hong Kong was the only place that was still relatively stable and immune to Chinese politics and Japanese invasion. Like other firms based in Guangzhou, I decided to relocate Li & Fung to Hong Kong while retaining its headquarters in Guangzhou to carry on with the trading business until the outbreak of the war."

—Fung Pak-liu

Early Years in Hong Kong

In the mid-1930s, Li & Fung was gradually moving its business operation and headquarters from Guangzhou to the British colony of Hong Kong in view of the unpredictable political situation and, hence, also laying the foundation for its century-old business empire. The leadership of the company also passed from the first to the second generation of the Fung family. Owing to the gift he demonstrated in managing the family business throughout the political and economic turmoil during this period, Fung Hon-chu became the key person in Li & Fung in Hong Kong.

Li & Fung's connection with Hong Kong dated back to the founding of the company in Guangzhou. At that time, Li & Fung used its Guangzhou headquarters as its base to source goods through its mainland network and then transported them to Hong Kong for consignment to overseas customers. In 1917, to facilitate expansion overseas, Fung Pak-liu set up a branch office in Hong Kong.

By the mid-1930s, the Sino-Japanese War and the war in Europe broke out, but Hong Kong's economy experienced unprecedented growth regardless. Because Shanghai suffered heavily from the Sino-Japanese War and later even fell to the enemy, large quantities of goods originally destined for ports along the Yangzi River were redirected to Hong Kong for consignment. As a result, Hong Kong's reexport trade boomed. In 1937, Hong Kong's trade with the Chinese mainland reached a record of HK$796 million. According to the statistics released by the China's Customs authorities, up to half of China's external trade went through Hong Kong. This robust reexport trade lasted until the fall of Guangzhou on October 21, 1938.

As the situation became increasingly tense in Guangzhou and as Hong Kong's economy continued to flourish, Fung Pak-liu decided in 1937 to relocate Li & Fung's core operations to the relatively safe and stable British colony. Fung Hon-chu recalled, "Father had a hunch that it wouldn't be long before the enemy's troops entered Guangzhou and so immediately sent people to Hong Kong to make preparations." The task of setting up a branch office in Hong Kong was entrusted to Hon-chu, who was just an office assistant then and was much lower in rank than his elder brother Mo-ying. Hon-chu's original ambition was to become a mining engineer but, as fate would have it, he was "conscripted" by his father to do trading work and now during an emergency, he had to stand in for his father to set up a new branch in Hong Kong.

Fung senior did not have too many options. He could have sent Mo-ying or a senior employee to Hong Kong to do it. But Mo-ying was already fully occupied in Guangzhou and the lesson Pak-liu had learnt from the Fung Yau-yen incident was too new and painful for him to even consider leaving the job to someone else. He decided to entrust this major task to Hon-chu. Pak-liu understood that although Hong Kong was still relatively safe for the time being, its prospects were far from predictable. However, to prepare for the worst, he thought Li & Fung should have a foothold offshore so that in the eventuality that it was no longer possible to remain in Guangzhou, they could still move immediately to Hong Kong.

At the same time, Pak-liu also felt that he was physically much weaker than before and it was necessary to retire from the forefront and let his off-spring take up heavier responsibilities. Hon-chu recalled that he would often let his father see the drafts of his English correspondence and correct his grammar. He said, "My English was far from perfect and I wasn't confident about writing letters in English on complicated matters, so I would write a draft and give it to my father. One day he said, 'Look here, don't bother me any more. I think you can now write better English than I can.' Ever since then I wrote all my own letters, no matter how complicated; I still write them with confidence."[1] While he was not sure of his English letter-writing skills, Hon-chu was very confident in composing cables and coding them. He called himself an expert in coding and decoding cables which he enjoyed. This not only saved expenses but also ensured secrecy.

Hon-chu arrived in Hong Kong in 1935 to take care of Li & Fung's business in the colony. His title was assistant manager because his father did not want to appoint him to too high a position yet.

In July 1937, Japan used the Lugou Bridge Incident as a pretext to launch its invasion of China. Guangzhou fell to the enemy in October 1938. As it was no longer possible to remain in that city, Li & Fung moved its entire operations to Hong Kong. In 1937, Li & Fung was registered as a limited company in Hong Kong under the name of Li & Fung (1937) Limited, with Fung

---

[1] Hutcheon (1991), p. 18.

Hon-chu as the manager. The company rented the eighth floor of Princess Building as its office. There were about a dozen employees, some of whom were old staff who came from Guangzhou on their own accord, and some were hired in Hong Kong. The Fung family also moved to Hong Kong and took residence in its property at 18–20 Connaught Road Central.

Li & Fung's new company in Hong Kong obtained the full financial support of National City Bank of New York (now Citibank), which had developed a close business relationship with Li & Fung since its establishment in 1906. At the celebration to commemorate the 75th anniversary of the firm, Fung Hon-chu said, "The Bank has been supporting us in various ways, including trade financing, deposits, foreign exchanges, and letters of credit. Its global service network is very useful to us because it covers all the major cities of the world. With its support, we have been able to meet our customers' needs and ensure our own financial liquidity." Senior Vice President Kent de M. Price, Citibank's senior officer in Hong Kong, also said, "We regard Li & Fung as an interesting company to work with. They are innovative and dynamic and their banking needs are never the same."[2]

During its early years in Hong Kong, Li & Fung was still exporting mainly bamboo wares, rattan wares, and locally-made redwood furniture, and was dealing with foreign hongs like Jardine Matheson and Dodwell. In Fung Lai-wah's recollection, business was more robust than in Guangzhou. Hon-chu was able to actualize his capabilities in business. Under his leadership, Li & Fung developed quickly in Hong Kong. Whenever he recalled his achievements during those hard times, he could not help feeling proud of himself.

The outbreak of World War II in 1939 cut off the supply of commodities from the United Kingdom (U.K.), Australia, and North America to German-occupied Europe. Countries in Europe had to look for new supply sources in the Far East, which unfortunately was also affected by the Sino-Japanese War. These circumstances, however, gave rise to more business opportunities for many trading firms in Hong Kong, and Li & Fung was one of them.

---

[2] *The Asian Wall Street Journal,* June 18, 1982, p. 7.

During this period, Hong Kong's export sector flourished. Torches made in Hong Kong were in great demand in Britain due to frequent air-raids and blackouts. To gain a share in this market, Li & Fung set up its own factory, Victoria Torch Manufacturing Co. Ltd., in Hong Kong in addition to sourcing from other factories. Victoria was a large factory that worked around the clock to produce millions of metal torch cases yet it was still unable to cope with the huge demand from the U.K. To ensure entry to the U.K. market, Li & Fung was buying tinplates an brass sheets from Canada to qualify for "imperial preference" and avoid U.K. import duties. This business generated substantial profits for Li & Fung and laid the foundation for its operation in Hong Kong. Part of the profit was used for property investment in Hong Kong.[3] With a solid base in Hong Kong, Li & Fung proceeded to expand to Guangdong, Guangxi, Fujian, and Hunan.

In 1941, Fung Hon-chu married Madam Li Pui-yiu. Their honeymoon in Qingdao was cut short by the imminent outbreak of the Pacific War. On December 8, 1941, Japanese warplanes launched an attack on Hong Kong. The Kowloon Peninsula was taken on December 13. At the refusal by the British army to surrender, the Japanese launches a massive attack and not long after, landed on Hong Kong Island. Governor Sir. Mark A. Young surrendered on December 25.

Resurgence and Development after World War II

At the outbreak of the Pacific War in 1941, the allied forces were dealt a serious blow by the Japanese army. On the one hand, Britain's colonial presence in the Far East showed signs of disintegration. The U.S. government, on the other hand, was badly in need of the support of China—its major Asian ally—in terms of military cooperation to enable it to fill the vacuum left by the western European powers that had retreated from the Far East and Southeast Asia after the war. To win the support of the Chinese

---

[3] Li & Fung Limited (1981), pp. 12–13.

government and people, the U.S. demanded that Britain should follow its example in withdrawing extraterritorial rights in China and should surrender its sovereignty over Hong Kong. During the Cairo Meeting in November 1943, President Roosevelt made Chiang Kai-shek understand that the U.S. would support China's resumption of sovereignty over Hong Kong, which would then be declared an international free port. However, Britain refused to consider this option after the war. Prime Minister Winston Churchill had made known his position that no country should cherish the thought of benefiting from Britain without going to war. Meanwhile, the British government had resolved to reoccupy Hong Kong by military means.

It was known that Hong Kong's postwar status depended largely on which country's army first entered the British colony after Japan's surrender. Research revealed that should a strong Chinese army or a U.S. army enter first, there was little Britain could do, except face the music. However, the Kuomintang government's policy was "to suppress internal troubles before embarking on any external aggression." With its priority to eradicate the communists, the Kuomintang government was basically indifferent to the sovereignty issue of Hong Kong. Besides lacking a strategic vision and totally unprepared for Japan's sudden surrender, it did not have a plan to enter Hong Kong ahead of the others.

On August 15, 1945, Japan declared unconditional surrender. The next day, its officers in Hong Kong made public the Japanese emperor's "Imperial Rescript on Surrender." On the same day, Franklin C. Gimson, Hong Kong's former Colonial Secretary, who had been imprisoned by the Japanese at Stanley Camp, met with Japanese officers there and demanded that a provisional British-Hong Kong government be set up under his leadership. The British government, in order to arrive in Hong Kong first, ordered Rear Admiral Cecil H.J. Harcourt of the British Pacific fleet then stationed in Subic Bay, the Philippines, to lead the Royal British Navy to Hong Kong. Under Harcourt's command, a powerful special fleet comprising a capital ship, some cruisers, and three aircraft carriers (one of which belonged to Canada) entered Victoria Harbor on August 30.

At an interview years later, Fung Hon-chu could still vividly recall the scene when the Royal British Navy entered Hong Kong: "Whilst the harbor thundered to the triumphant salutes of every warship, rubble, dissolution, and hunger could be seen everywhere on land. The harbor was jammed with sunken vessels. The retaliation of the Chinese and the animosity of the Japanese left the entire community in a chaos. As well, the population had been reduced by a million and most of the survivors were bereft of money, homes, food, and fuels."[4]

The British Navy set up a provisional military government as soon as it landed on Hong Kong Island. In May 1946, Mark A. Young, the governor of Hong Kong who had been taken prisoner by the Japanese for three years and eight months, returned to Hong Kong and took over the governance of the country from the provisional military junta by forming a civilian government. Upon reoccupying Hong Kong, the British government instituted a number of measures to restore political and economic order in the British colony, including disarming and imprisoning all the Japanese soldiers and impersonated police. In addition to ordering all the ninety-eight British police officers who had been released from Stanley Camp to report for duty immediately, the government also urgently recruited 1,000 provisional policemen to help maintain law and order so that the short-lived state of anarchy could be brought to an end.

"People understood instinctively that their survival lay in shedding the grim mantle of a war-torn city as quickly as possible," said Fung Hon-chu. He continued, "Soon warehouses were restocked; trams and ferries were running; shops and offices reopened; and factories restarted. A moratorium on foreign trade was enforced for a year after the surrender with the ordering of all goods needed for the British colony's rehabilitation in the hands of the government acting on the advice of local residents and former businessmen."[5]

Fung Hon-chu returned to Hong Kong the following day after the Japanese's surrender to recover Li & Fung's property and resume business at a temporary office at 18 Connaught Road Central. The British Navy had not yet entered Hong Kong and the streets were full of crestfallen Japanese soldiers. He recalled what he had seen the day he returned: "I almost died that day. The Japanese soldiers were extremely sad and demoralized, tak-

---

[4] Hutcheon (1991), p. 23.
[5] Hutcheon (1991), p. 23.

ing to drinking in the streets. Many local residents who were furious with them felt like stoning them to death. After I had arrived from Macau by boat, I sneaked back into Fung House. Regardless of the dilapidation of the office, I started restoring the place and typing a letter." A drunken soldier heard him and barged into his office, pointing a gun at him. Hon-chu froze, fearing that after surviving the Japanese occupation, he would perish on the day when Hong Kong was beginning to see the dawn of light again. By a stroke of luck, the soldier stumbled out, after just muttering some words in Japanese.[6]

The political situation in Hong Kong stabilized gradually in 1946 and private enterprises were reviving. Just around this time, the Third Chinese Civil War broke out, creating political and economic chaos, and an influx of migrants from China. As a result, Hong Kong's population was given an immediate boost and the economy began to flourish. Fung Hon-chu continued to use leased units in Princess Building for Li & Fung's head office, whereas the headquarters in Guangzhou were turned into a branch office, under the leadership of Fung Mo-ying and Li-Fung Lai-wah. In addition, the company also engaged in both import and export trading.

What Li & Fung imported was a new product that was unknown in Hong Kong—the ball pen. It was invented by the Americans toward the end of World War II and soon proved to be both innovative and successful. Soon after the end of the Pacific War, Li & Fung imported some ball pens for sale in Hong Kong, thus becoming the first local company to sell this new product. Li & Fung named this product "atomic pen" in Chinese, bringing to mind advanced technology and the atomic bombs that ended World War II. Consequently, this new product attained almost instant success and the Chinese name given by Li & Fung to the ball pen has since been commonly adopted all over the world.

Anticipating a bright future for the product, Li & Fung chartered Pan Am's large airplanes to fly in thousands of ball pens, which generated considerable profits for the company. The purchase price was US$1 each though

---

[6] Feng (1996), p. 23.

the wholesale price was only HK$300.[7] Several ball pens were either sold to trendy consumers or presented as gifts. Notwithstanding the enthusiastic response of customers, these ball pens needed to be improved in terms of product quality, despite being stocky in appearance since the ink was used up easily without a refill mechanism. Thus, according to Hon-chu, a large quantity of these substandard imports eventually found their way to the garbage can.

Li & Fung's management was restructured in 1946. In particular, Fung Pak-liu's two sons, Mo-ying and Hon-chu, became executive directors—Mo-ying was in charge of finance and administration, while Hon-chu handled merchandizing and sales. Their sister, Lai-wah, also became an executive director and was responsible for accounting and personnel management. However, the new management team soon faced enormous difficulties. For instance, Li To-ming, Li & Fung's other major shareholder, refused to maintain his former relations with the company after the death of his original partner, Fung Pak-liu, and resolved to set up his own firm. Li also requested the bank to freeze Li & Fung's accounts based on mismanagement under the new leadership, thus giving a hard time to the Fung brothers.

"It was a tragedy," recalled Hon-chu, "as the only thing we could do was to make use of whatever cash we had. We could have made a fortune during those years. Initially, the bank was willing to lend only on the basis of our personal guarantee until a year later when it found that Mr. Li's allegations was groundless and resumed its financing. Eventually, Mr. Li offered to sell out all his shares to the Fungs. It was unfortunate that he failed to understand the gap between the older and younger generations."[8]

On October 1, 1946, Li To-ming sold his entire 300 Li & Fung Limited shares to the Fung family and signed a document, declaring his intention of terminating all relations with the company after his retirement. Li's move to sell out his shares in the early postwar period was ill-conceived. By doing

---

[7] Li & Fung Limited (1981), pp. 16–17.
[8] Hutcheon (1991), pp. 25–26.

so, he not only gave up his share in a business with a bright future, but also brought to an end the forty-year old business cooperation between the Li and Fung families.

Despite the withdrawal of Li To-ming, the Fungs did not change the company's name, contrary to the common practice in the West. For example, Swire, the famous British hong in Hong Kong, was founded in Shanghai in 1867 as Butterfield and Swire Company, which signified the partnership between the Swire and the Butterfield families. After the withdrawal of the Butterfield family, it was renamed John Swire and Sons Limited in 1974. The Fung family, however, did not follow this example. To a traditional Chinese company, "Li & Fung" was an auspicious name—"li" means profit and "fung" means abundance. Any attempt to change the company's name at that juncture will only add to the pressure then faced by the Fungs. Moreover, the incident was not something they wished advertised.

Li & Fung gradually recovered from that devastating incident. Business returned to normalcy but there began a change in the range of products. The company found that it was no longer practical to rely on bamboo wares, which were being replaced by plastic substitutes invented in the U.S. Its reliance on Chinese porcelains also diminished due to the declining quality of these products followed the founding of the People's Republic of China (P.R.C.). Fung Hon-chu recalled that his father had paid a visit in 1910 to Jingdezhen in Jiangxi Province—China's porcelain-making center—to introduce to the makers a better way of controlling the burning temperature inside the kiln, that is, by using a thermostat. Unfortunately for Fung Pak-liu, the makers were too proud and conservative to accept his suggestions.

Through the generations, with the main focus to please the monarchs, Chinese porcelain makers had achieved near perfection in the production of various kinds of porcelain utensils, so it was not surprising that they were proud of their craftsmanship and artifacts. At the same time, they were also too self-complacent to accept new ideas and seek improvement. Under these circumstances, the quality of porcelains made in Jingdezhen gradually declined, and this had been so since the beginning of the 20th century. Porcelains overseas were already mass-produced in factories without emphasizing on unique designs and craftsmanship. Of course, porcelains made in Jingdezhen still commanded much respect all over the world, though the demand

The "Giraffe" brand of firecrackers sold by Li & Fung.

The second generation of Li & Fung's management,
Fung Pak-liu's youngest son, Fung Mo-ying (top),
and fourth daughter, Li-Fung Lai-wah (bottom).

Fung Hon-chu (right), Fung Pak-liu's third son, during a factory visit.

A family-styled cottage rattan factory in Hong Kong in the 1950s;
Li & Fung was already a major exporter of rattan goods then.

A plastic-flower factory; Li & Fung was the pioneer in Hong Kong.

One of the fine porcelain products made in China.

for these products was on the decline. Consequently, Li & Fung reduced its dependence on porcelains made in China. But handicrafts like bamboo wares, rattan wares, and porcelains were still among the 100-odd products traded by Li & Fung after the war.

In 1949, after the closure of Li & Fung's branch in Guangzhou, Fung Mo-ying, Li-Fung Lai-wah, and all the company's employees in Guangzhou joined the headquarters in Hong Kong. According to Madam Chung Hok-mei, who joined Li & Fung upon graduating from the Guangzhou Secondary School and had been working in the company's accounts department for forty-three years, Li & Fung was already a trading company with scores of employees operating on three floors leased at Princess Building in Queen's Road Central and having a few warehouses in Kowloon. It was mainly exporting to the U.S. bamboo wares, rattan furniture, and Chinese native products, such as ivory carvings and firecrackers. These products were made chiefly in Hong Kong and the company was doing better than during the Guangzhou days.

"The rattan wares exported by Li & Fung made up two-thirds of Hong Kong's total rattan exports," Madam Chung said. She added, "Every time we unloaded our stock, the streets around the warehouses were jammed-packed with a sea of rattan chairs and other rattan products, causing congestion." She also recalled that the "rattan guys" who supplied to Li & Fung would only accept cash, whereas the suppliers of firecrackers would accept bank checks, which were usually in the amount of tens of thousands of Hong Kong dollars each.

"Mr. Fung (Hon-chu) was highly energetic and got along superbly with the staff," added Madam Chung. "His management was systematic with a clear division of labor. The accounts department had four to five people. In contrast, the sales department had about twenty people, divided into two groups—one for Europe and the other for the U.S. Generally speaking, the company only recruits those who were proficient in English, having graduated from prestigious schools or even universities, and were in their thirties. She remembered that she was initially responsible for typing, letter writing, and other clerical work. She became the cashier in the late 1940s and was responsible for handling quotations and orders. Her salary then was approximately HK$300, which was far from low by market standards in those days.

Li & Fung thrived in the 1950s. In fact, in 1955, the company rebuilt its three residential properties at 18–20 Connaught Road Central and converted them into a twelve-story office block called Fung House. After moving the company's headquarters to this building, the company redeveloped its property at Magazine Gap Road into a four-story apartment block consisting of eight units with a total area of about 20,000 square feet. The property was originally the residence of the taipan of Cable & Wireless and purchased by Li & Fung in 1950. After the reconstruction of the building, the Fungs moved into the first two floors, which had a spacious garden; the remaining two floors were leased out. That building was later expanded into a twelve-story residential block with twenty-four units called Harbor View Mansions. In 1995, Mansions was again rebuilt into a thirty-three-story high luxurious apartment block by Sun Hung Kai Properties Limited. The Fungs made the top two floors their residence. Prior to World War II, the residence of the local Chinese was subject to restrictions. For instance, they were not allowed to take up residence beyond Caine Road at Mid-Levels. Interestingly, the Fungs were among the first Chinese families to break this rule.

Strategic Adjustment during Hong Kong's Industrialization

After World War II, Hong Kong soon resumed its status as an entrepôt in the Far East. In 1947, its total external trade amounted to HK$2.77 billion, more than doubled the prewar record set in 1931 of HK$1.28 billion. By 1951, it had reached HK$9 billion, up by 240% from 1947. The speedy recovery of trade was attributed to the huge increase in trade with the mainland which, after becoming the P.R.C., was obliged to foster stronger economic links with the world. Foreign firms like Jardine Matheson and Swire also returned to Hong Kong one by one and prospered by "trading with China" instead of "trading in China." Unfortunately for them, the outbreak of the Korean War in 1950 resulted in a trade embargo imposed on China by the United Nations (U.N.) under the direction of the U.S. In 1952, Hong Kong's reexport trade plummeted, thus greatly hindering the British colony's economic development. Because the status of Hong Kong as an entrepôt had been shaken all of a sudden, all the "hongs" (foreign companies in Hong Kong) and trading firms relying on the reexport trade as their mainstay suffered.

Luckily for Hong Kong, the manufacturing industry began to grow during this period. In the late 1940s, to escape from the political instability caused by the Third Chinese Civil War, a large number of industrialists from Shanghai and other industrial and commercial cities in China migrated to Hong Kong, bringing along with them the capital, technology, and equipment, as well as links with the international market that were crucial for industrial development. It was this group of industrialists who started building up Hong Kong's industrial foundations for the textile industry, followed by garment manufacturing. In those days, investors who fled the mainland took their capital to Hong Kong instead of Taiwan. In Taiwan, despite the favors offered by the Kuomintang government to the industrial and commercial sectors, businessmen were repelled by the strict controls imposed on them. In comparison, Hong Kong possessed a number of advantages that were conducive to industrial development—a stable and open economic policy, a simple and low tax regime, the absence of tight restrictions and controls, well-developed telecommunications, superior port facilities and services, and an abundant supply of cheap labor. The massive influx of people from China had already boosted Hong Kong's population to 2 million—a source of huge and cheap labor for industrialists.

In the mid-1960s, Hong Kong experienced serious social disorders as a result of various incidents, such as the spate of bank runs in 1965, the demonstration against Star Ferry's price increase in 1966, and the riots in 1967. Though industrial development was adversely affected, Hong Kong's industrial exports continued to grow strongly and contributed to economic prosperity, in general. By 1970, Hong Kong's industrial exports were 4.3 times that of the previous decade, representing an average compound growth rate of 16% per year. For the same year, the manufacturing industry's contribution to Hong Kong's gross domestic product (GDP) rose to 30.9%. From an entrepôt, Hong Kong had evolved into an industrial city—this was essentially the golden era for Hong Kong's textile and garment industries. Meanwhile, the manufacture of plastics, toys, watches and clocks, metal wares, and electronics also began to flourish. All these helped to foster the growth of sectors like import/export, shipping, finance, and real estate, as Hong Kong's economy entered a new phase of development.

In view of the structural transformation that was taking place in Hong Kong's economy, Li & Fung quickly adjusted its business strategy by redirecting its focus from reexports to domestic exports, and becoming actively involved in Hong Kong's industrialization. The domestic products exported by Li & Fung included plastic flowers, rattan wares, wood wares, firecrackers and fireworks, garments, toys, and electronics. The production of plastic flowers was a new industry in Hong Kong and, at one point, was only second to textiles in importance. As one of the pioneers in this industry, Li & Fung sourced large quantities of plastic flowers from factories in Hong Kong for overseas markets. Li Ka-shing, who started Cheung Kong Plastics Company, was also one of Li & Fung's suppliers. As Madam Chung Hok-mei, Li & Fung's former employee, recalled, Mr. Li himself came to her office to conduct business. Founded by Li Ka-shing in 1950, Cheung Kong Plastics Company became Cheung Kong Industries Limited in 1957. Its products were reputed for their high quality and low price. One of the leading wholesalers of the U.S. also bought from Cheung Kong, and Mr. Li, who was called "the king of plastic flowers," later became the richest man in Hong Kong.

At the height of the plastic-flower boom, Li & Fung set up a factory called Wai Dai Industries Limited under the management of Fung Mo-ying in Kwun Tong. Its experience in running Victoria Torch Manufacturing Company Limited before the war was valuable to Li & Fung in this new venture. Wai Dai was a semi-automated factory that employed a few hundred workers, most of whom were immigrants from China. In addition to self-production, the factory also contracted out its production on a piece-rated basis to various households where housewives and children would string together the flower petals, thus creating thousands of job opportunities.

Concurrently, Li & Fung continued to engage in its traditional businesses like rattan furniture, but it no longer reexported from China and instead sourced the products directly in Hong Kong and even manufactured some of them. During the 1950s, Li & Fung became the leading exporter of Hong Kong's rattan wares, delivering as many as 1,000 to 2,000 pieces each day. Even with many rattan craftsmen coming from China on its payroll, the company was still unable to meet the market demand and, therefore, had to farm out some of its orders to cottage factories. Two small but elegant-looking rattan chairs made by Li & Fung had been purchased by Prince Charles and Princess Anne and were to be used at Buckingham Palace in England. Li & Fung's business also extended to wooden products, including salad bowls and eating utensils. However, owing to the rise in production costs and competition from other Asian countries, it later switched to the manufacturing of metal eating utensils. Li & Fung built two multi-story factory blocks in the Kwun Tong industrial district to make plastic flowers and wood products; it also ran a number of factories. But with the continual expansion of its business, none of these factories can fully satisfy its needs. Eventually, it became a sourcing agent, purchasing from different manufacturers in Hong Kong and China, and providing merchandizing services for its clients at a reasonable fee.

After World War II, firecrackers and fireworks remained Li & Fung's major products. Trade involving these products dated back to the early days of Li & Fung's establishment. Toward the end of the 19th century, the weight of firecrackers and fireworks exported from Hong Kong was about 2.7 million pounds a year, of which three-quarters were shipped to the U.S., and the remainder to Europe and other parts of the world. Guangzhou, Hunan, and Macau were the centers of production in China. In addition to sourcing from these locations, Li & Fung also set up its own factory in Guangzhouwan to cope with overseas orders, of which 60% came from the U.S., and the remaining 40% came from other markets. This highly lucrative business continued until the outbreak of the Korean War and the U.N.'s trade embargo imposed against China.

However, the trading of firecrackers and fireworks was never suspended. During the Japanese occupation of Guangzhou, Li & Fung closed its factory in Guangzhouwan and relocated to Macau. In the 1950s and 60s, Li & Fung was the largest among the six Macau factories licensed to export to the U.S. In terms of quality control and product safety, Li & Fung had always enjoyed a good reputation and was thus able to secure more and more orders from the U.S. market. Gradually, it had to buy from and expand its scope of management to the other five factories in Macau. Even so, it was unable to satisfy the enormous market demand. In 1968, Li & Fung set up a large-scale modern factory in Taiwan called President Firecrackers & Fireworks Company Limited. That factory's products targeted the U.S. market. Statistics show that from 1967 to 1971, Li & Fung had been Hong Kong's largest exporter of fireworks. The visit of President Richard Nixon to China in 1972 resulted in improved Sino-U.S. relations and the lifting of U.S.'s trade embargo against China. In other words, pyrotechnic products made in China were again admitted to the U.S. market, which immediately posed a serious threat to Macau. Within a year, almost all the fireworks factories in Macau were forced to close down.[9]

Li & Fung then resumed its sourcing from China. In view of the influx of pyrotechnic products from China though Hong Kong, the U.S. government deemed it fit to tighten its control over the quality of these imports. To this end, the U.S. Consumer Products Safety Commission decreed that all such products had to be clearly labeled with registered trademarks, as well as warnings and explicit directions for use. Li & Fung responded quickly to the new requirements by further strengthening its quality control and management. Under the company's supervision, the "Black Cat" and "Giraffe" brands of products made in China had not for once been seized or ordered destroyed by the U.S. authorities. Moreover, Li & Fung actively participated in the safety promotion scheme organized annually by the American Pyrotechnics Association to ensure continued growth in the U.S. market.

Indisputably, among the wide range of products handled by Li & Fung, the most important category was textiles. A large number of Shanghainese entrepreneurs fled from China and arrived in Hong Kong in the 1950s, bringing with them machinery and equipment, as well as investment capital which, according to the estimates of an economist, was roughly equivalent to 40% of the British colony's total GDP from 1947 to 1955. A considerable percentage of these migrant entrepreneurs were from the textile industry. It was estimated that of the 5 million spinning machines that existed in China in 1949, approximately 200,000 ended up in Hong Kong. Most of these machines were of the latest models and highly efficient. These favorable circumstances spurred the growth of the textile industry in Hong Kong, which became the world's leading exporter of cotton fabrics, yarns, and bedclothes.

The volume of textile exports from Hong Kong was so enormous that Britain, one of the world's largest markets for textiles, had to resort to protectionism. Under the Lancashire Agreement in 1959, Hong Kong was forced to exercise voluntary restrictions over its textile exports to Britain. In 1962, the so-called Long-term Arrangement Regarding Trade in Cotton Textiles was established under the General Agreement on Tariffs and Trade (GATT),

---

[9] Feng (1996), p. 39.

allowing importing and exporting countries to arrive at export quotas through bilateral negotiations. Countries that had entered into bilateral agreements with Hong Kong included the U.S., members of the European Community, Canada, Norway, Sweden, and Australia. Upon the expiry of the said Arrangement at the end of 1973, the Multifiber Arrangement (MFA) took effect from 1974, allowing importing countries to impose textile quotas and thus violating the principles of GATT to the detriment of developing countries. Hong Kong was, however, the first signatory to MFA, and owing to its strong track record in textile exports, it enjoyed considerable advantage in terms of quota allocation.

At this stage, the textile industry in Hong Kong was basically dominated by a group of prominent Shanghainese industrialists, including Wong Toong-yuen of Hong Kong Cotton Spinning, P.Y. Tang of South Sea Textile, Chen Din-hua of Nan Fung Textiles, Chao Kuang-piu of Novel Enterprises, Cha Chi-ming of China Dyeing Works, T.K. Ann, Chou Wen-hsien, and H.C. Tang of Windsor Industrial Corporation, as well as the legendary Rong family. Statistics revealed that among all the textile factories in Hong Kong in the 1950s, only one did not belong to the Shanghai group. By 1978, approximately 80% of the spinning mills in Hong Kong were owned by the Shanghainese. These facts point to the significant contribution of migrant businessmen from China to Hong Kong's textile industry.[10]

The manufacture and export of textiles and garments were highly lucrative in the 1960s, representing 45–50% of Hong Kong's total exports. Li & Fung seized the golden opportunity then available to focus on the export of textiles and garments. Although the company's employees were predominantly Cantonese, they somehow managed to overcome the language barrier by conversing with the textile industrialists in Shanghainese, some Putonghua, English, and Cantonese, thus forging close relations with them and enabling Li & Fung to achieve exemplary results in textile exports and become one of Hong Kong's top garment exporters. "Li & Fung's garment exports grew stronger and stronger in the 1960s," said William Fung, "and we were almost

---

[10] *Hong Kong Economic Journal Monthly*, October 1988, p. 56.

second to none in Hong Kong." Their largest counterparts during this period were two British firms, Dodwell and Swire.

In those days, businessmen from the West searched for new opportunities everywhere. According to its own records, Li & Fung was inundated with appointments with these businessmen, who included importers, manufacturers and some prominent retailers; it thus greatly benefited by talking with them. Meanwhile, through a curious product mix of bamboo and rattan wares, fireworks and firecrackers, plastic flowers, and textile products, Li & Fung achieved steady growth in its export business and strong cash flow while maintaining firm and close economic relations with the world's fastest-growing market—the U.S.—thus laying a solid foundation for massive expansion in the future. Its customers now numbered a few hundred and its sourcing network comprised more than a thousand factories all over Hong Kong. It attained healthy growth year after year, with its total revenue for 1969 estimated at HK$71 million. By 1973, it had grown to HK$189 million, representing a high average growth rate of 28% per annum (Exhibit 2.1).

Exhibit 2.1   Li & Fung's business growth, 1969–1973

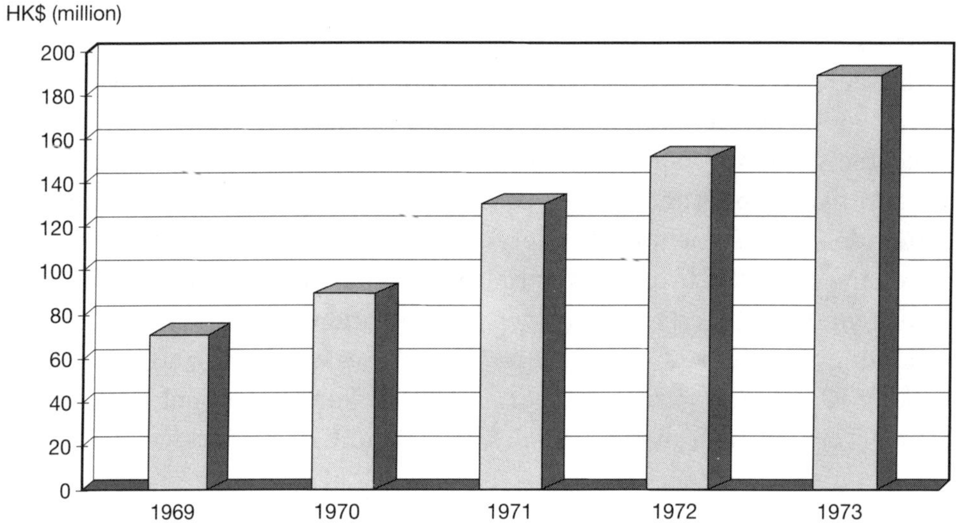

HK$ (million)

Source: Li & Fung 65th Anniversary Supplement.

Chapter 3

First Public Listing: 1973–1989

"Victor and William began to examine the company's organization, structure and manpower problems and put forward solutions. It was the very first time that the whole operating system of the company had been scrutinized from a professional perspective by applying modern management techniques. Having identified the problems, Victor and William next turned to devising solutions and implementing changes."

—Fung Hon-chu

Public Listing—First Step to a Modern Enterprise

By the late 1960s and early 1970s, the third generation of the Fung family had joined Li & Fung one after another, infusing into it the new blood and vitality essential for its long-term development.

Li & Fung's management team consisted of the following: Fung Mo-ying was the board chairman whereas his younger brother, Fung Hon-chu, was the managing director. Mo-ying was the head of internal administration and finance, while Hon-chu took charge of external affairs, including trade. In the early 1970s, Mo-ying, who also doubled as the chief executive officer, would normally work half the expected time for health reasons, relinquishing his major duties to Hon-chu. Now in his sixties and having been appointed by Governor David C.C. Trench as a Legislative Councillor, Hon-chu was devoting a lot of his time in the work of the Legislative Council, as well as the Urban Council, of which he was also a member. As a representative of the business sector, he had to put forward constructive ideas to the government. The two Fung seniors desired that their offsprings take up and continue the family business, spearheading its modernization with the management knowledge and skills learned from the U.S.

Fung Mo-ying had three sons and four daughters with his two wives, Wong Yeuk-hung and Shu Shui-man. The three boys were Kwok-fun, Kwok-hong, and Kwok-chor; the four girls were Yuen-sang, Suet-sang, Mei-sang, and Yim-sang. On the other hand, Fung Hon-chu and his wife Lee Pui-yiu had two sons and three daughters. The boys were Victor (Kwok-king) and William (Kwok-lun), and the girls were Pui-hei, Pui-kit, and Pui-ling. Among the third-generation descendants of the Fung family, Mo-ying's sons, Kwok-hong and Kwok-chor, as well as Lai-wah's son, Wing-hong, were the first to join Li & Fung; they were soon followed by their cousins, Victor and William. Together, they eventually formed the core of the company's business team by becoming heads of departments or directors. The third generation brought new ideas and momentum to the company and ensured that its business could be passed on smoothly.

Fung Mo-ying's eldest son, Kwok-hong, joined Li & Fung in the 1960s. He was chiefly responsible for sourcing plastic flowers and other products, like sundry goods and fire crackers, were added to his portfolio later. Eighteen years Kwok-hong's junior, Kwok-chor was Fung Mo-ying's youngest son. Having graduated from St. Stephen's College in Hong Kong, Kwok-chor studied biochemistry at Johns Hopkins University, New York. In 1971, the degeneration of his lungs caused by a long history of smoking confined Fung Mo-ying to bed. In order to be by his father's side, Kwok-chor terminated his studies and returned to Hong Kong to join Li & Fung.

As Kwok-chor recalled, "Li & Fung was already fairly well-established, occupying four floors (of about 5,000 square feet each) of Fung House in Central and employing a staff of one hundred. The main business consisted of the sourcing of garments, sundry goods, and toys. The company was then divided into several divisions or departments. Apart from the sundry-goods group, there were two other groups handling apparel for men and for women. Our largest customer then was not from the U.S.; it was rather C&A of Europe."

Li & Fung's organizational structure was still product-based. Kwok-chor remembered that he had joined the men's apparel group and learned to do business under its manager, Fong Yik-tuen. His monthly salary then was HK$1,200. His father advised him that it was essential to start from the lower ranks in order to gain a thorough understanding of the company's operation.

"When I first joined Li & Fung," said Kwok-chor, "it was still very much a family business. My father, one of my uncles, and one of my aunts, who were all directors of the company, handled all matters whether big or small. They went to work and came home together: you would see the same group of people either in the office or at home."

In those days, kickbacks were common in Hong Kong's business sector. Kwok-chor clearly recalled that he often went to the factories with his colleagues for the purpose of inspecting goods, although those colleagues would go before him to collect kickbacks. Once he walked very fast and his colleagues could not overtake him to tell the factory owner that he was the boss's son. There was embarrassment on both sides when the factory owner unknowingly thrust some money in his hand. Kwok-chor reprimanded the factory owner severely, but the latter retorted, "Competition is tough these days. Even if I don't offer kickbacks to your colleagues, other manufacturers will. What else can I do if I don't want to lose business?" At one point, some employees were going too far in demanding kickbacks, causing serious disaffection among the manufacturers. Kwok-chor stepped in and, as a result, fifteen employees resigned in protest. Because of the sudden shortage of staff and the increase in workload, he was forced to take care of everything by himself, even including the typing of contracts. Hence, he deeply felt a need for the company to reform its system of operation.

Following the footsteps of their cousin Kwok-chor, Victor and William also joined Li & Fung. In June 1972, William graduated with an MBA degree from the Harvard University. He wanted to find a job and stay in the U.S., given that his brother Victor, having attained a doctorate degree at Harvard, was already an employee of Citibank and was planning to return to Harvard for a faculty position. Meanwhile, Li & Fung's business was expanding fast. As the company's managing director, Fung Hon-chu was eager that one of his sons would return home to help him run the family business so that as he was advancing in years, he could devote more time and energy to public service. For Victor, however, a tenure offered by Harvard was hard to resist.

Eventually, the newly graduated William decided to forego the opportunity of working in the U.S. and joined Li & Fung. According to William, his mother had called him, urging him to return quickly because it was becoming increasingly difficult for his father to assume the Herculean task of running the company all alone. William had no choice but to return to Hong Kong first. Looking back, William called it a typical case of a family in need of drastic change. It is known that on his return, the first thing he told his father was that he did not believe in having a bright future in the family business; he did not realize then how mistaken he was.

Fung Hon-chu thought highly of his son who had been educated overseas. "Now that you possess the latest business administration knowledge from the U.S.," he said to William, "go and take a look at Li & Fung and figure out what its problems are and what improvement should be made." William was only a young lad of twenty-three without any working experience. Every time those words of his father's crossed his mind, he could not help hailing Fung senior as a visionary.

"Father was already a very experienced and successful businessman who enjoyed a prestigious social status," he said, "Yet, he wouldn't think twice about allowing a novice without practical experience to take on the colossal task of reforming the company. Unlike him, I still worry myself with various things about my son, though he is no longer a minor."

No doubt Fung Hon-chu belonged to the old school of Chinese businessman, but he was exceptional in that he was highly amenable to reforms. In a press interview when he was eighty-one, he remarked: "Professionalism is the norm of the day. Many of our employees are U.S.-educated. The times are changing. We cannot afford not to change with the times."

In recounting Li & Fung's history, he was affirmative about progress and change without betraying a modicum of nostalgia. He recalled: "When I joined Li & Fung before the 1960s, there was no airplane and absolutely nothing. Our customers took more than a month to arrive by ship; now it is very different. They may suddenly appear in front of you to see what you are up to. In the past, we could at best send telegraphs by using our code number; nowadays not only are facsimiles considered too backward but they are also making way for electronic mails."

William Fung joined Li & Fung as the manager of its textiles department in September 1972. Victor Fung also returned from the U.S. during Christmas in 1973. Drawing on their Western experiences and their knowledge of the newest theories of management acquired from the U.S., the two brothers conducted a Harvard-style case study of Li & Fung. Several months of observation led them to conclude that the company was beset with a number of problems. On the whole, there had been almost no fundamental change in the company's business mission as an intermediary between overseas merchandisers and local manufacturers. Until Victor and William joined the company, the company's management structure and model had remained basically the same.

In Fung Hon-chu's recollection, "Victor and William began to examine the company's organization, structure, and manpower problems, and put forward solutions. It was the very first time that the whole operating system of the company had been scrutinized from a professional perspective through the application of modern management techniques."[1]

Victor and William's scrutiny revealed that Li & Fung had several problems. First, there was no systematic organization within the company's internal structure to ensure high efficiency and good management. Specifically, the departments did not have to prepare business plans and financial budgets. In other words, the task of the accounts department was no more than the keeping of sales and profit records. There was also a serious shortage of professionals and experienced managers within the whole organization. The company's total employment size was around a hundred but their over-

---

[1] *Capital*, Hong Kong, February 1992, p. 70.

all quality was just mediocre. Though the departmental managers were all well-experienced on account of their long service, the majority did not have university education. Also, owing to the absence of a remuneration system, staff salary was below reasonable levels, thus causing high turnover rates and making it virtually impossible to retain outstanding employees.

"Having identified the problems," recalled Fung Hon-chu, "Victor and William next turned to devising solutions and implementing changes, one of the first being to stress the importance of setting business targets at the departmental level. The accounts department had to provide sufficient information, sales reports, gross profits by departments, and monthly reports for the departmental managers to assess their own performance and correct errors before they became serious.

"Departmental budgets were needed to enable each of the seven product groups to assess their sales, profits, personnel requirements, and cost control, as well as to allow each to see the roles they would be playing in the company's overall performance.

"Greater emphasis was given to staff remuneration, promotion, and training, which became more systematic in order to enhance efficiency. To improve the staff's overall quality, the company was given a transfusion of highly qualified, well-trained men and women. The implementation of these reforms took two years and in the mean time, the company prepared to go public in 1973."[2]

Both Victor and William felt that were Li & Fung to grow successfully from a traditional family business into a modern enterprise capable of taking up new challenges, the surest way was to become a public-listed company.

"When I first came back from the U.S.," said William, "the family members controlled the key posts and the shareholders were spread among the eight surviving members of the second generation of the founder of the company. But when the third generation came in, you couldn't benefit from the shareholding; you had to get involved. Some of my cousins joined the business but didn't have the interest."[3]

---

[2] Hutcheon (1991), p. 51.
[3] Hutcheon (1991), p. 53.

Li & Fung's shares were quite dispersed among the family members, with Mo-ying, Hon-chu, and Lai-wah holding a relatively higher percentage each. The company was not managed under an effective system; neither was there a fixed plan for paying dividends to the shareholders. Only those who worked in the company were entitled to salary and bonus. The majority of the thirty-five family members who belonged to the third generation were not interested in the company. Some had a vocation in banking or other professions. Still, others were planning to emigrate. Even those who were willing to succeed their forebears could not be said to be adept enough to cope with the volatility of the world market and other unforeseeable challenges.

In view of all these observations concerning the company, Victor and William proposed that Li & Fung should go public. "If you want the company to continue flourishing," said William to his father, "then you should separate its ownership and operation. To do that, you must turn it into a public-listed company." In fact, the two Fung brothers regarded public listing as a catalyst that would enable the company to dispense with its old management style, to distinguish between the company's ownership and management, and to embark on a professional and modern management.

"From Li & Fung's perspective," William pointed out, "public listing carries many advantages. First, the company will come under public scrutiny so that shareholders can benefit. Second, after going public, we can develop a long-term dividend payout policy to ensure a stable return to shareholders. Third, the company's shares will have a market price and shareholders' assets will become liquid. Last but not least, as a public-listed company, we will be in an advantageous position to attract talents to help upgrade our management." He added that the raising of capital from the market was never a major consideration for them because the company was already rich in capital.

A family meeting was convened to consider Victor and William's proposal. Despite opposition from certain members, the proposal had the support of both Fung Mo-ying and Fung Hon-chu, the board chairman and director, respectively. Though indisposed, Mo-ying attended the meeting and stood up to lend his support to the proposal. Many other members of the family also welcomed the decision to list the company because as priority shareholders, they would be entitled to bonuses. Through their shareholdings, they would receive dividends on a regular basis, though they would no longer take part in the management of the company.[4] The meeting resolved that Li & Fung should actively prepare for public listing.

Hong Kong's stock market was then undergoing a boom unequalled since the war. To Victor and William, it was an opportunity they could not afford to miss. On December 30, 1972, by an extraordinary resolution, 995,000 new shares were added to the share capital of the company at HK$100 each, thus raising the total share capital from 1937's HK$500,000 (with 5,000 shares at HK$100 each) to HK$100 million (with 1 million shares at HK$100 each). The next day, a resolution was carried whereby Li & Fung would split each of its 2,500 issued shares into 100 shares, resulting in a total of 250,000 shares at HK$1 per share. Concurrently, HK$47.75 million was to be taken from the company's capital reserves whereas HK$6 million would be taken from the profit-and-loss account—a total of HK$53.75 million—to make up the total share capital of the 53.75 million shares. These shares were to be allotted to the original shareholders proportionately. By so doing, Li & Fung increased its issued shares from 250,000 to 54 million at HK$1 per share.[5]

In March 1973, Li & Fung underwent a restructuring, leading to the setting up of Li & Fung Limited. On March 6, Li & Fung realigned its businesses such as trading, real estate, and finance by establishing six subsidiaries, namely, Li & Fung (Trading) Limited, Li & Fung (Taiwan) Limited, Li & Fung (Macau) Limited, Li & Fung (Properties) Limited, and Li & Fung (Finance and Investment) Limited. By then, Li & Fung and its subsidiaries had a total workforce of 150. Its total net asset value was HK$56 million, of which HK$51.65 million were due to the value of its properties in Hong Kong, comprising mainly Fung House in Connaught Road Central, and Harbor View Mansions in Magazine Gap Road at the Peak.

In March 1973, following the upturn since the fourth quarter of 1972, the end of the Vietnam War, and the Hong Kong government's announcement to build the mass transit railway, the trading volume mounted substantially at the local stock market as many local companies were paying generous dividends and bonus shares, and the financial markets in the West remained in

---

[4] *Business Week*, November 27, 1995, p. 70.
[5] *Li & Fung Limited IPO Prospectus*, March 27, 1973.

a state of turbulence. An increasing number of local people, including wage-earners and housewives, participated in stock trading and speculation.

Madam Chan Po-sum, a trading member of the Kam Ngan Stock Exchange, observed, "Not only housewives but also monks and nuns were buying stocks…Even amahs preferred to work only for those who would buy and sell stocks on their behalf…Stock brokers were looked upon as demigods, receiving special treatment even in restaurants."[6]

Almost everyone was involved in this state of frenzy where shares were preferred to cash. Against this backdrop, a large number of companies went public. In 1973 alone, there were no less than 110 newly listed stocks in Hong Kong. Fearing that the stock market was becoming overheated and speculation was going out of control, the Hong Kong government instituted a number of measures, with a view to letting off some steam. Regardless of those measures, the Hang Seng Index kept climbing, peaking at a historic 1,774.99 on March 9.

On March 27, 1973, Li & Fung started distributing the prospectus and application form for its shares. Its underwriters were the renowned Schroders and Chartered Limited, Wardly Limited, and Asia Pacific Capital Corporation Limited. According to the prospectus, Li & Fung was to offer for sale to the public 13.5 million existing shares, or 25% of its total shares, at the price of HK$1.65 each which, according to the Board's estimates, represented a price/earnings (P/E) ratio of 13.2, a dividend yield of 6.06% and a dividend cover of 1.25 times. "Because our company had always been making profit," said William Fung, "we had no need for raising new capital." Li & Fung was, therefore, offering its existing shares and not issuing new shares. The main purpose for its initial public offer (IPO) was to reform its outdated mode of operation and to chart a new course for its business strategy.

Li & Fung's IPO set a new record in terms of subscription due to overwhelming public response. When applications closed on April 3, the issue had been oversubscribed by 113 times, thus freezing banks' funds by a total of HK$2,308 million. Among nearly 55,600 applicants, only 3,954 succeeded. Most of them could only receive a percentage of the shares applied for

---

[6] *Capital*, Hong Kong, February 1996, p. 54.

through a ballot.[7] The oversubscription remained a record for the next 14 years. It owed partly to the then favorable market conditions, and partly to the company's reputation and business performance.

The Hong Kong stock market was peaking out at the time of Li & Fung's IPO. A crisis was in fact brewing because the buoyancy of the market was not in line with the economy. On March 12, 1973, forged share certificates of Hopeful Holdings Limited were discovered. Fearing that their stocks could turn into waste paper, many retail investors resorted to short-sell what they had in hand. Concomitantly, interest rates were on the rise and money supply was tightening. As a result, the Hang Seng Index nosedived, plummeting to 1,301.13 by the end of March. By the end of 1973, it had reached 438.68, down more than 75% from its peak. However, Li & Fung's IPO did not seem to have experienced any significant impact. The trading of Li & Fung stocks commenced on April 17, 1973. After the IPO, the amount of Li & Fung shares held by the Fung family decreased from 99.92% to 74.92%, of which Fung Mo-ying and Fung Hon-chu were each holding 9.29%, Li Fung Lai-wah was holding 8% and the estate of Fung Pak-liu was holding 14.99% (Exhibit 3.1).

Exhibit 3.1   Li & Fung's major shareholders, before and after public listing in 1973

Shareholder	Capacity	Number and Percentage of Shares	
		Before Issuance of New shares	After Issuance of New shares
Fung Hon-bong	Professor of civil	5.1 million (9.45%)	3.6 million (6.67%)
Fung Hon-chu	Director	7.12 million (13.18%)	5.02 million (9.29%)
Fung Hon-hing	Merchant	5.1 million (9.45%)	3.6 million (6.67%)
Fung Hon-yin	Medical doctor	5.1 million (9.45%)	3.6 million (6.67%)
Fung Lai-ngoi	Housewife	5.1 million (9.45%)	3.6 million (6.67%)
Fung Lai-sheung	Housewife	5.1 million (9.45%)	3.6 million (6.67%)
Fung Mo-ying	Director	7.12 million (13.18%)	5.02 million (9.29%)
Fung Pak-liu's estate	–	8.1 million (14.99%)	8.1 million (14.99%)
Li-Fung Lai-wah	Director	6.12 million (11.32%)	4.32 million (8.00%)
Sir. Albert Rodrigues	Medical doctor	20,000 (0.04%)	20,000 (0.04%)
Sir. Oswald Cheung	Barrister	20,000 (0.04%)	20,000 (0.04%)
Public	–	–	13.5 million (25%)
TOTAL		**54 million (100%)**	**54 million (100%)**

Source: Li & Fung Limited's IPO prospectus.

---

[7] Hong Kong Government Information Services, Feature Article 6004/2, pp. 19–20.

The Move from Traditional to Professional Management

Immediately after its public listing, Li & Fung began to establish a new management system, most importantly, by forming a new board of directors and appointing a professional management team.

The first drastic change for the company after its IPO was that its board of directors now became more accountable to the public. In an interview in February 1978, Victor Fung, the chairman of Li & Fung (Trading) Limited, gave his views on this change.

"I feel that this decision is important. In order for the company to continue to grow, it must go into this type of structure instead of remaining a very close-knit family concern."[8]

On the new board, there were three members from the Fung family: Fung Mo-ying, Fung Hon-chu, and Li-Fung Lai-wah. Mo-ying was the chairman, whereas Hon-chu was the managing director. Lai-wah retained the directorship which she had been holding since 1945. When Fung Mo-ying passed away on February 4, 1975, Fung Hon-chu doubled as both the chairman and managing director of Li & Fung. In April, Fung Hon-hing joined the board, filling the seat vacated by Fung Mo-ying. It was obvious that the core members of the Fung family were still at the helm of Li & Fung. The new board included two celebrities in Hong Kong—the Honorable Sirs. Albert Rodrigues and Oswald Cheung. Sir. Rodrigues was a leading physician who had served as the Senior Executive Councillor and the Council Chairman of the University of Hong Kong. Sir. Cheung was a renowned barrister-at-law in Hong Kong. Having served as the senior member of both the Executive Council and Legislative Council, he was made a commander of the British Empire (CBE) in 1976. Sirs. Kerry St. Johnston and Anthony Hayward later were also appointed to the Li & Fung board. The presence of these personalities on the board meant that the company's operation was now subject to a higher degree of public scrutiny. It also boosted Li & Fung's corporate image and reputation.

Reporting to the board, the management was led by Fung Hon-chu. Ho Chik-kong was appointed as Group Managing Director. Having been a

---

[8] *Hong Kong Trader* (1978), Vol. 2, p. 7.

manager of Citibank for many years, Ho was highly experienced in banking and finance. He became acquainted with Fung Pak-liu when he was a senior officer of Citibank's Guangzhou branch. Citibank had always been Li & Fung's bankers and Ho had been a close friend of the Fungs for generations. Retiring from Citibank in 1968, he joined Li & Fung the next year as a manager. In 1976, he was appointed as a director of Li & Fung (Finance & Investment) Limited and had since been devoted to the finance business of the group.

During the mid-1970s, Fung Hon-chu gradually moved to the backstage to handle the export of the traditional products that he had a penchant for, particularly fireworks and firecrackers. The company was in effect in the hands of his two sons, Victor and William. In 1977, Victor was appointed as the managing director of Li & Fung (Trading) Limited. He became a director of Li & Fung Limited in 1981 and replaced his father as its managing director. William was appointed in 1975 as a director of three of Li & Fung's subsidiaries, namely, Li & Fung (Trading) Limited, Li & Fung (Properties) Limited, and Li & Fung (Finance and Investment) Limited. He became the managing director of Li & Fung (Properties) Limited in 1982. In 1986, William succeeded Victor as the managing director of Li & Fung and doubled as chief executive officer. The succession of Victor and William signified the smooth handover of the management of Li & Fung from the second generation to the third generation of the Fung family.

By the early 1980s, Li & Fung was administered by a new generation of professional managers. Aside from Victor Fung, the company's managing director, and William Fung, the managing director of Li & Fung (Properties) Limited, the administrative structure of Li & Fung also consisted of Wong Chi-kei, the managing director of Li & Fung Trading; Fung Kwok-hong, the manager of the sundry-goods department in Li & Fung Trading; Chow Wing-hong and Cheung Kong Ching-yee, managers of the apparel department in Li & Fung Trading; Chan Kut-lap (later renamed Chan Chun-lam), the manager of the toys and stationery department in Li & Fung Trading; Lee Wing-hong, the director of Li & Fung (Properties) Limited; Kwan Yee-suet, the manager of LiFung Fidelity; Hui Kung-fa, the manager of Lifung Gap Stores Limited; Koo On-kei, the managing director of Minko Consolidation; Lau Kai-kwan, the managing director of World-Trade Merchandize Ltd. Lau Butt-farn, the finance manager of Li & Fung; and Victor Co, the managing director of Li &

Fung (Taiwan) Limited.[9] Among these members of the senior management, Wong Chi-kei warrants particular mention. Educated in the U.K. and the U.S., Wong had held a number of posts in the Hong Kong government, including the Department of Administrative Services, District Services Department, Labor Department, and also the Postal Services Department where he was the postmaster general. Bringing with him a wealth of administrative experience after retiring from the civil service in 1980, he joined the company as the managing director of Li & Fung Trading and a director of several Li & Fung subsidiaries. In 1994, Wong filed a lawsuit against Li & Fung for failing to pay him certain salary-related benefits. A vigorous debate between him and Victor Fung was staged in the courtroom. The case ended with Li & Fung paying Wong HK$900,000.[10]

The new generation of senior executives at Li & Fung Limited has all received either professional training or university education. The prominent representatives remain Victor Fung, William Fung, Chan Kut-lap, and Lau Butt-farn. Both Victor and William have postgraduate degrees from the Harvard University with strong academic training and are conversant with modern business administration. Joining Li & Fung in 1972, Chan Kut-lap graduated from the University of Hong Kong with a degree in social sciences and later also obtained an MBA degree from the Chinese University of Hong Kong. Chan is highly experienced in the sales of durable goods. Lau Butt-farn joined in 1981 with a first degree in physics. He is also a member of the Institute of Chartered Accountants of England and Wales. With this new management team exposed to Western business administration, the former traditional family business of Li & Fung now entered a new era of robust transformation and development.

At its 75th anniversary in 1982, the company established a fund for the Li & Fung Lecture on Commerce and Industry to sponsor an annual lecture jointly organized with the Chinese University of Hong Kong. Because the presenters invited from all over the world to the forum are either renowned business people or specialists in their respective fields and the topics they

---

[9] *Wah Kiu Yat Po*, June 18, 1982.
[10] *Next Magazine*, Hong Kong, September 18, 2003.

choose must contribute to the increasingly diversified economic development of Hong Kong, the lecture was well received by the community. The fund also signifies the high degree of importance that Li & Fung Limited's new management attaches to upgrading business administration.

Following Li & Fung's public listing, the new generation of managers, including Victor and William, proceeded to apply unsparingly their knowledge of modern management to the company's business. During an interview in 1978, Victor was asked whether, as a young Chinese with Western education and attuned to the Western way of thinking, he had found it difficult to adapt to the traditional business world of Hong Kong.

He replied, "I must admit that there were mild conflicts of opinion at times. But I must say too that the board of Li & Fung, which is made up of senior directors from outside and three family members, has been extremely receptive to new ideas. I have never tried to beat anybody over the head with a new idea and rather used the gentle, gradual approach. But sometimes my father would say 'that's fine on paper but it will never work.' And I accept this because I am talking to a man with some 40 years' experience in the business. On the other hand, I feel that the management of Li & Fung has accepted the idea that the organization must evolve with the times and that past methods, which might have been effective at that time, must now be modified."[11]

However, Victor also stressed that Li & Fung Limited's executives subscribed to the same view that an organization should change with the circumstances and should not shy away from modifying what used to be effective policies and measures. The most important underlying reason was that Li & Fung Limited was now a public-listed company. In the five years after its IPO, a revolution took place quietly within Li & Fung Limited. The management structure evolved from the old "one boss/employees system" into an effective management hierarchy. The other significant change occurred in the company's staff force. Before its IPO in 1973, none of Li & Fung's employees had university education. By 1978, of the company's 120 employees, 20 were university graduates. The management of the company had all received ei-

---

[11] *Hong Kong Trader* (1978), Vol. 2, p. 7.

ther professional or tertiary education, and was well-equipped with the latest business administration knowledge.[12]

In 1986, Victor resigned from the position of managing director and was succeeded by his brother William. Together with three partners, Victor founded an Asian investment and merchant bank—Prudential Asia Capital Fund, whose U.S. parent was Prudential Insurance Company. On this move, Victor had this to say in an interview with journalist Heung Shu-fai of *First Magazine*:

"According to the Chinese tradition, the eldest son inherits the family business. After my brother William and I took up Li & Fung Limited, theoretically I should have become the head of the company. But I wanted to go off the beaten track and leave it to my brother, who has a strong interest in trading, to develop and grow the family business. I have worked at Citibank and I know about finance. I was eager to enter the direct investment/venture capital fund business to actualize myself. I, therefore, withdrew from the day-to-day operations of Li & Fung Limited and, together with Chris Leung and Martin Tong, set up Techno Ventures. Martin left in 1986 and Chris is very gifted and independent. I moved on to partner with Prudential Insurance Company in establishing Prudential Asia Capital Fund."

In 1988, Victor became the founding chairman of the Hong Kong Venture Capital Funds Association, in which during his tenure, he actively promoted the development of venture capital funds in Hong Kong. Toward the end of the 1990s, Hong Kong was gradually solidifying its status as the venture-capital center in Asia. The venture-capital funds managed by companies based in Hong Kong amounted to over US$1,000 billion. Of these companies, the ones managed by Victor Fung and Chris Leung stood out in terms of both funds size and return rate. Li & Fung Limited, meanwhile, has become a prominent multinational trading group under the leadership of William Fung. Heung Shu-fai, a veteran journalist, commented that "the decision taken by Victor Fung in 1984 was extremely rare among Chinese families"

---

[12] *Hong Kong Trader* (1978), Vol. 2, p. 7.

and that "Victor's decision made thirteen years ago has proven to be indisputably wise."[13]

Hence, in the hands of the two U.S.-educated youngsters belonging to the third generation of the Fung family, the old family business founded by Fung Pak-liu and Li To-ming in 1906 began to change and landed on the road to modernization. Of course, not every traditional family business in Hong Kong can boast of the same success story. Undoubtedly, those who fail to change would soon fade away.

Planting the Customer-oriented Structure

Soon after Li & Fung's IPO was established, Hong Kong faced the harshest economic difficulties since the war. In February 1973, the third U.S. Dollar crisis exploded, leading eventually to the collapse of the Bretton Woods system. The ramifications of this were far-reaching. The global financial market became highly volatile. Inflation was raging high. Stepping into 1974, the Middle-East oil crisis sparked off the most severe global economic downturn after the war. The U.S., West Germany, and Japan plunged into a state of recession, which was disastrous to world trade. For Hong Kong, its export trade faced increasingly intense competition from Singapore, Korea, and Taiwan in the international market. Li & Fung Limited, therefore, also had to struggle for survival. Detrimentally, because overseas buyers were becoming more experienced and hence harder to please, while more local suppliers were emerging, the profit margin for trading firms was narrowing. The days were counted for trading firms who merely played an intermediary role between overseas buyers and local manufacturers.

In March 1973, the Board of Li & Fung Limited stated in the company's first annual report after going public: "1973 is generally acknowledged as a most difficult year for international trading. Uncertainties and fluctuations in the world monetary situation, widespread inflation and acute shortages of essential raw materials afflicted every sector of the economy and every

---

[13] *Next Magazine*, Hong Kong, September 26, 1997.

traditional overseas trading partner of Hong Kong." Despite all that, the company's financial performance for 1973 was quite good. Its trading volume reached HK$189 million, up 14% from 1972. Total net after-tax profit and special charges was HK$7.266 million, exceeding the forecast of HK$6.75 million in its IPO prospectus and increasing by a hefty 93% from 1972.

However, under the impact of the global recession and the system of textile export quotas imposed by Western governments, Li & Fung's Limited business performance declined significantly in the ensuing years. In 1974, the company's trading volume and after-tax profit dropped to HK$83,719,900 and HK$1,751,700, respectively, down by 56% and 76%, respectively. Trading volume continued to plummet in 1975, falling by 26% to HK$62,175,200, despite a modest rise in after-tax profits. The drastic reduction in trading volume was due mainly to the loss of a major U.S. customer, C&A.

Recalling this incident in an interview in 1979, Victor Fung said, "They've been with us for 12 years. But the problem was they demanded exclusivity. It was taking us all our time, just handling this one big account. It was just too big. I feel very strongly that when a company is big enough to set up its own buying office, they don't need us, unless we are willing to tailor our operation to their specific needs."[14]

Because of that, it was not until 1979 that Li & Limited Fung was able to outdo its 1973 business performance (Exhibit 3.2).

Exhibit 3.2   Li & Fung's business performance (HK$ million), 1973–1979

Year	Revenue	Operating Profit	After-tax Profit
1973	189.0000 (+14%)	8.6505	7.2660
1974	83.7199 (−56%)	1.8067	1.7517 (−76%)
1975	62.1752 (−26%)	2.2092	2.0923 (+19%)
1976	77.1184 (+24%)	4.7313	4.0388 (+93%)
1977	86.4000 (+12%)	4.4080	3.5900 (−11%)
1978	178.5189 (+107%)	8.2983	6.8772 (+92%)
1979	252.5555 (+41%)	11.0232	9.2148 (+34%)

Note: Figures in brackets represent percentages of change year-on-year.
Source: Li & Fung Limited Annual Reports, 1973–1979.

---

[14] *Hong Kong Trader* (1979), Vol. 5.

In its early years as a listed company, Li & Fung's scale of operation was still quite limited. According to people like Danny Lau Sai-wing (currently an executive director of Li & Fung Limited) and Lam Chuen-lai (currently a director of Li & Fung (Trading) Limited), the company was then headquartered at Fung House at Connaught Road Central with a staff of about 200 and was engaged mainly in the merchandizing business. Within the company, there were a number of product groups classified by market and product, including two textile-apparel groups in charge of sales to the U.S. and Europe, respectively. There was also a sundry-goods group handling mainly the export sales of non-apparel items such as toys. Apart from these, the company was also involved in other non-trading businesses, including finance, real estate, shipping, etc.

Owing to the C&A incident, Li & Fung Limited realized the risk of relying too heavily on individual large customers and continuing to be an intermediary. In an interview in 1979, Victor Fung said, "I could see that we need to develop the U.S. market—and quickly. We approached the problem very methodically, almost with a do-or-die attitude. Our strategy was to narrow down the market segment we wanted, to go after the top people, the right people, even if it meant giving up people if they weren't the type of better ready-to-wear that we wanted. That was probably the hardest time for me, the first one or two years. I was making one or two trips to the U.S. a year."

"The thing was," he continued, "we were offering business relationship—an entirely new concept. That was our strategy. In the past, Li & Fung had always acted as a buying office, functioning as the Chinese middleman. In the old days this was necessary; but not any more. I could see that buyers wanted a little more than mere interpreters. They were after production management and that was what we were offering.

He also added, "To me, the answer is specialization. The people that we have in our group cannot be just general traders, they must be product specialists and that is really the direction we have turned our organization in the last five years. Within our garments or sundries divisions, we have them broken down into different product groups which are again segregated into more specialized categories."[15]

---

[15] *Hong Kong Trader* (1979), Vol. 5, p. 7.

Victor was even more explicit a little earlier. He said, "It is a well-known fact that trading as a business has been under pressure for a number of years. While the trading company's former function as a mere broker between two interested parties has not gone, it is on the decline because over the past 10–20 years, the market had become increasingly perfect. The larger manufacturing concerns are now doing more direct exporting and the overseas customers have become more adapted to the ways of the 'mystic' Orient through constant visits to this part of the world. That being the case, I feel there is now a need to reexamine the fundamental role the export industry can play."[16]

Back in the old days, Li & Fung Limited's internal organizational structure was already centered on its major customers. This approach became all the more dominant in the late 1970s when Victor and William reaffirmed the customer-oriented approach as a corporate policy. Under this approach, the company was to match customers' needs by offering comprehensive high-quality service and to delivering its best. To achieve this goal, the company set up various product groups by centering on its major customers. Each product group was to serve specific customers by offering comprehensive consulting service, identifying suitable suppliers, and becoming a consultant for these customers through the provision of market information and the introduction of new production models and new product lines, etc. It was to go so far as to offer new product concepts, implement product quality control, and provide financial support. As described by Victor, Li & Fung Limited was entering a period when it began "to involve itself in both the front and back ends of the whole production process." At the front end, Li & Fung Limited was "marketing, designing, and managing" whereas at the back end it was "inspecting, packaging, and transporting."

In 1977, Li & Fung Limited partnered Leslie Fay, one of the largest ladies' apparel groups in the U.S. by forming a 50/50 joint venture—Leslie Fay International Limited—as the U.S. company's merchandizing office in Southeast Asia for coordinating all matters regarding the sourcing of apparel in the Far East. This joint venture was essentially one of Li & Fung Limited's specific

---

[16] *Hong Kong Trader* (1979), Vol. 5, p. 7.

product sales groups. With an annual turnover in the region of US$200 million, Leslie Fay was the second- or third-largest ladies' apparel retailer in the U.S. "Leslie Fay already enjoyed a long presence in Hong Kong," said William Fung, "and had their own merchandizing department. However, their management team kept changing and those in charge of the overseas desk were all gone. Leslie Fay's headquarters in New York felt that its relationship with manufacturers in Hong Kong was not close enough. The company therefore, found it advisable to enter into partnership with Li & Fung Limited so that we could identify and manage Chinese manufacturers for them and allow them to focus on merchandizing."

During this period, Li & Fung Limited made a number of major breakthroughs in the U.S. and European markets. Several leading chain stores from the U.S., including Gap Stores Incorporated and Lewis Galoob, became its key customers. In 1978, with a view to strengthening its service to Gap, Li & Fung Limited set up a wholly-owned subsidiary, Lifung Gap Stores Limited, as Gap's sole merchandizing office in Southeast Asia. In 1979 and 1981, Li & Fung partnered with Peek & Cloppenburg, a Dutch apparel chain, and Combined English Stores of England, to set up Hillung Enterprises Limited and Lifung CES Limited, respectively. The former was 30%-owned by Li & Fung Limited whereas the latter 50%. Not only were these two joint ventures formed to become the sole merchandizing offices of the two European importers, but these joint ventures were essentially Li & Fung's product sales groups that served to generate considerable turnover and profits.

After the establishment of Lifung Gap Stores Limited, Li & Fung Limited embarked on open recruitment for staff. Lam Chuen-lai and Danny Lau Saiwing were among those who joined the company during this period. Large customers like Gap Stores Limited depended very much on Li & Fung's agency service because technology back then was not as advanced as today's. In accordance with the specifications sent in by Gap, Lifung Gap Stores would provide various agency services, ranging from the selection of fabrics and manufacturers, price negotiation, order placement, product inspection, and management. Taken together, all these services essentially constituted an embryonic form of "supply chain management." As a manager of Lifung Gap Stores back then, Danny Lau considered this company to be the first of its kind to offer comprehensive agency services to a single customer through a devoted team. This model was an innovative approach that was infinitely important for Li & Fung's future development.

The year 1979 marked the inception of China's economic reforms and open-door policy to foreign investors. In those days, many foreigners still harbored reservations about doing business with China. As a reputable U.S. chain-store group, Gap was among the first companies to source products from China. In Lam Chuen-lai's recollection, Li & Fung went with Gap to Shanghai in 1980 to purchase fabrics from Shanghai Textile Import/Export Company. The prices quoted by this Shanghai supplier were low and the fabrics were of reasonable quality. However, China obviously still had to catch up with international trade practices. The buyer had to provide the chassis to the supplier; otherwise, the products might vary with that of the former. This would never happen with Hong Kong suppliers. Notwithstanding their numerous difficulties, Li & Fung and Gap succeeded in breaking into the China market.

By the early 1980s, Li & Fung's reputation and customer base were growing steadily in China. Some new customers were introduced by Gap whereas many others, including those from Europe and the U.S., came of their own accord after hearing about Li & Fung. Besides Gap, the company's clientele now included names like The Limited, Express, Lerner, and Petrie stores. Hong Kong's major markets, particularly the U.S., were then experiencing a slowdown and the rise of trade protectionism in world trade caused many countries to turn their back on the GATT (General Agreement on Tariffs and Trade). As a result, Hong Kong's export trade was shrinking. Notwithstanding the unfavorable circumstances, Li & Fung was able to sustain growth— registering conspicuously outstanding business results due to its solid experience and track record.

Li & Fung recorded a total turnover of HK$449 million in 1981, up by 58% from 1980. If the results of the joint-stock companies under its control were included, it could reach HK$520 million. The company was emerging as the leader of Hong Kong's export sector. In the same year, Li & Fung's after-tax profit and minority shareholders' rights was HK$14,431,100, representing a growth of 25% year-on-year. In 1982, the company set a new turnover record of HK$544 million, up by 21% from the previous year. Should the results of the joint-stock companies under its control be taken into account as well, it would have amounted to HK$706 million.

The mid-1980s was a period when Gap's business in Hong Kong underwent fast expansion. The staff force of Lifung Gap Stores grew to fifty-sixty. Gap also purchased 20% of Lifung Gap Stores' shares. Under the agreement between the two parties to this joint venture, Gap had the option to purchase from Li & Fung the remaining 80% so that it could assume full control of its vast merchandizing business in Hong Kong. Realizing Gap's increasing intention to go its own way, Li & Fung recalled Danny Lau in 1985 to set up another sourcing group to cater specifically to a new U.S. client—The Limited Incorporated—another major retail chain group. Danny remembered that the new sourcing group under him had continued to adopt the model of Lifung Gap Stores in serving The Limited, by providing comprehensive agency services, thus helping this retail chain to develop and grow.

Li & Fung's major export product lines were textiles and apparel. To a certain extent, related products such as fashion accessories were also included. In 1982, Li & Fung formed a joint venture with a leading jewelry retail chain in England. The joint venture was later acquired by Li & Fung. It was engaged in the distribution of fashion accessories, including handbags, leather shoes, trendy wristwatches, scarves, and leather belts. The latest products that came under this sourcing group were all high-priced branded items that were popular among major U.S. customers. The group was headquartered in Hong Kong with branches in Southeast Asia, including Korea, Taiwan, and Thailand. The market information network thus established was highly valuable for Li & Fung, which was becoming an integrated supplier for customers.

The subsidiary products handled by Li & Fung's trading business were non-apparel items, mostly toys. Its major customer was Lewis Galoob, a U.S. toy distributor. In 1978, Li & Fung formed a 50/50 joint venture with Galoob called Galoob International Toys Limited that acted as a merchandizing office in Southeast Asia. The toy items distributed by this joint venture included GI Joe, Micro Machine, Ninja Turtle, Cabbage Patch dolls, Star Wars, Spacemen, E.T., Baby Talk (a talking doll), and Disney cartoon characters, which were highly popular among American and European consumers. Having built up cooperative relationship with Galoob, Li & Fung went further by offering it financial assistance, including funds for two of its R&D projects. In 1981, through a US$500,000 investment, Li & Fung became one of Galoob's shareholders. Galoob was the first overseas company that Li & Fung invested in. In 1986, Galoob was successfully listed on the New York Stock Exchange. The relationship between Li & Fung and Galoob was maintained until 1988. In 1989, after its successful privatization, Li & Fung sold all its Galoob shares, thus deriving a profit of US$14 million (approximately HK$10.9 billion) from this investment.

Toward the end of the 1980s, Li & Fung established a wholly-owned subsidiary, Toy Island, for the distribution of toys. Toys had always been the company's largest hard goods item insofar as export trading is concerned and this situation lasted for 50 years. Following the model for textile and apparel products, Li & Fung became involved in all the aspects of the supply chain for toys, ranging from being the merchandizing agent for overseas toy companies, supervising and assisting Hong Kong and offshore manufacturers, devising R&D, packaging and design plans, and through its joint venture, Toys 'R' Us, embarked on the retail business. The person in charge of this department then was Chan Kut-lap (alias Chan Chun-lam), now a director of Li & Fung (Trading) Limited.

During the same period, the products distributed by Li & Fung expanded from handicrafts to textiles, apparel, fashion accessories, toys, electronic products and metal wares, of which the most important category was U.S.-bound apparel products. At one point, the company's trading business was heavily concentrated on a few major customers, especially those large retail chains or department stores. Li & Fung also had to pay the price for this hugely successful business structure it created. After some years of cooperation with Li & Fung and business growth, many of the large American and European customers would set up their own merchandizing office in Hong Kong to cut cost. Naturally Li & Fung suffered from such initiatives, thus becoming a victim of its own success, but its former customers benefited from its success formula.

In May 1987, Gap, Li & Fung's largest apparel client, decided to exercise its option prescribed in the joint venture agreement by acquiring the remaining 80% of Lifung Gap Stores Limited's shares, thus gaining full control of the joint venture. Although Li & Fung continued to be the merchandizing agent of Gap's branches in Taiwan and Singapore, its trading business in Hong Kong was dealt a serious blow. Turnover dropped sharply from HK$2.194 billion in 1986 to HK$1.453 billion in 1987, shrinking by 34% (Exhibit 3.3). Fortunately, the company's consolidated after-tax profit and minority shareholders' rights fell only slightly—from HK$40.94 million in 1986 to HK$40.01 million in 1987.

Exhibit 3.3 Li & Fung's business performance in the 1980s (HK$ million)

Year	Revenue	Operating Profit	After-tax Profit
1980	283.408 (+12%)	13.872 (+31%)	11.521 (+25%)
1981	449.321 (+59%)	16.960 (+22%)	14.431 (+25%)
1982	544.061 (+21%)	12.234 (–28%)	10.522 (–27%)
1983	774.777 (+42%)	26.554 (+110%)	21.137 (+101%)
1984	1,151.812 (+49%)	39.208 (+48%)	33.200 (+57%)
1985	1,314.454 (+14%)	31.045 (–21%)	30.799 (–7%)
1986	2,194.036 (+67%)	57.740 (+86%)	63.846 (+208%)
1987	1,453.088 (–34%)	44.342 (–23%)	45.029 (–29%)

Note: Figures in brackets represent percentages of change year-on-year.
Source: Li & Fung Limited Annual Reports, 1980–1987.

In 1987, Li & Fung's export trade business entered a period of consolidation after years of phenomenal growth. It was the year of the October global stock market crash. The uncertainty looming over the U.S. retail market and the major change in fashion trends then taking place had significantly curtailed buyers' desire to stock up. Moreover, orders for Li & Fung were sluggish. In view of these circumstances, Li & Fung adopted a more pragmatic strategy by strengthening its contacts with more importers while devaluing or provisioning for some of its investments and loans.

"Little Jardine"—Going International and Diversified

In the first one hundred years since its opening as a port, Hong Kong has always been positioned as an entrepôt for the Chinese market. Foreign companies in Hong Kong engaged in reexport trade—commonly known to the locals as "hongs"—were in control of a large portion of China's external trade and enjoyed a privileged status mainly by virtue of their connections in the West, their branch networks throughout the China, and the support of Chinese compradors.

The outbreak of the Korean War which entailed the U.N.'s trade embargo against China in the mid-1950s had caused Hong Kong's entrepôt trade to shrivel all of a sudden and, thus, for the first time, the hongs found their position no longer secure. Hong Kong's manufacturing industry was still at its nascent stage. Without adequate capital and lacking the knowledge

In 1995, Li & Fung rebuilt three properties into a 12-story office block, named Fung House, located at 18–20 Connaught Road Central.

Fung Mo-ying's sons, Kwok-hong (top left) and Kwok-chor (top right), and Li-Fung Lai-wah's son, Li Wing-hong (bottom), joined Li & Fung as the third-generation management between the late 1960s and early 1970s.

Mr. and Mrs. Fung Hon-chu with sons, Victor (back right) and William (back left).

Victor (second from left) and William (second from right) at Li & Fung Limited's relisting ceremony at the Stock Exchange of Hong Kong in 1992.

Workers assembling toys at Toy Island, Li & Fung's full subsidiary, set up in the late 1980s.

A corner at Li & Fung's showroom for fashion accessories.

A garments factory operated by Li & Fung (then one of Hong Kong's leading garment exporters) in the 1960s.

of and connections with the international market, Chinese entrepreneurs had to rely on the hongs for receiving orders, purchasing raw materials, and reselling their products to overseas markets. For that reason, the hongs were still able to maintain their status as a whole. However, by the 1970s, Hong Kong industrialists had built up their own strengths. They now had their own export departments to deal directly with overseas buyers and did not rely any more on the service of intermediaries who charged them a fee. Against that backdrop, the position of the hongs took a nose-dive.

P.G. Williams, who had been both chairman of the Inchcape Group and deputy chairman of Hong Kong & Shanghai Bank since the late 1970s, felt deeply about the changes faced by the hongs in the development of the Hong Kong economy. Asked by a reporter in an interview in November 1978 what he considered to be the biggest change Hong Kong had undergone since the war, he gave the following answer:

"I was deeply impressed by how the trading firms' status had changed with the development of the Hong Kong economy, which had always been in a state of flux. When I first arrived in Hong Kong, there were various kinds of trading firms. They were mostly doing reexport trade with China, which is their major market. They would ship to China goods coming from Europe and America, and then reexport Chinese raw materials to the West. Their status was extremely high. Such firms were actually in control of a large part of China's foreign trade. However, things took an about-turn in 1949 when the Communist Party took over China, triggering the U.S. embargo, soon followed by the Korean War that led to the U.N. embargo. As a result, Hong Kong's reexport trade collapsed, forcing many trading firms to close.

Fortunately the manufacturing industry began to grow in Hong Kong with a promising future. The trading firms redirected their attention from the traditional reexport business to import and export. Because there was fierce competition, many firms that failed to cope with the new circumstances were weeded out. Those that remained merged with each other to form a few large firms. To build up their own strength and size, they began to diversify into other businesses such as manufacturing, eventually becoming some of the largest enterprises in Hong Kong today. In this process, naturally some old firms became extinct while new ones sprang up. But those that could withstand the challenges and remain were extremely rare, which is a pity."[17]

Many of the century-old hongs and large companies that could not cope with the new situation became victims of mergers and acquisitions. They include the famous Gibb & Livingston, Gilman, Dodwell, Lane Crawford, Watson's, and Whampoa Dockyards. Amidst the intense competition, a few leading British hongs were able to outshine the rest. With their unique political and economic advantages, they gradually turned into conglomerates that controlled the economic lifeblood of Hong Kong. Among them, the best known were the so-called "Big Four," namely, Jardine Matheson, Hutchison Whampoa, Swire, and Wheelock Marden.

Among the Big Four, Jardine Matheson was considered the most powerful. An article in the U.S.'s *Fortune* magazine once wrote that Hong Kong was ruled by the Jockey Club, Jardine Matheson, Hong Kong & Shanghai Banking Corporation, and the Governor—in that order. Jardine's ranking spoke volumes about its strengths. At any rate, in the 1960s and 1970s, Jardine was increasingly wary that Hong Kong as a borrowed place in borrowed time could end up returning to China. It was, therefore, actively pursuing a strategy of diversification and internationalization, spending billions in acquiring overseas assets, including Reunion Properties in Britain, H. Davies Ltd. in the U.S., Rennies Consolidated Holdings in South Africa, and TTI in the Middle East. Its business portfolio now covered wholesale and retail, warehousing, air transport, as well as finance and insurance. Other British hongs were also adopting very much the same strategy. In 1977, Hutchison and Whampoa Dockyard merged into one company, Hutchison Whampoa, whose business ranged from import/export trade to wholesale and retail, business services, container transport, dockyards, warehousing, transport, real estate, mining, construction, and investment. The Swire Group became a diversified conglomerate by expanding its business scope from mainly trading and shipping to air transport, real estate and other areas. For Wheelock Marden, its business interests expanded to cover trading, department stores, shipping, and property development.

---

[17] *Hong Kong Economic Journal Monthly*, Issue 8, Vol. 2, pp. 52–53.

Internationalization and diversification were keenly pursued by Hong Kong enterprises in those days. As a Chinese hong, Li & Fung was no exception. Back in the late 1960s, to cope with the development of its export business, Li & Fung's sourcing network had already been extended from Hong Kong to other parts of Southeast Asia, Taiwan being its first destination. Li & Fung (Taiwan) Limited was set up in 1969. Its head office in Taipei, Lifung Tower, was the product of Li & Fung's collaboration with a Taiwanese construction company that offered it advice on sourcing in Taiwan. According to Fung Hon-chu, Li & Fung was attracted to Taiwan by its low-cost labor. Soon after this development, Li & Fung (Singapore) Limited, Li & Fung (Macau) Limited, and Li & Fung (Malaysia) Limited were set up in the early 1970s, forming a regional sourcing and distribution network. Li & Fung (Taiwan) commenced business with only five employees, but by 1999, its staff size had reached 300. In 1998, it generated a revenue of US$300 million (approximately HK$2.34 billion), which constituted 15% of Li & Fung Limited's total revenue of US$2 billion for the same year and made it one of Taiwan's best-performing export firms.

Recounting Li & Fung's development in the Asian region, William Fung said, "Costs in Hong Kong were already too high for us to stay here. To maintain our competitive edge, we had to move elsewhere—first, to Taiwan; and when Taiwan was losing out to Korea, we landed in Korea. When it was no longer viable in Korea, we headed for Thailand and Indonesia. Hong Kong has, therefore, become our regional headquarters with branches in Taiwan, Korea, and the rest of Southeast Asia." To him, it was like engaging in guerilla warfare but it was crucial as a means to adapt to external circumstances.

Li & Fung was actively seeking diversification to support the development of its core sourcing business. As early as the 1950s, it had already begun investing in the manufacture of plastic products, rattan wares, wood wares, etc. In the 1960s, it opened a plastic-flower factory—Wai Dai Industries Limited, and other factories making rattan furniture and wood wares. In 1968, a large modern factory, President Firecrackers & Fireworks Company Limited, was set up in Taiwan. In 1977, Li & Fung entered into a joint venture with the world's largest trademark system manufacturer in the U.S. to set up Soabar Systems (Hong Kong) Limited, which opened a factory in Hong Kong for supplying trademarks and trademark printing systems to the Asian textile industry.

Hong Kong entered a property boom in the 1970s. Many trading firms and manufacturing companies were into property development and investment as well. When Li & Fung went public in 1973, its rental income derived from its investment properties amounted to HK$1,735,800. These properties included Fung House at 18–20 Connaught Road Central, apartments at 11 Magazine Gap Road, a warehouse at 15–19 Lam Tin Street, Kwai Chung, and a building in Taipei, with a gross area of 82,800 square feet. The net rental income of Fung House was HK$1.53 million per year.

On becoming a publicly listed company, Li & Fung set up a wholly-owned subsidiary, Li & Fung (Properties) Limited, devoted to property development and investment. In 1979, Li & Fung partnered Li Ka-shing's Cheung Kong (Holdings) Limited in forming a joint company to redevelop Fung House in Connaught Road Central. During the redevelopment, Li & Fung purchased two units in Worldwide House, Des Voeux Road Central, for its provisional headquarters. The other departments of the company were housed in a leased building in Tsim Sha Tsui on the other side of the Victoria Harbor. In 1983, the new twenty-two-story Fung House was completed. The top three floors of the building were reserved for the company's headquarters whereas the other floors were sold. Basically, property investment constituted only a very small part of Li & Fung's business. In 1987, the profit derived from property investment was HK$3,453,000, representing just 6% of the company's total profits.

Meanwhile, investment in shipping was another major development for the company. In 1973, through its subsidiary, Li & Fung (Finance and Investment) Limited, it bought a secondhand freighter, "Kwong Fung," by borrowing US$1.8 million from a bank. The profit generated by this ship in the first year was HK$400,000. In 1978, another freighter, "Man Fung," was bought. In view of the sluggishness of the world's shipping business, the company adjusted its strategy by only chartering out the two ships. To expand its market for shipping lines, Li & Fung also invested in Sea Horse Shipcharterers Limited, the main business of which was in chartering and in shipping lines. By the early 1980s, anticipating the downturn of the global shipping industry, the company sold the two old oil-inefficient freighters just before oil prices inflated fourfold and shipping prices declined sharply, hence avoiding the risk of incurring huge losses. Two years later, through a joint venture in Singapore, Li & Fung bought a ship for servicing deep-sea oil-drilling projects, thus resuming its investment in shipping. In 1982, Li & Fung entered into cargo consolidation and forwarding by acquiring Minko Consolidators Limited.

In the meantime, Li & Fung expanded its business scope to areas like finance and insurance. In 1977, it bonded with Hong Nin Bank and a trade-financing company in Thailand to set up Lihong Finance Limited that offered financing services chiefly to small and medium-sized manufacturers. In 1982, Li & Fung partnered Groups des Mutuelles Du Mans of France in setting up a 50/50 joint venture, Norman (Hong Kong) Insurance Co. Ltd.

By the late 1980s, Li & Fung Limited was already a diversified enterprise engaged in a wide range of businesses encompassing import/export trade, real estate, warehousing, shipping, finance, insurance, and investment, and was thus known as "Little Jardine" as well.

Chapter 4

Going Into Retail—Circle K, Toys "R" Us

"We are basically a novice when it comes to retailing. We enter into this business for no other reason than to keep up with the times. Being Chinese, our roots are planted here. Frankly it is difficult for exporters like us, as intermediaries, to survive in any other ways. The making of garments, for example, is already well taken care of by garment manufacturers. In comparison, retailing seems to offer us a better chance of surviving."

—Fung Hon-chu

Circle K—Setting Foot in the Convenience Store Market

The Fung brothers, Victor and William, were of the view that Li & Fung's export business should be followed closely by retail development. They thought that with the maturity of an economy, its exports would gradually lose competitiveness. Such an economy should, therefore, turn its focus inward by developing its retail sector. In 1973, Li & Fung Retailing Group was set up through Li & Fung (1937) Limited—Li & Fung's holding company—with a view to developing retail in Hong Kong and the Asian region. In the mid-1980s, the company was convinced that the time was ripe. By cooperating with several multinationals through Li & Fung Retail Group, Li & Fung proceeded to enter Hong Kong's retail sector. Its first project was the Circle K Convenience store chain.

By the 1980s, Hong Kong's manufacturing sector was faced with intense competition from overseas, particularly new industrialized economies in the neighboring Asian region, and was aggravated by rising labor cost. The opening of the Pearl River Delta in southern China to foreign investors since the late 1970s attracted a large number of manufacturers to relocate their labor-intensive production lines northward. Hong Kong was gradually being transformed from an externally-oriented export economy into a service economy, playing multiple roles as a servicing center for the industrial sector in southern China, an entrepôt (again) for reexport trade, and a financial services center in the Asia Pacific region, respectively and concurrently. From the middle to the end of the 1980s, the Hong Kong economy experienced double-digit growth. As inflation mounted, labor income continued to rise. The local retail market was fast becoming a new territory where fierce competition was rife.

The Japanese department stores were the first to explore this territory—retail market. In the mid-1980s, Hong Kong's retail sector attracted a large number of Japanese investors who not only opened large department stores in the key commercial districts like Causeway Bay and Tsim Sha Tsui but also extended their reach to residential districts like Shatin, Tuen Mun, and Quarry Bay. By the early 1990s, nine different Japanese department stores had opened a total of fifteen shops in Hong Kong. Although in terms of numbers, the Japanese stores made up only a small minority among the 200 or so sizable department stores in Hong Kong, their strength and experience, as well as more advanced marketing strategy and scientific management posed

A Circle K Convenience store in Tseung Kwan O, Hong Kong.

Retailing in Hong Kong in the mid 1980s.

Ready-to-eat food and beverages, and freshly baked breads sold in Circle K.

The Babies "R" Us zone at a Toys "R" Us store.

Toys "R" Us was the pioneer of the U.S.-style "warehouse store" in Hong Kong.

a major challenge to their local counterparts. In 1989, the revenue recorded by all the Japanese department stores in Hong Kong accounted for 40% of the total industry.

Concurrent with the Japanese endeavor, two leading supermarket chains—Wellcome and PARKnSHOP—were actively expanding their branch networks in Hong Kong. Statistics show that from 1982 to 1992, Wellcome's branches expanded from sixty-two to 185, whereas PARKnSHOP's branches also increased from forty-three to 160. The two supermarket giants were always engaged in price wars throughout the years. At one point, the retail price was 10–20% lower than the wholesale price and 20–30% lower than the original retail price. In other words, they were cheaper than those in the traditional grocery stores and other retail outlets by 30–40%.[1] This kind of cut-throat price wars shocked the suppliers, including distribution agents, wholesalers, manufacturers, and importers. Although competition was only between the two supermarket chains, in reality, the smaller supermarkets and grocery stores were the ones being driven out of the market. A large number of independent supermarkets and retail outlets simply could not withstand the competitive pressure and closed down one after another.

During this time, a new force—the 24-hour convenience store—emerged in the local retail market. Performing the roles of the mini-store, dispensary, fast-food restaurant and supermarket while opening round-the-clock, it is a highly convenient retail outlet for consumers because it caters to the needs of people from all walks of life. As a result, it enjoyed considerable market following. In 1981, Jardine Matheson first introduced to the Hong Kong market the 7-Eleven shops, which quickly took root and grew at an unimaginable speed. The number of 7-Eleven shops reached forty-seven in 1982 and shot up by a staggering 563% in ten years to 285 by 1992, accounting for about 70% of the total number of convenience stores in Hong Kong (Exhibit 4.1).

The success experienced in the 7-Eleven shops inspired the Fung brothers. Victor was already toying with the idea of going into retail in the early 1980s. Back then Li & Fung planned to cooperate with UNY Co Ltd, a Japanese department store, to open shop in Hong Kong and also enter the Japan market.

---

[1] Economic Information & Agency (1986), pp. 148–149.

Exhibit 4.1   Growth in the numbers of supermarkets and convenience stores in Hong Kong in the 1980s

Year	PARKnSHOP	Wellcome	7-Eleven
1981	34	50	8
1982	43	61	43
1983	78	75	62
1984	91	86	79
1985	107	95	145
1986	136	124	183
1988*	129	135	221
1992	160	185	285

* As at April 1988.

Source: *Hong Kong Economy Yearbook*, various issues.

For that purpose, Victor had asked Lau Butt-farn, who joined Li & Fung in 1980, to conduct market research to identify a suitable location in Hong Kong for a new department store. Unfortunately, the Hong Kong economy reacted negatively to British's prime minister Margaret Thatcher's visit to Beijing in 1982, and Li & Fung shelved its plan. Eventually, after twenty-two rounds of difficult negotiations, the Sino-British Joint Declaration regarding the future of Hong Kong was successfully concluded, and Hong Kong entered a phase of transition. In 1987, UNY Co Ltd opened a store in Taikoo Shing.

A few months after UNY Co Ltd had decided to shelve its plan to cooperate with Li & Fung, a manager from UNY Co Ltd indicated to Lau Butt-farn that UNY Co Ltd was interested in partnering Li & Fung to develop the Circle K Convenience store business. UNY Co Ltd was a large retail group in Japan. In addition to operating department stores and supermarkets, it also ran the Circle K Convenience store business under a joint venture with the U.S. firm, Conoco Phillips. "The Circle K business is very successful in Japan," said a Japanese manager, "it is certainly worth a try in Hong Kong too." After reporting to Victor, Lau was authorized to negotiate on behalf of Li & Fung. A tripartite agreement for cooperation was reached with Conoco Phillips and UNY Co Ltd after two to three months' negotiation.

The Circle K brand name was originally owned by Conoco Phillips, one of the largest oil-refineries and petrochemical groups, as well as convenience store chains in the U.S. with a presence in over forty countries worldwide. At one point, it was among the top 300 in the Fortune 500 list. Circle K

Corporation, one of its subsidiaries, was the second-largest convenience store chain in both the U.S. and the world, next only to 7-Elelven. It had 6,300 shops all over the world, of which 2,400 were located in twenty-three states in the U.S. Under a franchising arrangement with UNY Co Ltd, there were around 170 Circle K shops in Japan. In January 1985, in cooperation with Circle K Corporation and UNY Co Ltd, Li & Fung opened its first Circle K shop, known to the locals as "OK Convenience Store." Initially, Li & Fung's shareholding was 50%. Hong Kong's convenience-store market was basically dominated by 7-Eleven under the Jardine Matheson Group. 7-Eleven operated as a franchise, whereas Circle K was centrally managed by the new joint venture.

"In the past, our main business in Hong Kong and China was the export of apparels, toys, and other consumer goods," Victor said, "but we believe it is only natural that we take part in developing the Circle K store chain so that we can grow our retail business as a whole. We also strongly believe that there is great demand for such kind of retail outlets in Hong Kong." Victor also felt that the joint venture was ideal for the three parties who were all striving toward the goal of consolidating their business and penetrating international market at the same time. In a grand ceremony officiated by Victor together with the representatives of Circle K Corporation and UNY Co Ltd in 1985, the first OK shop in Hong Kong was opened at Fenwick Street. Circle K Corporation had high expectations for its joint venture with Li & Fung in Hong Kong. Its representative, William Remmers, the senior vice president of Circle K Corporation and chairman of Circle K International announced that with the 1997 handover smoothly resolved, the Hong Kong economy was expected to rebound. He was, therefore, very confident about the prospects for the development of the Circle K joint venture in Asia.

Regarding Circle K's entry, Michael Radmore, the managing director of the 7-Eleven Group, said, "We have encountered no direct competition since we commenced operation four years ago." There were ninety-five 7-Eleven shops in Hong Kong, 80% of which were profitable. Expressing surprise that Circle K came in so late, Radmore thought that the local market should be big enough to accommodate two convenience store chains. He also felt that the entry of Circle K would by no means affect the 7-Eleven Group's original plan to open 500 shops in Hong Kong in the coming seven to eight years.

In the U.S., convenience stores are run in conjunction with petrol stations but this is obviously not feasible in Hong Kong where people like doing their shopping near where they live or work. Particularly in the rainy summer months, housewives prefered to shop in the neighborhoods. With these considerations, convenience stores are ideally located either in densely populated residential areas or in the business centers, particularly the former, or, better still, near schools. Because Wellcome, PARKnSHOP, and 7-Eleven had already entered the densely populated areas, the biggest problem for Circle K was to find suitable shop space; even if it could be found, fierce competition was unavoidable.

Confronted with such a competitive environment, Circle K's focus from the onset was the housing estates in the new towns. Lau Butt-farn became the managing director of the Circle K business by the time the fourth OK shop was opened. He recalled: "Victor has demonstrated his vision by asking me to concentrate on housing estates in the new towns." Lau spared no effort in tendering for shop space in the housing estates, including the eleventh shop in Tin Ma Court, Wong Tai Sin, and the twelfth shop in Sui Wo Court, Shatin. The development of the satellite towns, including Shatin, Tuen Mun, and Cheung Kwan O, was taking off. Circle K focused almost exclusively on these new districts and succeeded in attaining its targets within two to three years. According to Lau's analysis, the success was due to the fact the Hong Kong economy was booming and the new housing estates had to be located away from the urban center, thus making it inconvenient for shopping. Moreover, as supermarkets and convenience stores in those locations were few, competition was not severe for Circle K.

However, the problem with doing business in such locations was that hooligans would often linger in the shop, threatening the staff and scaring away customers. And thefts were common. Lau recalled that he once received a phone call late at night from an employee who had to quit because there were troublemakers in the shop. Lau had no choice but to arrive at the shop immediately and man it with the assistance of the shop manager from eleven o'clock at night till the next morning.

One of the convenience store's important strategies was to supply daily necessities that are in line with the preferences of old customers and local residents. Similar to the 7-Eleven shops, the range of products sold at OK stores covered no less than 3,000 items, including snacks that appealed to students and youngsters, bread, ice-cream, milk, hot beverages, cigarettes, health and beauty aids, proprietary medicines, newspapers, magazines, videos, and groceries. To attract more customers, Circle K started an in-store bakery in the early 1990s that offered a variety of freshly baked breads, pastries, and cakes.

The OK store operates three shifts with two employees in each shift, including the store manager. That means each store requires at least six employees to run round-the-clock. Given Hong Kong's full-employment situation in the late 1980s and early 1990s, labor was in short supply. Like other sectors, convenience stores also found it very difficult to recruit and retain employees, who could be no older than sixteen or seventeen with only primary school education and spoke a little English. To make it convenient to both its staff and customers, Circle K began to sell more products containing Chinese instructions. "The main difficulty is not so much the product as its English brand name and instructions," Lau Butt-farn explained. "As English facilitates the input of data in the computer, we will continue to use it with little chance of shifting to Chinese. But the stores must keep a list of products in Chinese."

Toward the end of 1980s, afflicted by the economic downturn, the Nagoya Railway Company decided to sell its convenience-store business in Hong Kong. Li & Fung bought all the ten or so shops and received HK$1 million from the seller as compensation. By the early 1990s, Circle K was running roughly 100-odd stores in Hong Kong. It then extended its business to Taiwan by forming a joint venture with Lai Lai Department Store. In 1991, Li & Fung acquired the Fotomax chain and appointed Lau Butt-farn to take charge of this new business. A former general manager of PARKnSHOP was also recruited to manage Circle K.

It was worth noting that by the late 1980s, Li & Fung's two foreign partners in the Circle K business were in financial difficulties. The U.S. Circle K Corporation was in financial trouble after acquiring some 1,000 stores from 7-Eleven and overexpanding in the U.K. On the other hand, UNY's department store in Taikoo Shing had all along been operating at a loss. These two big shareholders therefore withdrew their support for Circle K in Hong Kong. Li & Fung increased its shareholding annually and by 1997, it became the sole owner.

Understandably, Circle K had always faced strong competition from 7-Eleven. Owing to sluggish local consumption after the mid-1990s, Circle K suffered some losses after some fast growth initially; from 1985 to 1998, it incurred a total loss of HK$1.7 billion. Analysis revealed that a number of negative factors were at work. First, it lacked economies of scale because it had too few stores. Second, the cost of operation was high due to inflation and the rise in rent and staff costs. There was also fierce competition in the market. On top of these factors, high staff turnover was also a concern. Many of the new recruits would leave even before the completion of training.

Although Li & Fung intended to go public with its Circle K business in the early 1990s, it was forced to delay this plan due to the bearish stock market in Hong Kong. In 1997, there were again rumors that Circle K would go public, but this was denied. Interviewed by Bloomberg, William Fung said that because 1997 was the worst year for retail, Circle K's public listing would have to wait for five years.

Toys "R" Us—Pioneer of the Hypermarket Model in Hong Kong

The other major move taken by Li & Fung to enter the local retail market was the setting up of a 50/50 joint venture in 1986 with the world's leading toy supermarket chain, Toys "R" Us, Inc. from the U.S., to open large-scale toy supermarkets in Hong Kong. The overseas franchise of Toys "R" Us was extended only to Hong Kong and Taiwan.

Toys "R" Us, Inc. was founded by Charles Lazarus in 1957, that is, at the peak of the postwar baby boom. The huge demand for toys as parents were keen to buy toys for their kids inspired Lazarus to go into the toy-shop business. Lazarus' first toy shop was opened in 1957 under the name of Toys "R" Us, which combined "Toys" with the last three letters of "Lazarus." The trademark has a backward "R," the way many children in the West write when they first start learning to write the alphabet "R." By featuring the inverted "R" in his trademark, Lazarus meant to show the lively and mischievous side of kids.

When Toys "R" Us was first established, discount sale was still uncommon in the U.S. Because Toys "R" Us was run in the form of a self-served supermarket offering the widest selection of toy products at the lowest prices, it became a household name in no time. With the help of its "bargain-of-the-day" strategy and high-quality image, it redefined the market position of toys. In the past, customers would only buy toys for kids as gifts during festive seasons like Christmas. The high-quality yet low-priced toys offered by Toys "R" Us encouraged customers to spend and see toys in a different light. Toys "R" Us, Inc. operates on a unique philosophy. Charles Lazarus believed that the self-served and cash-and-carry model found in supermarkets not only lowered the price but also appealed to customers. Owing to its speedy growth, the share price of Toys "R" Us, Inc. on the New York Stock Exchange shot up 159 times in nine years—from US$0.25 per share in 1975 to US$40 in 1984. By 1998, Toys "R" Us was running 698 shops in the U.S. and enjoying a market share of 20%.

Given its phenomenal success in the U.S. market, Toys "R" Us planned to enter the global market in 1993. Its first shop outside the U.S. was opened in Canada in 1984, followed by twenty-seven overseas markets, including the U.K., Germany, France, Spain, Japan, Singapore, Malaysia, Taiwan, and Hong Kong. Twenty years of development has rendered Toys "R" Us, Inc. as the world's largest retail group for toys. By the end of 2001, Toys "R" Us had a total of 1,599 chain stores worldwide, of which 701 were under Toys "R" Us in the U.S., and 507 were under Toys "R" Us, International, supplying mainly toys, games, and sporting goods; 184 were under Kids "R" Us (in the U.S.) and 165 were under Babies "R" Us supplying mainly child's wear and baby's wear; and also 42 under Imagin-arium (in the U.S.). Toys "R" Us, Inc.'s annual report revealed that between 2001 and 2002, the group's total revenue was in the region of HK$12.63 billion (Exhibit 4.2).

Exhibit 4.2   Business performance of Toys "R" Us, Inc. (US$ million)

Year	1992/1993	1994/1995	1996/1997	1998/1999	2000/2001	2001/2002
Turnover	7,232	8,819	10,113	11,459	12,774	12,630
Net Profit (Loss)	438	532	427	(132)	404	67
Total Assets	5,323	6,571	8,023	7,899	8,003	8,076
No. of Stores	918	1,115	1,372	1,481	1,581	1,599

Source: Toys "R" Us, Inc. Annual Report 2001.

The relationship between Toys "R" Us, Inc. and Li & Fung can be traced back to the days when Joseph Baczko, the international director of Toys "R" Us, Inc., and Victor Fung, the chairman of Li & Fung, were both studying at the Harvard Business School. "I like to personalize joint ventures," Baczko once said, "and as far as Li & Fung is concerned, I know who are in charge."

When Li & Fung first started Toys "R" Us in Hong Kong, they still did not have a Chinese name for the shop. To come up with a corresponding and innovative Chinese name, William Fung, managing director of Li & Fung, racked his brain and his consultants suggested names such as "Toys Kingdom" and "Toys Empire," but William found none of them satisfactory. One day, looking at the inverted "R" in Toys "R" Us, William suddenly hit upon the idea of using the Cantonese term "反斗" (*fan dao*), which means playful and mischievous, and corresponds closely to what is symbolized by the inverted "R" in the original English name. That was how the Chinese name "玩具反斗城" came into being.

It has been proven that this cute Cantonese name has gone down well not only in the Hong Kong community, but also in Taiwan. William was reported to have had second thoughts initially about using it in Taiwan but somehow he decided to go ahead with it. Its success in the non-Cantonese community of Taiwan in a sense attests to the importance of innovation and risk-taking for Li & Fung's achievements.

Toys "R" Us' first shop in Hong Kong was located at Ocean Terminal in the boisterous commercial district of Tsim Sha Tsui in Kowloon Peninsula. Prior to the 1960s, Tsim Sha Tsui was a place where the old terminal warehouses of Kowloon Wharf, a British firm, were located. However, with the revolutionary changes in the 1970s when the Kwai Chung Container Terminals commenced operation, Tsim Sha Tsui began to lose its original functions. From the mid-1960s to early-1980s, Tsim Sha Tsui gradually evolved into a commercial hub where modern office buildings, residential blocks, and hotels sprang up one after the other from where terminals and warehouses used to be. These redevelopment projects comprised of the Ocean Terminal, Ocean Center, and Harbor City, among which the Harbor City commercial complex had been reputed as being "the largest and most successful commercial complex in Asia." It embraces the interlinked shopping malls of Ocean Center, Ocean Terminal and Harbor City, with over

600 boutiques, three hotels and around fifty restaurants, together with some high-class office blocks and residential property, making it one of the best-known business hubs in Hong Kong.[2]

In 1985, Hong Kong entered the transition phase prior to its reunification with China. The property market was still recuperating from a severe crash that lasted between 1982 and 1984, and many shop spaces remained unoccupied, including those in primary locations like the Ocean Terminal. Optimistic about the long-term prospects of the Ocean Terminal shopping mall, Li & Fung decided to lease the basement of Ocean Terminal for the first Toys "R" Us shop in Hong Kong. Lau Butt-farn still recalled that when he accompanied Victor Fung to meet with Kowloon Wharf's manager in charge of property management, they found that the basement was dirty, untidy, and packed with goods. Elevators had to be installed before it could be leased out and government approval was needed for changing the use of the property concerned. Because the Kowloon Wharf manager believed it could not be done, the negotiation came to a stalemate. Later, Lau called the manager, asserting that if he did not have a definite answer by ten o'clock the next morning, there would be no further negotiation. In response, the other party immediately consented and Li & Fung obtained the shop space it was looking for at an extremely low rent rate. The Ocean Terminal shop has a floor area of over 40,000 square feet, three-quarters of which are used for the selling of products. This is in line with Toys "R" Us' principle—that its shops must all be spacious.

The Toys "R" Us shop in Ocean Terminal officially opened on November 7, 1986. Because of its location in a large-scale shopping mall, its spaciousness that enables customers to shop in comfort, and its policy of offering the widest range of products at the lowest prices, Toys "R" Us was a sensation from the start. At its opening, a crowd of over 50,000 turned up in a queue that extended 200 meters from the shop front to Star Ferry Pier outside Ocean Terminal. The shop recorded a turnover of HK$1 million on its opening day and was once Toys "R" Us, Inc.'s top sales outlet outside the U.S. in terms of turnover. Toys "R" Us soon became a household brand in Hong Kong.

---

[2] Feng (1996), p. 158.

At the beginning, Toys "R" Us in Hong Kong mainly adopted the U.S. business strategy for a "toys hypermarket" and was under the management in the U.S. This strategy is characterized by spaciousness, self-service, and the supermarket style of operation. The Ocean Terminal shop occupies an area of over 40,000 square feet and is stocked to a height of twelve feet with all kinds of toys, including large items like the plastic slide. To minimize staff costs, it adopts a flexible approach in recruitment. During peak months in November and December, it is staffed by thirty full-time and 150 part-time employees. At normal times, the staff force consists of twenty-five full-time and sixty part-time employees.

The products sold at Hong Kong's Toys "R" Us shop came mostly from the U.S. Toys "R" Us participates in the American International Toy Fair held in New York by the American Toy Industry Association at the beginning of each year. About 2,000 toy manufacturers, distributors, and importers are invited as exhibitors of new products. Toys "R" Us, Inc. also stages the annual Dallas International Toy Import Show at Dallas Market Center with participation of toy manufacturers from all parts of the world. In recent years, as more and more American toy manufacturers are using China as their production bases, Toys "R" Us in Hong Kong also sources its toy merchandizes from China.

The product items sold in Hong Kong numbered more than 10,000, ranging from different kinds of toys and games to baby products, children's apparels, books, and confectioneries. Customers are given infinite choices, including famous global brands that suit different age groups. Toys "R" Us also provides an exchange and refund service. Toys "R" Us has a strong appeal to the local people by localizing traditional Western games like Scrabble and Monopoly with menus in Chinese and by having Chinese and English books on its shelves. "This is a great help in marketing these products in Hong Kong and Taiwan," said Shek Hing-lun, Manager of Toys "R" Us.[3] According to him, sales have been robust since the opening and customers are not restricted only to the local people.

The Hong Kong retail market has been hard-hit by the American way of running retail outlets. As pointed out by Tang Wing-kei, the former managing

---

[3] Hutcheon (1991), p. 61.

director of Toys "R" Us, Hong Kong, at an interview, Toys "R" Us is distinguished by "having the largest variety of product offerings at reasonable prices and also a spacious and comfortable shopping environment. Customers can try all the products personally and children will find themselves in paradise where they are free to choose what they like without being coerced by salespeople. Families can come and enjoy a good time together in our shop." Tang also added: "In my experience of over ten years in the toy retail business, I keenly felt the impact created by the American retail concept. When we first opened in 1986, our branded imported items were priced 30–40% lower than the prices of the other major toy retailers. Apart from that advantage, we were always at the forefront, be it in product offerings, refund policy, or customer service."[4]

Since 1986, Toys "R" Us has set up four stores in locations with a high concentration of either business activities or residential blocks, namely, Ocean Terminal in Tsim Sha Tsui, New Town Plaza in Shatin, Windsor House in Causeway Bay, and Tsuen Wan Plaza in Tsuen Wan. It was a major event in town when the Shatin store opened in 1988. Officiating the opening ceremony were William Fung, managing director of Li & Fung; Harry Oppenheimer, chief executive of De Beers; and Larry Bouts from Toys "R" Us, Inc. The new store was crowded with customers from all parts of Hong Kong. Toys "R" Us entered Taiwan in 1989 by setting up a store in Hsin Sheng Road, Taipei. Its opening ceremony also created a sensation, setting a record-high sale on the first day. At present, there are sixteen Toys "R" Us stores in Taiwan, spread out in major cities like Taipei, Taoyuan, Taichung, Chiayi, Tainan, and Kaohsiung.

Fotomax and Fun Fun World

Due to the experience gained from running Circle K and Toys "R" Us, Li & Fung further diversified its retail business by acquiring Fotomax and Fun Fun World. Li & Fung acquired Fotomax (Far East) Limited from the Shui

---

[4] *Li & Fung Retailing Forum*, Issue No. 7, May 1999, p. 3.

On Group in Hong Kong in 1992. Formerly known as Fotomax Color Photofinishing, Fotomax was established in 1982 as a photofinishing shop and
video-rental outlet.

After acquiring Fotomax, Li & Fung proceeded to expand its sales network
aggressively. When it was eventually sold in 2001, there were fifty-two Fotomax shops all over Hong Kong. It should be mentioned, however, that the
business performance of Fotomax, especially the video-rental part, had not
been up to expectations. The video tapes of locally-produced movies were
then controlled by two or three distributors who sold at high prices. But the
video-rental market was fiercely competitive and operators had to offer club
membership and coupons to attract customers. Even so, the coupons became
increasingly cheaper so that on average, each video had to be rented out
thirty times to break even. During this period, the quality of locally-produced
films was on the decline and many movie lovers switched to foreign films,
making it even tougher for video-rental stores to survive. Li & Fung therefore
terminated Fotomax's video-rental service after the mid-1990s. During 1998
and 1999, the video-rental industry in Hong Kong virtually collapsed. Fotomax fortunately escaped from that, thanks to Li & Fung's earlier decision.

Upon terminating its video-tape business, Fotamax focused on the development of digital photofinishing. In the past, Fotomax had relied on Kodak's
equipment and would only sell Fuji films. In 2000, Fotomax invested HK$30
million in acquiring the Fujifilm digital laser-printing technology from Japan
and launched a new digital imaging service at all its outlets in Hong Kong. By
including digital laser-printing, Fotomax Imaging CD, and a website (www.
fotomax.com), Fotomax set a new trend in imaging service. In February 2001,
Fotomax partnered with eolasia.com to launch an on-line photofinishing service. Customers could order the photos of movie stars or their idols through
the Fotomax website.

With the advent of the 21st century, the operating environment for the
retail sector became increasingly difficult, prompting Li & Fung to restructure its retail business. In July 2001, it was announced that Li & Fung Retail
Group had reached a sale-and-purchase agreement with China-Hong Kong
Photo Products Holdings Limited whereby, in return for the former's Fotomax shares, the latter would issue 70 million new shares to the former at
HK$1.25 per share, 78.5% higher than the closing price of the latter's share
that day, representing a P/E ratio of 12:1. The new shares made up 6.4%

of China-Hong Kong Photo's issued shares. China-Hong Kong Photo had been the sole distributor of Fuji products in Hong Kong and Macau since its establishment in 1968 and in China since 1980. It operated an extensive network of sales outlets in Hong Kong and China and, for many years, the Fujifilm digital-printing systems and the digital imaging products under its sole distributorship had been best sellers in those markets. By the end of the 1960s, it became the major supplier of photo-processing equipment and materials for Fotomax.

"We are very delighted to invest in China-Hong Kong Photo," said William Fung, managing director of Li & Fung (Retailing), "as we believe Fuji digital products are revolutionizing the digital imaging world with advanced technological development. Fotomax shares the same vision as China-Hong Kong Photo on its China strategy. With Fotomax's track record catering for the upper-middle consumer segments, we are confident that this will bring value to China-Hong Kong Photo and expand its retail network in the Greater China region."

Dennis Sun Tai-lun, the chairman and managing director of China-Hong Kong Photo Products Holdings Limited, said: "This acquisition is in line with our broader strategy to develop retail opportunities. Fotomax has an extremely valuable position as Hong Kong's premium provider of quality imaging services. We are very excited about adding this successful company to our group, especially as it will add synergy to the group's existing strategies and strengthen our operations. After the acquisition, we believe that Fuji products will take up more than 50% of the film-processing market in Hong Kong, ousting our competitors."

Fun Fun World was a retail joint venture set up in 1996 by Li & Fung and Fun World (Hong Kong) Limited, a subsidiary of Sun Hung Kai Properties Limited. It was 70%-owned by Li & Fung. Positioned as "a playground for the whole family," Fun Fun World offered mainly a range of exciting games and rode in its outlets in all parts of Hong Kong, including the commercial districts on Hong Kong Island and the new towns such as Shatin, Taipo, Yuen Long, and Sheung Shui. Each Fun Fin World center had its unique features. For example, the center situated in Phase 1 of Causeway Bay Plaza, for instance, occupied an area of 5,600 square feet with sixty-eight machines of different types that appealed to the younger generation, particularly the baseball game machine that amplified the liveliness and excitement of the center. This center was also characterized by its impressive glass signboard extending 135 feet from Percival Street to Hennessy Road. The center in Grand Century Place, Mongkok, with a mosaic of twenty-five 28-inch televisions to form one gigantic television screen wall, was the first indoor game center in Hong Kong with such a large television screen. The center at Wan Tsui Plaza in Chaiwan had especially imported from Japan premium items with popular cartoon characters like Hello Kitty, Mickey Mouse, and Doraemon for customers to redeem. The center at Sunshine City, Ma On Shan, was decorated like a plush palace and customers could play games that befitted kings and queens.

However, under the impact of Hong Kong's persistent economic downturn, Fun Fun World did not perform as satisfactorily as expected and was sold in September 2001. By then, there were twelve Fun Fun World centers in Hong Kong. In fact, in just two months, Li & Fung had withdrawn from Fotomax and Fun Fun World. Under the fiercely competitive retail environment in Hong Kong, it adjusted its retail business development strategy from one of diversification to one of focus on two core businesses, Circle K and Toys "R" Us.

Chapter 5

Privatization — The Key to Modernization

"In those days, there were divergent views within the family. Victor and I could see that a great opportunity was emerging but the other family members disagreed. As it turned out, China continued with opening up her economy. However, some family members were losing their interest in Li & Fung and chose to sell all their stakes to Victor and me. Too preoccupied with his new venture with Prudential Asia at that particular juncture, Victor suggested the privatization of Li & Fung."

—William Fung

Li & Fung's Privatization—The First Management Buyout

Toward the end of the 1970s, Hong Kong's future has increasingly became a major issue. In 1983, negotiations commenced between the British and Chinese governments over this issue. On December 9, 1984, British's prime minister Margaret Thatcher arrived in Beijing to join Chinese Premier Zhao Ziyang in signing the Sino-British Joint Declaration on the future of Hong Kong whereby the P.R.C. government would resume sovereignty over Hong Kong from July 1, 1997 and, in accordance with the principle of "One Country, Two Systems," the Hong Kong Special Administrative Region (HKSAR) would be set up under the policy of "Hong Kong people ruling Hong Kong with a high degree of autonomy." Hong Kong's original social and economic system and way of life were to remain unchanged for 50 years. From then on, Hong Kong entered into the transitional period to the 1997 handover.

During this period, the Fung family started discussing internally the shareholding of Li & Fung Limited. In October 1987, the U.S., stock market crash devastated stock markets around the world. Hong Kong was also dealt a serious blow. The Hang Seng Index (HSI) took a nosedive from its peak of 3,949.73. On October 26, when the Hong Kong stock market reopened after a four-day suspension, panic short-selling drove the Index down by 1,120.7 points or 33%. The stock market's slump sparked off a crisis in the HSI Futures Market. As a result, the Hong Kong government had to step in to stabilize the market by using the Foreign Exchange Fund. The temporary closure of the stock market also led to the restructuring of the Stock Exchange of Hong Kong and the imprisonment of its former chairman, Li Fook-shiu.

Amidst these economic shockwaves, the Fungs convened a full-scale family meeting in Boston to discuss the future of Li & Fung and particularly its shareholding. It is understood that there were serious disputes at the meeting. As Li-Fung Lai-wah recalled, "Different views were raised during the meeting." Fung Hon-hing, one of the board members, was said to have objected violently to the privatization of Li & Fung. After thorough discussion, however, most of the family members agreed to sell their shares to the management of the company, i.e., Victor and William, so that the two could proceed to privatize the company.

The main objective of privatization was to enable those who were interested in and capable of running the company to become its controlling shareholders so that they could do it effectively and, at the same time, allow those who were uninterested to liquidate their shareholding. According to Fung Hon-chu, Li & Fung could only succeed with a lot of hard work over a long period. Even then, it had to reinforce its foundations on a continuous basis. It would make life so much easier for the management if the company was under its control.

At an interview in 1992, William Fung was asked to comment on the privatization. He said, "We had serious reservations about family-style management. In the past, all our family members had a share, which also meant a position, in the company. The purpose for Li & Fung to go public in 1973 was to root out the conflicts in such a style of management. After that, the management made various attempts to restructure the company and do away with 'vicious internal competition.' Unfortunately before the implementation of major reforms, some members had already backed out." The Sino-British negotiations over the future of Hong Kong were concluded at the end of 1984.

"Views were diverse within the family as regards the conclusion," William continued, "Victor and I were of the view that it would open up golden opportunities whereas the others thought otherwise. After that, China continued with the implementation of an open-door policy but some of our kinfolk were no longer interested in retaining their shares and opted for selling them to me and Victor. At that point, Victor was occupied with the business of the newly established Prudential Asia and so suggested to privatize Li & Fung."[1]

On September 12, 1988, Li & Fung announced that it was in negotiation with certain shareholders that could have significant implications for all shareholders. On October 10, the company announced that it would propose to undertake a complete buyout of all its share and turn it into a wholly-owned subsidiary of King Lun Company Limited (KLCL), which was registered in British Virgin Islands and equally owned by Victor Fung and William Fung, respectively. However, Consolidated Resources Limited (CRL) was given the priority to acquire 25% of KLCL's issued shares. CRL was a wholly-owned subsidiary of Eastern Investment Limited, an investment

---

[1] *Capital*, Hong Kong, February 1992, p. 65.

holding company whose interests were in Asia and Australasia and whose shareholders included Anglo American Corporation of South Africa Limited (AAC), De Beers Centenary AG, Minorco SA, etc.

This management-initiated buyout was the first of its kind in Hong Kong. Under this buyout plan, KLCL would purchase by cash the 54 million issued and paid-up Li & Fung Limited shares from shareholders at HK$8.50 per share. After the completion of the buyout, Li & Fung Limited would give up its listing status in Hong Kong and become a full subsidiary of KLCL. For the purpose of the buyout, Prudential Asia was engaged as financial advisers. On September 9, 1988, the last trading day prior to the initial announcement on September 12, Li & Fung Limited's share was traded at HK$5.05, which implied that the buyout price of HK$8.50 would be at a premium of 68.3%. The P/E ratio would be 20.7 times. In the past six months, the price of the share ranged from HK$6.30 to HK$4.75. Should it be calculated on the basis of the consolidated net asset value of each share, which was at HK$5.14, the buyout price was at a premium of 65.4%.

According to Schroder's documents on Li & Fung's privatization, the initiative to privatize was adopted due to the inactive trading of the company's shares on the stock exchange. In the six months ended on August 31, 1988, the average monthly transaction volume was 576,000 shares. The proposal to privatize would enable public shareholders to liquidate their shares at a higher price than recently recorded.[2] Together Victor and William were holding 7.471 million or 13.8% of Li & Fung shares. Coupled with CRL's 3.15 million shares, they altogether were holding 10.621 million shares or 19.7%. In other words KLCL, would have to buy the remaining 46.529 million shares with a total sum of HK$369 million. Funds were to be raised from the sale of KLCL's shares to CRL and bank loans.

William Fung recalled, "The biggest issue with this buyout was to borrow money from banks. For decades, Citibank has been our major corresponding bank, so we approached them first. However, Citibank's lending procedure was very complicated, involving first credit analysis and then approval by

---

[2] Schroders Asia and Prudential Asia (1988), November 14, p. 7.

their headquarters in New York. That resulted in the leakage of the buyout and caused Li & Fung's stock price to go up, forcing us to put it on hold—not once, but twice." After that, Victor and William turned to HSBC by contacting chairman William Purves and sending in all the information by fax. The next day, they sat down for half an hour and came to an agreement. "HSBC is very different from Citibank in that they look at who they are dealing with first," said William. Subsequently, KLCL borrowed HK$250 million from HSBC and HK$180 million from Anglo American, CRL's large shareholder. Together with their own injection of HK$60 million, the Fung brothers now had a total of HK$490 million to execute their buyout plan.

The board of Li & Fung then announced the formation of an independent committee comprising two independent directors, Sir. Anthony Hayward and Sir. Albert Rodrigues, to offer advice to public investors regarding the buyout proposal. The board also appointed Schroders as an independent financial adviser to the independent committee and public investors. After their assessment, the independent committee and Schroders publicized a document on November 14 that stated that the buyout plan was fair and reasonable, and recommended that it be voted for by shareholders. At that time, Fung Hon-chu, Li-Fung Lai-wah, and Fung Hon-hing were materially holding 13.624 million shares, of which 11.016 million shares and some other shares held jointly with certain members of the Fung family (other than those on the management of the company) were held by a trust fund. These shareholdings constituted 51% of Li & Fung Limited's issued shares, which meant that the percentage held by minority shareholders was only 29.3%.

On December 7, 1988, in accordance with a court order, a meeting for Li & Fung's public shareholders and an extraordinary general meeting were held consecutively to vote for the management buyout, which was completed in January 1989. This successful leveraged buyout initiated by the Fung brothers would be recorded as the first of its kind in Hong Kong.

After the buyout, AAC who supported the Fung brothers acquired 27.5% of Li & Fung's shares through its subsidiary, CRL, and became the second-largest shareholder of Li & Fung (1937). When Li & Fung Limited was spun off from Li & Fung (1937) to go public again in 1992, CRL was holding 12.8% of Li & Fung Limited's shares through KLCL. In September 2000, AAC sold all its 27.5% of KLCL's shares back to the Fung brothers and in return, KLCL allotted 117 million (8.51%) Li & Fung Limited's shares to AAC.

Through Goldman Sachs Asia and Casenove, AAC immediately placed 49.75 million shares (3.62%) with a number of institutional investors. Together with 1.4% sold through direct channels, AAC had parted with 5.1% of Li & Fung Limited's share at a placement price of HK$32.75 per share, representing a discount of 7.48%. The unsold 4.89% went into a joint venture with the Fung brothers and would remain there for no less than three years.

AAC is South Africa's premier mining company. Its shares are traded in both London and Johannesburg stock markets with a market cap of over £16.5 billion. Its assets are distributed in all parts of the world, including several platinum and precious metal mines in South Africa; De Beers being one of its subsidiaries.

In early 2000, AAC decided to restructure its business empire and started selling its non-core assets to concentrate on the development of its mining and natural resources businesses. The sale of KLCL was a part of its new strategy. On the completion of this deal, AAC pocketed HK$2.259 billion or US$300 million. Some commentators in Hong Kong pointed out that without spending a cent, the Fung brothers had increased their Li & Fung shareholding by 4.3% and achieved a paper gain of HK$1.9 billion at the expense of AAC. An AAC spokesman from South Africa responded, "AAC invested only US$3 million in KLCL in 1989, which was minimal compared to the US$300 million realized in the current deal…The HK$1.9 billion is not a big amount to us. The outstanding 4.3% of Li & Fung's shares has in fact been sold to the Fung brothers, but because of a confidentiality agreement between us, we do not deem it fit to disclose what we have gained in return." Through this deal, the shareholding of Victor and William increased from 38.11% to 42.4%.

The Management Model of Chinese Family Firms

In Hong Kong's 150 years of existence as a trading post, many Chinese family firms have emerged and flourished with amazing success generations after generations. This success can be contributed to a number of factors. Apart from a favorable external environment, their management models also deserve credit. This model is characteristically Chinese and diametrically opposite to its Western equivalent for it stems primarily from a traditional Chinese culture that embraces Confucianism.

The entrepreneurial spirit cherished in the West implies the separation of ownership and management. The major shareholder(s) may not necessarily get directly involved in the company's day-to-day decision-making and operations. Instead, the running of a company is entrusted to professional managers under a system established to serve the company's interests. Chinese family firms may aspire to adopt the Western management model but, given their cultural roots, they would still take a very unyielding approach when it comes to actual control and management. To them, the idea of owning a company without controlling and running it is simply unpalatable. Since the 1970s, an increasing number of successfully-run Chinese family firms in Hong Kong have gone public listed but, in many cases, the "family" remained in control in both shareholding and board business.

For the Chinese firm, the family is not only its creator and owner, but also its operator and manager. The family's interests always represent the top consideration and goal. Even for companies that have gone public listed, the primary goal is still to increase the family's investment and control. Given this scenario, it is almost without exception that the founder of the business or the head of the family will be the commander-in-chief. The management structure will be such that it converges on him and the positions of his subordinates will depend on their blood relations with the family. Moreover, generally, the patriarch is at the top of the hierarchy. At the next level is a management team made up of close relatives who are destined to be his successors. They may make suggestions to the patriarch on the firm's business strategy and management. More distant relatives and friends further down the hierarchy are responsible for the firm's daily operations. Under them are the general staff members.

The situation described above has been quite common among Chinese family firms. For example, the Wing On Group of department stores founded by the Kwok brothers, Kwok Lok and Kwok Chuen, was managed together with their two other siblings, Kwok Kwai and Kwok Shun, in Hong Kong, Shanghai, and Australia. Among the textile firms founded by Shanghai industrialists in Hong Kong in the 1950s, the management was almost entirely in the hands of the Shanghai clan. Yet, it should be noted that the large firms were beginning to hire professional managers and specialists. According to an article in *The Economist*, many leading Chinese firms, such as the business empires of Li Ka-shing in Hong Kong and Charoen Pokphand in Thailand, have successfully enlisted professionals in their management structure without undermining the family's control.[3] That was exactly the situation with Li & Fung after its first public listing in 1973.

In managing its internal relations, the Chinese family firm values unity, harmony, and forbearance. Under the family head and the influence of the Confucian precepts of loyalty and filial piety that have been in existence for 2,000 years, internal relations have in general been relatively harmonious despite occasional conflicts and tensions. Particularly where external dealings are concerned, there is always a high degree of unity within the firm. Its business thrives on a myriad of social connections built on personal relations and on the Confucian doctrine of trust, which is usually the guiding principle. Obviously, it is very different from the practice in the West where business transactions are conducted in accordance with the letter and spirit of the law.

As proven time and again, the Chinese management model is full of vitality. Its biggest advantage lies in its ability to arrive at decisions quickly and react to market conditions with infinite flexibility. It is, therefore, conducive to capturing new business opportunities that usually engender high profits. In a Chinese firm where power and connections are highly concentrated, the insight and experience accumulated by the patriarch through the years enables him to respond promptly to changes with quick decisions and strategic adjustments. He can also make use of his well-established personal connections in the interests of business development. In this respect, it apparently has some advantages over the Western model. Furthermore, under the leadership of a potent and charismatic patriarch, a firm's vertical integration is propelled by a strong centrifugal force. Family members at the key positions will all have a strong sense of identity, loyalty, and commitment. Even in the event of a change in business direction, there is seldom violent objection, which no doubt facilitates ready adaptation to any new market environment. In terms of horizontal integration, personal connections

---

[3] *The Economist,* July 18, 1992.

and trust, instead of the law, are relied on to drastically reduce the transaction cost and enhance the firm's resilience.

The virtues of this management model are usually manifested to the fullest in the first one or two generations. With the vision and judiciousness of the founding patriarch and the cohesiveness within the family, it is possible for a small firm to rise and become a business empire in just a matter of decades. Such examples abound in Hong Kong. Among the Chinese firms that emerged in the 1950s, many have become business giants in just one single generation. Li Ka-shing, for instance, has turned his humble plastic-flower factory into a business empire covering Asia, Europe, and North America within four to five decades. While being in the right place at the right time is certainly a paramount factor, the entrepreneur's clairvoyance and the unique management model he follows must be given due credit.

As expected, this model also has some inherent weaknesses, which become most conspicuous during succession. For a Chinese firm, success or failure often depends on the founder and his successor's judgment, experience, potency, outside connections, and ability to iron out internal differences. Under the traditional rule, the father is succeeded by his son. He who founds a business empire naturally yearns for an heir who can equal or even outshine him. For this reason, the fostering of potential successors is a major enterprise in itself. Nowadays, it is common to find the offspring of many old entrepreneurs join the family firm with a doctor's or master's degree. That, of course, is a positive development in itself but the issue is the capabilities required of an entrepreneur often cannot be acquired even at the most eminent universities.

Very often the successor's incompetence can lead to the downfall of a business empire. Hong Kong's 150-year economic history is replete with numerous such cases. There is an old Chinese saying: "The prosperity of a family can seldom be sustained for more than three generations." Zheng Guo-fan, a Qing scholar and senior court official also said, "Non-indulgent children are not born to a wealthy family." Indulgence and extravagance are condemned by traditional Chinese moralists as the main cause of a family's downfall. However, with the rise of financial management as a profession and the availability of financial advisory services in the market, it is rare for the riches of a prominent family to evaporate in one or two generations. Nowadays, a family business seldom fails due to individual's action. More often than not, it fails because the descendants are too shortsighted, expanding too rashly and thus undermining the very foundations of the firm. On the other hand, internal conflict and strife could also destroy a family firm quite easily. That explains why Chinese entrepreneurs consider the fostering of their successors to be of paramount importance. For Li & Fung, its second-generation helmsman, Fung Hon-chu, fully appreciated the importance of succession. He enlisted his sons, Victor and William, to work for his firm and learn from the job as soon as they completed their university education overseas. In this respect, Li & Fung can be considered an outstanding example.

Another family business's weakness lies in the deep-rooted tradition that only male descendants are entitled to equal shares of their father's estate. This "binary fission" style of inheritance not only undermines the control of the family over its firm, but also breeds internal conflict. In addition, it renders the accumulation of capital impossible, thus hindering expansion. Some scholars have pointed out that an enterprise, is not necessarily handicapped in its development simply because it is a family firm. If a family is a company that can hold assets and its asset value is not reduced by the inheritance problem, it can still expand and continue its operation. Many large and century-old enterprises in Japan are also family businesses. In these cases, the original families have all undergone the process of corporatization whereas unfortunately, for Chinese enterprises, it is usually the other way round, with the family gaining greater and greater control over the firm.

Yet, the Chinese family firm can find a way to circumvent this inherent weakness, as demonstrated by Li & Fung's privatization by the end of 1988. In an almost unprecedented move, Victor Fung and William Fung, who were at the top management of the company resolved to buy out the shares held by their family members, thus solving the thorny problem of ownership and setting a successful example for Chinese family firms. It should be borne in mind, however, that not all such firms can follow the same approach.

A further challenge for a Chinese family firm is to adapt to changes in the operating environment. To do that, it must overcome the restrictions imposed by tradition and imbibe the positive elements of Western management and by doing so, become modernized. Traditional Chinese family firms are invariably subject to some serious restrictions. First, their management system is such that the biggest decision-maker has the final say whereas those under him only execute the decision made. As a result, the initiative and creativity of the middle to lower management are stifled. Non-family members, in particular, are seldom promoted to senior positions. Another problem concerns external relations. Since Chinese family firms thrive on personal relations instead of contractual relations, they often find it hard to cope beyond the sphere of the former.

In fact, major changes have already been creeping in surreptitiously. Since the 1980s, many Chinese family enterprises have been recruiting managers formerly working with Western corporations. In 1979, after acquiring Hutchison Whampoa, Li Ka-shing, the chairman of Cheung Kong Holdings, deliberately steered clear of the oriental style of management by appointing a considerable number of professional managers. With the coming in of the second and third generations, changes like that will surely be accelerated. Descendants with an overseas tertiary education will also tend to apply what they have learnt from the West to their family enterprises.

In an article written in 1993, Victor Fung said, "The traditional family firm encounters all sorts of obstacles when trying to shake off the reins of the family. However, the entrepreneurs today learn fast how to free themselves from the constraints they face. I can see that a totally new Chinese management model is in the making; such a model not only embraces traditional values like industry, thriftiness, and social harmony, but also borrows from the West qualities such as flexibility and innovation in doing things, as well as the readiness to assimilate foreign elements. This model is championed by the second and third generations of Chinese businessmen, many of whom have been educated overseas. The fact that some of them still have to listen to their family does not stop them from successfully acquiring from the West new management skills and recruiting foreign managers to expand their businesses and sustain growth."[4] Privatization has become Li & Fung's key to modernization.

---

[4] Chinese General Chamber of Commerce, Hong Kong (1993), p. 128.

From Diversification to Specialization

With the privatization of Li & Fung, all the Fung family members (including Hon-chu), except Victor and William, resigned from the company's management. Kwok-chor left the company in 1974 upon the death of his father, Mo-ying, to study law in the U.K. He developed an interest in law when assisting in Li & Fung's public listing in 1973, thereby allowing him to come into contact with legal issues like IPOs and family trusts. He graduated from Lincoln's Inn in England and later became an eminent barrister-at-law with his chambers at Prince Building, Central. Kwok-chor's wife, Chan Siu-wai, is the youngest daughter of Chan Chun, the founder of Crocodile Garments. When Mr. Chan passed away in 1997, most of his offsprings migrated to Canada; but Siu-wai was among the few who remained in Hong Kong. Kwok-hong, Kwok-chor's elder brother, who was once the manager of the sundry-goods department in charge of firecrackers and fireworks in Li & Fung Trading, opened a handicrafts company after the privatization project. Li Wing-hong, a former director of Li & Fung (Properties) Limited, chose to migrate to Vancouver.

Victor and William became the biggest shareholders and top decision-makers of Li & Fung. Their priority was to sort out the company's diversified business portfolio and improve its management. In the 1980s, there was a common belief among business managers in the U.S. that specialization should be preferred over diversification. In privatizing Li & Fung, the Fung brothers were motivated by a wish to take control of it so that they could restructure its business in a professional manner.

On that, William once said at a meeting of fund managers organized by Goldman Sachs in New York, "We were reading all the relevant books, such as *In Search of Excellence*. We knew we should strive to do our best in our business. Before privatization, Li & Fung was like a mini-Jardine Matheson Group. We were all over the place, doing real-estate development, insurance, and so on and so forth. We even had a sizeable team for transporting timber from Indonesia to Japan. After privatization, these non-core businesses either became part of the private firm or were simply sold. Since then, our focus has been on only two segments, namely, trading—by being the buying agent for companies in Europe and the U.S.—and retail."

As soon as the privatization of Li & Fung was completed in early 1989, Victor and William decided to part with the non-core businesses in order to reduce their loan burden. As told by William, Jones Lang Wootton was appointed to conduct a valuation of all Li & Fung properties, including Fung House in Connaught Road Central, found to be worth HK$191 million. Regardless of the surveyors' advice, they decided to sell those properties after much consideration. The sale generated an extraordinary profit of HK$145 million, which was used to pay off bank loans. After the sale, the "June 4 Incident" occurred, leading to the collapse of Hong Kong's property and stock markets. Like any traditional Chinese, William always ascribes his good luck to the benevolent deeds performed by his ancestors.

After parting with all the non-core segments, Victor and William proceeded to streamline Li & Fung's businesses which were then grouped under two main streams—export trading and retail. They also reinforced and restructured the businesses. Offices with a floor area of about 80,000 square feet were leased at LiFung Tower, China Hong Kong City at 33 Canton Road, Kowloon, as their new headquarters. The traditional role of export traders was basically that of an intermediary between local manufacturers and overseas buyers. Since the 1970s, the liaison between overseas buyers and manufacturers in Asia has been much closer than before. Their knowledge of the market has also increased. Victor and William realized that there was a need to change or reinforce the nature of their trading business to meet customers' demands and adapt to the new situation.

So during the 1980s, apart from playing its traditional role of a sourcing agent for overseas buyers, Li & Fung was also actively expanding its service range by extending its supply chain. Its new services included:

(1) Offering product designs and production plans, and the management of production processes, through which customers' concepts could be developed into feasible production plans;

(2) Sourcing raw materials, as well as parts and components;

(3) Providing the latest market and technical information to manufacturers, as well as information on productivity in the Far East to buyers;

(4) Offering financial assistance in the form of short-term loans to selected small and medium-sized manufacturers for use as operating capital upon order placement;

(5) Bridging the communication gap between buyers and manufacturers to ensure that the latter can fully understand the former's specifications; and

(6) Ensuring production and quality control, timely delivery, and compliance with buyers' requirements.

In addition to expanding its range of services and the scope of its supply chain management, Li & Fung also realigned its organizational structure. Under the new structure, its export business was divided (by product) into different groups: textiles (in the U.S.), textiles (outside the U.S.), fashion accessories, plastic wares, sporting goods, and handicrafts. All these groups were based in Hong Kong, except the sporting-goods group, which was based in Taiwan. Each product group was in charge of several departments and each product group and department was headed by a manager. To promote a company-wide entrepreneurial spirit, all the major duties in connection with export trading, including purchasing, merchandizing, shipping, and quality control, were all delegated to the departments under each product group. Only functions like finance, accounting, IT-system management, and human-resources management were centralized at the corporate headquarters. Under this system, each product group operated as an independent profit center, and the group managers and departmental managers could enjoy a high degree of autonomy.[5]

Among the various product groups, the largest revenue earner was the textiles group, which covered weaving products and garments, and was subdivided into three smaller groups. Two were in charge of garment exports to the U.S. Certain major customers were served individually by special departments under these two product groups, which had merchandizers stationed in offices in Hong Kong, Korea, Singapore, Taiwan, and Thailand. The third product group catered to customers outside the U.S., that is, mostly in Europe and Australia, and had merchandizers stationed in Hong Kong and Thailand. Each product group was staffed by professional merchandizers who were conversant with the fashion trends, technical requirements, and textile quota system of the markets they served. At the time of the privatization, Li & Fung's textile exports were experiencing robust growth. In just three years, this increased from HK$767 million in 1988 to HK$2,318 million in 1991, which

---

[5] *Li & Fung Limited IPO Prospectus*, 1992, pp. 12–13.

Exhibit 5.1   Li & Fung's export trade by product at the time of privatization
(HK$ million)

Product Group	1988	1989	1990	1991
Textiles	767.17 (58%)	961.87 (79%)	1,256.22 (79%)	2,318.21 (82%)
Fashion accessories	79.47 (6%)	106.21 (9%)	142.44 (9%)	200.33 (7%)
Plastics	513.52 (39%)	65.08 (5%)	84.94 (5%)	186.65 (7%)
Handicrafts	86.56 (7%)	86.10 (7%)	91.87 (6%)	117.63 (4%)
Sporting goods	–	–	7.46 (<1%)	3.53 (<1%)
Total turnover	**1,446.72 (100%)**	**1,219.27 (100%)**	**1,592.95 (100%)**	**2,826.30 (100%)**

Source: Li & Fung Limited IPO Prospectus, 1992.

represented a hefty rise of 202%. In terms of contribution to the company's total turnover, this represented an increase from 58% to 82% (Exhibit 5.1).

The fashion accessories group covered a large variety of products, including sporting bags, handbags, suitcases, briefcases, costume jewelry, wristwatches, footwear, and premium items. The U.K. was the major buyer of bags, costume jewelry, and wristwatches, while the largest demand for footwear came from the U.S. In 1989, the fashion accessories group started sourcing gifts and premium items. In 1990, Li & Fung acquired 50% of Cyrk International Inc., an U.S. firm specializing in the design, sale, and distribution of premium items for corporate customers, including the major sponsors of the Summer Olympics in 1992. For Li & Fung, the export of fashion accessories was also growing fast during the privatization period. It increased from HK$79.47 million in 1988 to HK$200.33 million in 1991, up by 152%. The contribution of this category to total turnover was in the region of 6–9%.

In the late 1980s, the plastics group was Li & Fung's second-largest export group after textiles. Its turnover in 1988 amounted to HK$513.52 million, representing 39% of the company's total turnover. After the privatization exercise, its turnover plummeted to HK$186.65 million in 1991, which was equivalent to just 7% of the company total. This decline was primarily due to the move taken by Gap to assume full control of its joint venture with Li & Fung and to operate on its own. The plastics group handled the export of mainly toys and games for U.S.-toy brands. In 1988, a department was set up specifically for the distribution of toy products under Li & Fung's "Toy Island" brand.

The handicrafts group was responsible for products that had been traded by Li & Fung for decades, including fireworks, artificial flowers, Christmas decorations, handwoven baskets, copperwares, porcelain, and other household utensils that were produced mainly in the Chinese mainland, Taiwan, and Korea. This product group was divided into three departments for the sale of fireworks, the sourcing of handicrafts for Albert Kessler, and the sourcing of handicrafts and household utensils for other clients, respectively. Li & Fung had been exporting fireworks since 1906. The export of its "Black Cat" brand of products was later extended from the U.S. to markets in Europe. Albert Kessler was an U.S. importer of gift items like handwoven baskets and porcelain Li & Fung acquired its ownership in 1989 in a bid to further diversify its product mix. During the period of privatization, the turnover of the handicrafts group increased, but its contribution to Li & Fung's total turnover dropped from 7% to 4%.

There was also the sporting-goods group set up in Taiwan in 1990 to take charge of sportswear, racquets, and golfing products.

Li & Fung's sourcing network was initially based in Hong Kong. In the early 1990s, it was expanded to cover Southeast Asia and the Chinese mainland with offices in Hong Kong, Taiwan, Thailand, the Philippines, Malaysia, Singapore, Indonesia, Korea, as well as Shanghai, Shenzhen, and Zhanjiang in China. These offices were buying various types of products from some 500 manufacturers in the region. The major sourcing centers were Hong Kong, China, and Korea, which accounted for 48%, 29% and 16%, respectively, of the company's total operating cost for trade. This extensive sourcing network enabled Li & Fung to profit tremendously from the region's burgeoning industrial sector by identifying the best manufacturers and raw material suppliers for its clients.

Concurrently, Li & Fung's customer base was enlarged to cover about 350 accounts in the U.S. and Europe, with the former being the major market. From 1988 to 1991, Li & Fung's exports to the U.S. grew 95% from HK$1.074 billion to HK$2.089 billion. The U.S. market accounted for 66–74% of the company's turnover. Germany was Li & Fung's most important market in Europe. Sales to Germany more than tripled from HK$95.27 million to HK$311 million in the same period (Exhibit 5.2). As well, Li & Fung's clients were mostly large companies. In 1991, the top four clients accounted for 59%

Exhibit 5.2   Li & Fung's export-trade markets during privatization (HK$ million)

Market	1988	1989	1990	1991
USA	1,073.75 (74%)	805.83 (66%)	1,063.17 (67%)	2,088.60 (74%)
Germany	95.27 (7%)	154.46 (13%)	207.45 (13%)	310.52 (11%)
Other European countries	106.57 (7%)	120.69 (10%)	139.60 (9%)	236.87 (8%)
Australia and New Zealand	60.07 (4%)	75.85 (6%)	90.57 (6%)	111.82 (4%)
Hong Kong	71.68 (5%)	29.60 (2%)	43.75 (3%)	34.15 (1%)
Canada & Mexico	23.54 (2%)	15.82 (1%)	23.20 (1%)	21.30 (1%)
Other countries	15.83 (1%)	17.02 (1%)	15.21 (1%)	23.09 (1%)
Total turnover	**1,446.72 (100%)**	**1,219.27 (100%)**	**1,592.95 (100%)**	**2,826.30 (100%)**

Source: Li & Fung Limited IPO Prospectus, 1992.

of the company's total export turnover. They were all garment importers, including three U.S. retailers—Express, County Seat Stores, and The Limited Stores, and Public Bekleidung Design GmbH, a German importer. Among them, Express was the largest. Express and The Limited Stores were both subsidiaries of The Limited, Inc., the top U.S. female apparel and mail-order group.

During the privatization period, Li & Fung's business grew steadily across the board. In 1989, the first year after privatization, the textiles group recorded a growth of 25% in turnover after securing a large number of orders from major clients. The fashion accessories group started sourcing premium items and its turnover also increased. Unfortunately, under the impact of the U.S. economic slowdown, the termination of its agency by Gap—the largest client of its plastics group, and the loss incurred by its strategic move to acquire Albert Kessler, Li & Fung's total turnover dropped by 15% in 1989. However, there was improvement in the next few years. The aggressive expansion of its two key clients in the U.S.—Express and County Seat Stores—resulted in a substantial increase in orders. Fuelled also by other favorable factors, Li & Fung experienced illustrious growth, in both revenue and profit. Its total turnover and after-tax profit grew from HK$1.46 billion and HK$27.16 million respectively, in 1988, to HK$2.855 billion and HK$86.92 million, respectively, in 1991, up 96% and 2.2 times, respectively (Exhibit 5.3).

Exhibit 5.3   Li & Fung's business performance during privatization (HK$ million)

Year	Total Turnover	Export Trade	After-tax Profit
1988	1,460.42	1,446.72	27.16
1989	1,240.52 (–15%)	1,219.27 (–16%)	217.19 (+421%)
1990	1,611.28 (+30%)	1,582.95 (+30%)	37.59 (–68%)
1991	2,855 (+77%)	2,826.35 (+79%)	86.92 (+131%)

Source: Li & Fung Limited IPO Prospectus, 1992

Relisting after Restructuring in 1992

In spring 1992, Deng Xiaoping, who is in his nineties, inspected the southern province of Guangdong and delivered a historic speech regarding the pace of China's economic reforms after the June 4 incident in 1989. Thereafter, China's open-door policy entered a new phase as foreign investors were allowed to enter not only the coastal regions in the South but also the Yangzi River region and further inland. The more liberal policy gave significant impetus to the Hong Kong economy whose GDP increased by an average of 5% annually between 1992 to 1997.

In view of the new economic climate, Victor and William decided to restructure Li & Fung's trading business, with a view to relisting. On October 25, 1992, through Li & Fung (1937) Limited, a private company wholly-owned by King Lun Holdings Limited (jointly owned by Victor and William), Li & Fung's trading operation was restructured and incorporated in Bermuda under the name of Li & Fung Limited (hereafter called Li & Fung Trading).

On June 2, 1992, an extraordinary general meeting convened by Li & Fung Trading resolved to increase its authorized share capital of HK$100,000 to HK$70 million, which was equivalent to 700 million shares at HK$0.10 per share, of which 500 million shares were issued or to-be-issued shares. These 500 million shares included 400 million issued shares and 100 million new shares to be issued. The company was to appoint Prudential Asia Investments and Wardley Finance as guarantors to prepare for relisting. On June 9, Li & Fung made a public offer of 100 million new shares valued at HK$0.10 each at a price of HK$2.20 each, implying a P/E ratio of 8. It was estimated that the yield would be in the region of 8%. After the deduction of costs, approximately HK$207 million would be raised from the relisting, of which HK$80 million would be used to purchase offices and warehouses in Hong Kong or

China, HK$80 million would be invested in some marketing or distribution companies in the U.S. or Europe, and HK$30 million would be reserved for acquiring some trading houses in the Far East. The remaining HK$17 million was to be retained as additional operating capital for the company.

Of the new shares issued by Li & Fung Trading, King Lun Holdings held 75% through its subsidiaries whereas the remaining 25% was held by the public. Li & Fung Trading then had tangible assets after adjustment valued at HK$83.81 million, a staff force of 733, of whom 504 were in Hong Kong and 229 from overseas. Apart from a 75% share of Li & Fung Trading, King Lun Holdings also wholly owned Palmyra Holding Pte. Limited, a leading toy distributor in the U.S. and Japan, and was engaged in the toy-retail business in Hong Kong, Singapore, Malaysia, Taiwan, and the mainland of China. It also held 75% share of Li & Fung (Retail) Limited, the operator of Circle K and Toys "R" Us in Hong Kong and Taiwan.

On July 1, 1992, Li & Fung Trading's shares was again traded in Hong Kong's stock market. An entirely new management team of professionals has been in place until today after the relisting. Victor Fung is the (non-executive) board chairman while William Fung is the managing director. Henry Chan, an executive director, joined Li & Fung in 1972, bringing with him fifteen years of experience in the toy industry. He was also made chairman of Toy Island Manufacturing Company Limited, a subsidiary of Li & Fung. Danny Lau, another executive director, joined Li & Fung in 1981 and has been in charge of the textiles (U.S.) product group.

Interestingly, most members of the management team have received tertiary education either in Hong Kong or overseas and are highly experienced in their respective fields. For example, Lam Chuen-lai, a manager of the textiles (the U.S.) product group, graduated from Hong Kong Polytechnic (now Hong Kong Polytechnic University) with a high diploma in cotton-spinning technology. He joined Li & Fung in 1978 with more than seventeen years of experience in garment exports. Wong King-wai, a manager of the fashion accessories group, graduated from Hartnell College in the U.S. with a bachelor's degree and has over twenty years of experience in export. Jin Hai-de, a manager of the sporting-goods group, graduated from Christ's College in Taiwan and has a bachelor's degree. He joined Li & Fung in 1970 with over twenty-four years of experience. Yip Po-yuen, a manager of the plastics group, joined Li & Fung in 1982 with a bachelor's degree in biophysics from the University of Hong Kong and an MBA degree from the Chinese University of Hong Kong. Tse Chung-wai, who is responsible for the company's overseas investment, graduated from Harvard University with a first degree in economics and an MBA conferred by Harvard Business School.

Li & Fung Trading spent HK$225 million, raised partly from its relisting and partly from borrowing, to purchase an industrial block at 868 Cheung Sha Wan Road, Kowloon. In 1994, it purchased the adjacent building at 888 Cheung Sha Wan Road. The two buildings had a gross floor area of about 200,000 square feet. Li & Fung had them fully refurbished and, with the government's approval, turned it into a composite industrial-commercial building before renaming it Lifung Center. In early 1998, Li & Fung's head-quarters were moved to Lifung Center, which has since been the base for its export-trading business. With its base in Hong Kong and having broadened its sourcing network in the region with offices in countries like Sri Lanka, the Philippines, and Vietnam, Li & Fung Trading went on to invest in a distribution project in Panyu and a project called "Food Town" in Heshan, Guangdong. By then, the company had fifteen branches in twelve countries or regions in the Asia Pacific.

After Li & Fung's relisting, the U.S. economy remained in a slump whereas Europe was beset by a currency crisis in 1992. Notwithstanding these adversities, Li & Fung was able to benefit from its regional sourcing network and the advantages peculiar to different markets in the region by offering high-quality services and merchandizes to its customers in the U.S. and Europe, thus growing its turnover and profit substantially year after year. In 1994, Li & Fung Trading posted a total turnover of HK$6.125 billion and a after-tax profit of HK$553 million, up by 115% and 536%, respectively, from 1991 (Exhibit 5.4). The strong growth in 1994's profits was also due to the extraordinary profit derived from the sale of Cyrk, Inc.'s shares. By the mid-1990s, Li & Fung Trading had already established itself as a leading and highly reputable export-trading firm in Hong Kong and the Asia Pacific.

Exhibit 5.4 Li & Fung Trading's business performance (HK$ million), 1992–1994

Year	Total Turnover	After-tax Profit	Net Asset Value
1991	2,855	87	84
1992	3,980 (+39%)	133 (+53%)	346 (+312%)
1993	5,382 (+35%)	196 (+47%)	527 (+52%)
1994	6,125 (+14%)	553 (+182%)	804 (+53%)

Source: Li & Fung Limited Annual Reports, 1992–1994.

The Passing of a Giant

By going into uncharted waters without discarding everything of the past, Fung Hon-chu as the second-generation helmsman of the Fung family had made invaluable contribution to the development and prosperity of Li & Fung. Just before the war outbreak, he was given the colossal and daunting task of transplanting Li & Fung from Guangzhou to Hong Kong. But nothing would make him shrink.

After the war, he boldly redirected Li & Fung's business focus in accordance with the then prevailing economic climate in Hong Kong and, by doing so, sustained the growth of his company. Mr. Fung was very open-minded and flexible in handling Li & Fung's business transactions. His motto was: "There are no less than 101 different ways of doing business." Above all, he had a high regard for knowledge and learning. As a well-respected personality at an advanced age, he was still humble himself to take heed of the views of his two U.S.-educated young sons and allow the family firm to be public listed and modernized. More importantly, he ensured that the family business was successfully passed on to the third generation, which in turn enabled the restructuring of Li & Fung's ownership and provided a solid foundation for future growth.

Fung Hon-chu did not aspire to be a businessman at first. As he admitted himself, his interest was in mining. Yet, when he was entrusted with the mission to take on the family business, he did not budge from the challenge but faced it head on. He was very serious about his work. According to Lam Po-yuen who joined Li & Fung in 1982, Fung Senior would always do his homework before meeting with his guests. In fact, he would memorize the names of his guests' family members and prepare all the questions to be asked. He considered each meeting to be a business opportunity that should not be missed. He also had a way of playing safe, that is, by calling his guests "boss." That is, Fung Senior was nice to all his business partners, customers, and employees. As Lam said, no one would even dream of bad-mouthing Mr. Fung.

Fung Hon-chu considered marriage and family to be vitally important. He loved his wife, Pui-yiu, and was often seen taking a walk with her.

Mr. Fung came down with polio when he was still a boy but he was strong-minded and determined to be independent. Even when he was in his seventies, he would walk by himself using a cane without any help. In his last days, he retreated to the backstage in favor of his heirs and devoted himself to the firecrackers and fireworks businesses he was so fond of. Fung Hon-chu passed away in August 1994 at the ripe old age of eighty-three. The memorial held on August 19 was attended by Hong Kong's business leaders who paid their homage to the much-loved and respected entrepreneur. In attendance include many representatives from prominent organizations—the Li & Fung Group, Prudential Asia Investments Limited, Lung Kong World Federation School, Fung Clan's Association, Hong Kong Red Cross, South China Athletic Association, Tung Wah Group of Hospitals, Hong Kong Shippers Council, Textile Council of Hong Kong, Federation of Hong Kong Industries, Hong Kong General Chamber of Commerce, Hong Kong Trade Development Council, as well as the Municipal Governments of Jiangmen, Heshan, and Panyu.

Sir. Chung Sze-yuen, Hong Kong's veteran political leader, delivered a eulogy of Mr Fung:

"We have gathered here today to pay our last tribute to former Legislative Councillor, Mr. Fung Hon-chu. I have known Hon-chu personally for more than thirty years. It is with much sadness that I take this opportunity to highlight some of the numerous achievements he has chalked.

A native of Heyi, Guangdong, Hon-chu was born in 1911 in Guangzhou to a merchant's family. He was initially inclined to start a career in mining but at the behest of his father, Mr. Fung Pak-liu, he joined the family business, that is, the early Li & Fung Company, upon graduating from King's College. In 1937, he was sent to Hong Kong to set up a branch company at 18–20 Connaught Road Central. Under the leadership and hard work of Hon-chu, the company grew fast and laid the solid foundation it still enjoys today.

During the Second World War, Guangzhou and Hong Kong fell one after the other and Li & Fung's business was adversely impacted. As soon as the war ended, Hon-chu returned to Hong Kong to resume business and strive for success. Given his strong determination and effort, Li & Fung has grown into a leading and highly reputable Chinese business empire encompassing import/export trade, investment, manufacturing, and shipping.

Hon-chu was also highly committed to public service. He was the Urban Councillor from 1960 to 1966. He was appointed a Legislative Councillor in 1964 and served in that capacity for six years. During his tenure of office, he spoke out intelligently for Hong Kong's economic, financial, and social development; and his views were all taken seriously by the government. He was made a Justice of the Peace in 1960 and an OBE in 1965 for his distinguished contributions to the community. Hon-chu was a founding member of the Federation of Hong Kong Industries and the Hong Kong Exporters' Association, and he was the first Chinese to become a member of the General Committee of the Hong Kong General Chamber of Commerce. Hon-chu was also committed to social welfare and charity. He was an honorary adviser of the Tung Wah Group of Hospitals and he was deeply respected by his colleagues for his devotion. Hon-chu's contribution to Hong Kong's economy and society will be sadly missed by us all.

Our condolences go to Mr. Fung's widow, Pui-yiu, an excellent wife and mother who has also devoted herself to social service, particularly the welfare of women. Mr. Fung's sons and daughters are all elites of the Hong Kong society. The Fung brothers, in particular, have been highly successful in growing the family business and serving the community by becoming the leaders of key organizations like the Hong Kong Trade Development Council and the Hong Kong General Chamber of Commerce. With these brilliant heirs, I have no doubt that Hon-chu will rest in peace."

Chapter 6

"Filling in the Mosaic"

"The merger of Li & Fung Trading and IBS—the first and second largest trading groups in Hong Kong will create for us an extensive and powerful sourcing network worldwide consisting of 28 branch offices in 20 countries with over 2,000 employees. The existing clients of both companies will benefit, and for Li & Fung Trading, turnover would be doubled to HK$18 billion."

—William Fung

The Rise of Inchcape in Hong Kong

During the 1990s, there began a wave of mergers and acquisitions (M&A) in the U.S., which also found its way to Europe and Asia. Such M&A involved major sectors such as aviation, telecommunications, financial services, petroleum, and automobiles. This global trend was characterized by a common conviction that "big is powerful." Of all the numerous cases of M&A worldwide, there was one in Hong Kong that did not attract as much attention as it probably deserved—the acquisition by Li & Fung Trading of Inchcape Buying Services (IBS). By this particular acquisition, Li & Fung Trading succeeded in elevating itself from a regional trading firm to a multinational entity virtually overnight.

Inchcape was in fact a latecomer to the group of prominent British hongs in Hong Kong, despite its long history of more than two centuries. In the 17th century, Mackinnon Mackenzie & Co. built its trading business in the coastal regions of India, Persian Gulf, and East Africa. A Scottish merchant, James Lyle Mackay, who joined that company, started the navigation business with investments all over the British colonies to the east of the Suez Canal. In 1911, Mackay was made Baron Inchcape, becoming the first Earl of Inchcape in 1929. Soon, Mackay acquired control of the Mackinnon Mackenzie Group and became the world's leading navigation magnate. The partition and independence of India in the mid-20th century however, greatly undermined the Inchcape Group's strength and retarded its growth. In 1958, the third Earl of Inchcape set up a holding company, Inchcape & Co., Ltd., in London, which later became public listed. From then on, the Inchcape Group entered a phase of rapid development and expansion.[1]

Attracted by the prosperity experienced by European companies in Hong Kong, Inchcape came to the british colony toward the end of the 1960s. It immediately initiated a number of acquisitions through Inchcape (Hong Kong) Limited. It first acquired Gibb Livingston & Co., Ltd., one of the oldest trading firms in the colony. Founded in Guangzhou in 1836, Gibb Livingston

---

[1] Jones (1986), p. 255.

expanded to Hong Kong in the 1840s and also set up branches in Shanghai, Fuzhou, Hankou, and Jiujiang. In the 1870s, its head office was moved to Shanghai, exporting silk, tea, and sundry goods. It was also engaged in shipping and insurance.[2] Gibb Livingston's business and influence gradually declined after World War II.

Inchcape's second target was Gilman & Co., Ltd., which was founded by British merchant, R.J. Gilman, in 1841 in Guangzhou. It attained the status of a prominent trading firm in Hong Kong in the 1860s with branches in Shanghai, Fuzhou, Guangzhou, and Hankou in China, as well as Yokohama in Japan. It was engaged mainly in imports and exports. It also provided commission-based agency services. Gilman's business performance, with an annual profit of nearly HK$4 million, was far from impressive since the 1950s. A local company, Whampoa Dockyards, at first intended to acquire Gilman, but the latter was averse to the idea of being taken over by a Hong Kong firm. By then, Inchcape had already built up a reputation worldwide and was planning to expand its operations in Hong Kong. Eventually, Gilman became a subsidiary of Inchcape.[3]

After acquiring Gilman, Inchcape turned its attention to Dodwell & Co., Ltd. Dodwell's history dated back to 1858 when W.R. Adamson, a British silk manufacturer, established W.R. Adamson & Co. in Shanghai. Taking advantage of the opening of China to foreign trade, it rose rapidly by setting up branch offices in Hong Kong, Fuzhou, Hankou, and Japan, trading in items like silk and tea. The company's sideline businesses included shipping and insurance agency services. In 1872, the company appointed G.B. Dodwell, an English sailor, to take charge of its shipping business in England. Dodwell's capabilities contributed significantly to the company's business pursuits in the Far East. When Adamson retired in the early 1890s, the company was in deficit. To avoid the loss of agency rights to competitors, Dodwell set up Dodwell & Co., Ltd. in 1891 to take over the trademark and businesses of W.R. Adamson.[4]

---

[2] Huang (1992), p. 12.
[3] Jones (1986), pp. 273–274.
[4] Andrew Liardet, *Dodwell & Company Limited*, March 1994, p. 1.

Dodwell & Co.'s headquarters were located in London. Even before the outbreak of World War I, it had already built an enormous branch network across the globe, covering Hong Kong, Shanghai, Hankou, Fuzhou, Guangzhou, Tianjin, Chongqing, Yokohama, Nagoya, Tokyo, San Francisco, New York, Los Angeles, and Seattle. During the war, Dodwell's business continued to develop. After the outbreak of the World War II, nearly all the trading companies in the Far East suffered, with the exception perhaps of only Dodwell which, through its branches in London, Colombia, and New York, was able to stay afloat. Dodwell withdrew from China in 1949; to make up for the loss of business due to this move, Dodwell strengthened its presence in Australia, East Africa, and India.

When Inchcape tried to acquire Dodwell in the early 1970s, the main difficulty encountered was that Dodwell was not public listed in Hong Kong and its memorandum and articles of association had placed restrictions on the sale of 60% of its shares that were held by the Dodwell family and its key staff. At first, Dodwell was averse to the proposed acquisition for it was still hopeful that its investment in North America would generate good results. However, that investment turned out to be a letdown and its business in Japan also suffered from a setback. Under these circumstances, it gave in to Inchcape's acquisition. Moreover, Dodwell's chairman, J.H. Hamn, was on good terms with Inchcape's leadership, which made things easier.[5] Dodwell also had a host of subsidiaries, including Dodwell Trading, Dodwell Boutique, Dodwell (International) Merchandizing, and Dodwell (Hong Kong) Merchandizing.

By the mid-1970s, Inchcape had established itself as a leading trading firm in Hong Kong, with over thirty subsidiaries and joint ventures. Among these companies, eight major ones were owned directly by the U.K. parent, including Inchcape (Hong Kong), Inchcape (Far East), Inchcape Enterprise, Dodwell, Gilman and Gibb Livingston, whereas the rest were joint ventures of these eight companies. Inchcape's businesses in Hong Kong covered trading, car distribution, shipping, advertising, insurance, and manufacturing. In 1977, Inchcape purchased some floors at Elizabeth House for its headquarters in Hong Kong. Except for Dodwell that remained in Tsim Sha Tsui to

---

[5] Huang (1992), p. 7.

maintain close contact with its clients, all the subsidiaries moved to Elizabeth House.

In the 1980s, the decline of the Inchcape Group became apparent mainly due to the increased pressure on Asian governments to localize. Like other British hongs, Inchcape had been engaged in trading, shipping, and even mining in the British colonies in Asia since the 19th century. With the advent of the 20th century, this advantage gradually diminished. Again, like other well-established business empires, overexpansion had inevitably led Inchcape to lose its strategic focus and control over its subsidiaries. Paul Cheng, who later became Executive Director of Inchcape Pacific Limited, described those subsidiaries as "mini hongs." Each had its chairman, board of directors, and management. Owing to the overly diverse nature of the Group's business, overall planning was absent and there was even duplication and internal competition.[6]

Lord Inchcape, the chairman of the Inchcape Group, retired in 1983 and was succeeded by Sir. David Orr. To overcome the Group's problems arising from the lack of strategic focus, the new chairman formulated a series of business strategies, an important one among which was to profit from the emergence of the Pacific region by supplying Asian products to markets in Western Europe, and by expanding the Group's presence in China, as well as Central and South Americas. Two core areas were identified, namely, professional sales and professional services. Modern sales methods would be used to penetrate the traditional trade and retail markets. The transfer of technology and knowledge would also be sought. At the same time, the scope of services would be expanded from insurance, shipping, and harbor services to integrated transportation and consultancy services.[7]

To align with its strategic changes, the Group restructured its business and organization in Hong Kong in 1987 by setting up Inchcape Pacific Limited as its regional headquarters and holding company for strengthening the management of its subsidiaries. The Group's business mix was also adjusted to some extent, with the sales of loss-making or low profitable businesses like

---

[6] *Capital*, Hong Kong, July 1993, pp. 56–59.
[7] *Capital*, Hong Kong, July 1993, pp. 56–59.

Dowell Stores, and the allocation of more resources to focus on three core businesses (i.e., car distribution, marketing services, and business services). As a subsidiary of the Inchcape Group, Inchcape Pacific Limited was chiefly responsible for the parent's businesses in Hong Kong, the Chinese mainland, Taiwan, Macau, the Philippines, Vietnam, Laos, and Cambodia. Hong Kong commanded a central position in this company's regional presence and was very proactive in developing its local businesses.

The business services of Inchcape Pacific were offered through a number of subsidiaries, including Inchcape Insurance, Inchcape Buying Services (IBS), Inchcape Inspection and Testing, as well as Inchcape Shipping Services. IBS was the former Dodwell; Dodwell was split in 1976 so that its business in Hong Kong and Japan could merge with IBS while markets in Canada, Kenya, and Panama were merged with Inchcape Shipping Services and IBS.

IBS was founded in the early 1970s with Hong Kong as its headquarters. It conducted mainly buying services for the export of products such as toys, electronics, textiles, and garments. By the early 1990s, its global network encompassed some twenty offices in seventeen different countries or regions, including India, Pakistan, Bangladesh, and Sri Lanka, with a total staff force of 1,000. In those days, Hong Kong's three top export-buying houses were IBS, Li & Fung Trading, and Swire Trading, with a turnover of US$700 million, US$500 million, and US$400 million, respectively, as recorded in 1992.

The Acquisition of IBS

During its relisting exercise in 1992, Li & Fung Trading revealed its future plans and prospects in its IPO prospectus:

"The directors believe that Asia will continue to be a major area for the manufacturing of mass-produced consumer products for the world and that Hong Kong will continue to play the role of a major trading center in this region. The directors expect Thailand, Indonesia and, in particular, the P.R.C. to become increasingly important manufacturing centers for these consumer products due to their abundant and low-cost labor supply and the encouragement given by their governments to the export sector...In addition, different countries in the Far East specialize in different industries, as a result of factors such as dissimilarity in raw material availability, levels of labor skills and governmental regulations. This favors export-trading companies with the expertise to source components and products from different countries…Due to sourcing in the Far East becoming increasingly complex, the directors believe that major overseas buyers have realized that it is more beneficial to use export agents with a regional presence than to establish their own buying network. The directors believe that the Group's coordinated regional network can enhance the Group's ability to secure new customers and strengthen relationships with existing customers."[8]

After relisting, Li & Fung Trading formulated its first three-year (1993–1995) plan, aiming to surpass its major competitor, IBS, and to become Hong Kong's leading export firm. To achieve that, it actively built its regional sourcing network in order to reinforce its competitive position worldwide. During this three-year period, it set up a number of offices in various regional markets, including Jakarta, Indonesia (1992); Shah Alam, Malaysia (1993); Manila, the Philippines (1994); Hanoi, Vietnam (1994); and in several major cities in China, namely, Shenzhen (1992), Zhanjiang (1993), Changsha (1994), Guangzhou (1995), Shantou (1995), and Qingdao (1995). Together with those set up earlier in other markets, including Taipei (1968), Singapore (1973), Seoul (1987), Bangkok (1988), and Shanghai (1988), Li & Fung Trading now enjoyed a comprehensive sourcing network in the Far East.

Li & Fung Trading's business performance was impressive during this period. According to a research report published by Sun Hung Kai Research Limited, between 1991 and 1994, Li & Fung Trading grew at an average rate of 30% per year. Furthermore, its rate of return was 3.5%, outperforming its peers by 2–3%.[9] By 1994, Li & Fung Trading's turnover had reached HK$6.1 billion and its pre-tax and after-tax profits were HK$572 million and HK$553 million, respectively. In comparison, Inchcape's turnover derived from its buying services was HK$512 million and its pre-tax and after-tax profits were HK$52 million and HK$40 million, respectively. Before the completion of its first three-year plan, Li & Fung Trading already outdid IBS. In his company's 1994 annual report, William Fung proudly declared, "After eighty-eight years of history, 1994 saw the consolidation of he Company's

---

[8] *Li & Fung Limited New Issue and Offer for Sale 1992*, pp. 24–25.
[9] *Li & Fung Limited Annual Report*, August 8, 1994.

reputation as the pre-eminent export-trading company in Hong Kong and the region."[10] In July 1995, Li & Fung Trading was included in the fifty companies chosen for Hang Seng Hong Kong MidCap Index launched by HSI Services Limited.

Despite its distinguished status as Hong Kong's top trading firm, Li & Fung Trading had one very obtrusive weakness—its over-reliance on the U.S. as its export market. This imbalance could hardly be considered healthy. Export trade accounted for 99% and 92% of the company's turnover and profit, respectively. Of all its exports, apparels accounted for 75%, fashion accessories 12%, toys 10%, and handicrafts and sporting goods the remaining 3%. In terms of market size, the U.S. was the company's largest buyer, accounting for 84% of its exports, whereas the other markets made up the remaining 16%, of which 14% was from Europe.

The early 1990s was a difficult period for export traders. Sino-U.S. relations deteriorated after the June 4 Incident in 1989. The U.S. economy itself was underperforming, thus leading to trade protectionism. The U.S. government would frequently threaten to withdraw China's most-favored nation (MFN) trade status on the pretext of political issues like human rights. Such a climate at the international trade scene naturally created much difficulty for Li & Fung Trading's core business. With a view to driving market diversification, Li & Fung Trading embarked on its very first acquisition, the target of which was none other than its old rival—IBS.

For decades, IBS was the largest merchandizing company in Hong Kong. In 1994, its profit margin was 0.8% versus Li & Fung Trading's 3.3%. Li & Fung Trading's management believed that IBS's human resources could be better utilized to ensure considerably higher profits. IBS had more than 1,000 employees who were all professional buyers. What it lacked was an effective business strategy to propel profit growth. If IBS's profit margin could catch up with that of Li & Fung Trading's, then the latter could double its profits in three years after the acquisition. Furthermore, assuming that the P/E ratio of Li & Fung Trading's shares was to remain constant, the market capitalization of the company would be doubled from HK$300 million to HK$600 million. More importantly, while IBS resembled Li & Fung Trading

---

[10] *Li & Fung Limited Annual Report 1994.*

in terms of its business orientation, it had very different export markets. IBS relied more on Europe, which accounted for 71% of its business, whereas the U.S. accounted for only 29%. IBS had a total of twenty branches in eighteen countries. After acquiring IBS, Li & Fung Trading could achieve a more balanced market portfolio with the U.S. accounting for 59% and Europe the remaining 41%.[11]

"The merger of Li & Fung Trading and IBS—the first- and second-largest trading groups in Hong Kong—will create for us an extensive and powerful sourcing network worldwide consisting of twenty-eight branch offices in twenty countries with over 2,000 employees," said William Fung. "The existing clients of both companies will benefit. For Li & Fung Trading, turnover would be doubled to HK$18 billion." In addition, Li & Fung Trading could, upon acquiring IBS, make use of the latter's buying services in the Indian subcontinent, including India, Pakistan, Bangladesh, and Sri Lanka, to achieve geographical expansion. With a population of 1.4 billion, the Indian subcontinent possessed immeasurable market potential, which could contribute significantly to Li & Fung Trading's development.

According to a research report published by Goldman Sachs, after acquiring IBS, "The new Li & Fung will be a dominant player in export trading in the region, with no other entity near this size. The export trading, or 'sourcing' industry is normally characterized by a large number of small local players in each market, with very few with a regional network of any size, and none as large as Li & Fung following the IBS acquisition. The group will grow to a total of twenty-seven sourcing offices in eighteen countries, with supplier relationships at over 2,000 factories. The advantages to this network strength include: a wide range of sources for goods procurement, thereby providing customers with the best value for money; and, added efficiency as customers need only to deal with one regional sourcing agent. In addition to boosting the regional sourcing capacity, the enlarged Li & Fung will be better balanced in terms of the geographical mix of customers and product mix…The reduced dependence on the U.S. market and on textiles as the main product line should be viewed positively by investors."[12]

---

[11] *Li & Fung News*, No. 22, August 1995.
[12] Sachs (1995), pp. 3–4.

Based on Goldman Sachs' analysis, after the merger, Li & Fung's turnover by geographical location from the contribution of the U.S. would decrease from 80% to 56%, whereas that of Europe would increase from 20% to 44%. The company's reliance on soft goods like apparels would also drop from 79% to 72%, whereas the weight of hard goods would rise from 21% to 28%. Investors, therefore, would take a long position in Li & Fung's shares (Exhibit 6.1).[13]

A certain degree of risk, however, was also inherent in the acquisition. Li & Fung had never attempted a major acquisition before and so it lacked real experience. More importantly, IBS was a typical British firm whose management was predominantly Westerners. Obviously, there were fundamental differences in corporate culture between the two firms; cultural integration, therefore, could be a major challenge. Then, there was the wide gap in profit margin between the two firms, which stemmed from their different approaches in operation and management. The merger would almost inevitably lower Li & Fung's profit margin. Moreover, as a trading firm, IBS's tangible assets amounted to just over HK$30 million. The difference between the acquisition price and those assets would be ascribed to IBS's goodwill. In other words, after the acquisition, Li & Fung Trading had to write off the amount in relation to IBS's goodwill, thus reducing shareholders' interests.

Exhibit 6.1   Li & Fung Trading's export market and product turnover after acquiring IBS

	Li & Fung Trading (Before acquisition)	IBS	Li & Fung Trading (After acquisition)
Export market	100%	100%	100%
USA	80%	29%	56%
Europe & others	20%	71%	44%
Product	100%	100%	100%
Soft goods	79%	65%	72%
Hard goods	21%	35%	28%

Source: Goldman Sachs.

---

[13] Sachs (1995), pp. 3–4.

At that particular juncture, Inchcape was facing the same uncertainty as its British counterparts like Jardine Matheson and Hong Kong & Shanghai Banking Corporation in view of the imminent reunification of Hong Kong with China in 1997. As a multinational enterprise, Inchcape's core business involved car distribution. Buying services only constituted an extremely small part of its total turnover. The selling of this non-core business would give it more room to restructure itself and reinforce its core business. Against this backdrop, when Li & Fung Trading approached Inchcape with its intention, the latter reacted positively. The only key issue to be decided was the price.

On July 1, 1995, Li & Fung Trading and the Inchcape Group entered into a sale-and-purchase agreement after a few months' negotiations. Li & Fung was to acquire IBS at a cash consideration of not more than HK$450 million, representing a P/E ratio of 8–9. This was lower than the HK$475 million initially agreed in early May as Li & Fung subsequently decided not to acquire certain minor businesses under the IBS banner. According to the agreement, Li & Fung Trading was to pay Inchcape HK$275 million upon the completion of the acquisition but this amount was subject to IBS's shareholders' funds being not less than HK$60 million and the completion of certain business restructuring. The balance of HK$175 million would then be payable after the acquisition in two installments following the 1995 and 1996 results of IBS. These two payments could be adjusted, subject to IBS meeting the agreed gross income targets for these two fiscal years. This acquisition was partly financed—to the amount of HK$225 million—by Li & Fung Trading's internal cash reserves and partly by bank borrowings.

Upon the completion of the acquisition, Li & Fung Trading assumed management over IBS, including its brands and trademarks—mainly those of Dodwell. IBS was renamed Dodwell Company Limited, signifying the restoration of its heritage. In May 1996, Li & Fung Trading announced its financial results for 1995, the first year after acquiring Dodwell. Turnover soared 50% to HK$921.3 million, of which Li & Fung Trading accounted for HK$653.5 million and Dodwell HK$267.8 million. Operating profit was approximately HK$258 million, to which Dodwell contributed 15.5% (approximately HK$40 million). Since its acquisition by Li & Fung Trading in July 1995, Dodwell had already doubled its profits recorded in 1994.

William Fung expected Li & Fung Trading's business to be further strengthened in 1995. After acquiring Dodwell, he believed that profit would continue to grow in the next three years and that Li & Fung Trading would maintain its leading position in the industry. As 1995 would be the last year of his company's first three-year plan after relisting, William was confident that upon the completion of this plan, it would become a highly profitable and well-managed company based in Hong Kong. He also pointed out that the acquisition of Dodwell had allowed Li & Fung to enter the European market, extend its sourcing network to the Indian Subcontinent and almost double its professional workforce.

In its annual result release, Li & Fung Trading also announced the placing of 5.6 million existing and new shares, representing about 10% of its issued shares, to institutional investors at HK$6.55 per share or a discount of 5% on the closing price the day before. Part of the proceeds from the placing to the amount of HK$250 million would be used to pay off the bank loans for acquiring Dodwell and the rest would be reserved as operating expenses. After the placing, King Lun Holdings Limited (jointly owned by the Fung brothers) would have its holdings of Li & Fung Trading's shares reduced from 66.9% to 60.8%. Li & Fung Trading's gearing ratio would also drop substantially from 120% to the healthier level of 68–69%, thus reducing interest expenses by HK$20–30 million a year.

"The decision to acquire Dodwell was made within a short time," said William Fung. "There was no urgent need then to raise funds because we had gained a substantial amount of extraordinary profits from selling the shares of Cyrk Inc. Because the board wished to maintain a high dividend payout ratio of 70% of net profit and to share the proceeds arising from the sale of Cyrk Inc., we ended up in a relatively high debt ratio. We were of the view that it was in the best interests of shareholders to initiate the placing of shares rather than lowering the dividend payout ratio."

He pointed out that the placing would achieve the dual purpose of reducing the company's liabilities to pave the way for further acquisitions while increasing the circulation of the company's shares.

"The proceeds from the placing of 10% of our shares were roughly equal to the price we paid for Dodwell after excluding its assets," William stressed. "In other words, we have acquired a competitor whose turnover was more or less the same as ours for only 10% of our equities. It was without a doubt an excellent deal."

Implementing the "Filling in the Mosaic" Strategy (1996–1998)

Li & Fung Trading's second three-year plan commenced from 1996. The main strategy for this period was "filling in the mosaic." What "mosaic" meant, according to the group's research analysts, consisted of two parts. First, "by absorbing Dodwell's clients and overseas buying offices, Li & Fung Trading aimed to boost its supply-chain network for market expansion and for solidifying its core competitive strengths." Second, "by managing Dodwell in a better way, it aimed to raise its profit margin."[14] Victor and William's strategic focus was to unearth and make use of Dodwell's potential fully while raising its profit margin from below 1% to Li & Fung Trading's 3% level. By doing so, they aimed to enhance Li & Fung Trading's overall profitability and achieve the goal of doubling profit in the three-year period, from 1996 to 1998.

To achieve that goal, Li & Fung Trading embarked on an integration program with Dodwell in 1996. First, Dodwell had to be amalgamated properly with Li & Fung Trading through reorganization. Following the acquisition of Dodwell, Victor and William immediately set up a transitional working group made up of senior managers. This working group was entasked to ensure the smooth merging of the two companies, taking into account their respective organizational procedures and implementing a step-by-step merging process. Toward the end of 1995, in his capacity as chairman of the Group, Victor informed Dodwell's staff in Hong Kong through a circular that after careful consideration, the Group had decided to carry out certain organizational reforms to support its strategy for sustainable growth and ensure that the merged entity could continue to develop and move forward.

The restructuring process entailed a number of measures:

(1) Dodwell's organizational structure was required to be changed from "location-based" to "customer-based," as in the case of Li & Fung Trading. The circular said: "The first change is that our focus will be on products and customers. You all appreciate the importance of customer service and how it relates to profit. After careful strategic

---

[14] Li & Fung Research Center (2003), pp. 139–141.

analysis, we have decided to change Dodwell's former location-based organizational structure to that of product/customer-based, which has been proven to be highly successful by Li & Fung...It can raise the levels of profit and customer service across the Group's product lines and networks." After the restructuring exercise, Dodwell was internally divided into seven groups, including three product/customer groups, two sourcing groups, and one operation support group. To better manage the company's extensive sourcing network and facilitate the coordination of products and customers in various locations, there would still be a country and branch managers in each country/region, who would also double as the product group manager and company director. Their roles were to coordinate the operations of product and customer groups in their respective countries.

(2) Dodwell and Li & Fung Trading's respective offices in the same country or location would be merged. The circular said: "The second step we are taking is to merge the two companies' offices in the same country. This should enhance our overall operational efficiency and demonstrate our team spirit and internal cooperation, thus boosting our corporate image and assuring customers of consistent service quality. The removal of the merged office will be implemented in phases, having regard to the tenancy agreement, usable floor area, and timing. For Hong Kong, the implementation of this plan is expected to be completed in the first half of 1996."

(3) The two companies' finance, accounts, personnel, administration and IT departments were to be merged with a view to provide a more efficient and responsive support infrastructure to the frontline components. During the transitional period, these support services would be provided jointly by Li & Fung Trading and Dodwell.

The first obstacle for merging came from the general managers of Dodwell's offices in various countries and regions. They were at first resistant to the change from their location-based organizational structure to a product/customer-based one. Each country's general manager wanted to have the sourcing and production process of the entire product done in his country.

"Basically," said William Fung, "the senior management was psychologically prepared for the merger but the general managers in the various countries found it hard to adapt to regional cooperation. Our acquisition came as a shock to them. After the merger, we assigned Dodwell's general managers to different customer groups regardless of location. We also told them to focus on products and source from, not just one country, but regionally, by making use of Li & Fung's network."

The company's organizational restructuring commenced from January 1996. It was essentially a project to mold and integrate Dodwell with the Li & Fung model. After this integration, the interregional competition that existed under Dodwell's former business model diminished. The sourcing managers were given access to more information on different markets in order to achieve cost savings for clients by means of more efficient supply-chain management. "The merging of the two companies' back-office support also resulted in substantial benefits. With the centralization of the finance, personnel, and administration functions, a higher percentage of employees could be deployed to take up customer service at the frontline. Since better customer service depends on a well-developed information system, the merged company also achieved greater economies of scale in its information system."[15]

Frank Leong, former chief financial officer (CFO) of IBS, remarked in an interview: "This move was important for Li & Fung, as it took over a company that was the same size as it. In some cases, in some countries, it was more like a reverse takeover. In Bangkok during that time, there were only 10 to 15 people from Li & Fung, but there were some 40 Dowell people."[16]

In 1995, Frank Leong was invited by Victor to become Li & Fung Trading's CFO. To him, taking up this new position was not easy because the company's scale of operation had nearly doubled overnight with its total turnover reaching HK$10 billion. He found himself having to handle not only an expanded team of accountants but also the IT and human resources departments. In the first three years after Frank became Li & Fung Trading's CFO, the number of accountants fell by twenty although the company's total staff force doubled. After the restructuring, the Group's finance, administration, and IT departments were centralized in its Hong Kong headquarters.

---

[15] Li & Fung Research Center (2003), p. 141.
[16] *Finance Asia*, February 2001, p. 11.

Moreover, the ranking, salaries, incentive schemes, and fringe benefits of all the former Dodwell staff were adjusted in accordance with Li & Fung Trading's systems. As a major trading firm, Li & Fung Trading attaches a great deal of importance to the accumulation and deployment of human resources. It understands thoroughly well that the entrepreneurial spirit, the ability to communicate with clients and discover their needs, the relevant knowledge of products and their qualities, and an understanding of manu-facturers required of a trade professional cannot be acquired at school but have to be accumulated over time by practical experience. "We can't possi-bly recruit from the market because *we* are the market," said William Fung. "Sometimes, we have to acquire certain smaller trading firms to bring in experienced people." To have a stronger foundation for growth, it is crucial for his company to attract the talents it needs.

In an attempt to retain Dodwell's former staff after the merger, particu-larly the senior managers, Li & Fung enforced some new employment terms as from January 1, 1996. This measure applied only to the Dodwell office in Hong Kong. The new terms of employment covered mainly these points:

(1) *Rank and salary*. Dodwell's original ranking system was to be aligned with the Li & Fung model. Since this alignment and the change in employment terms could possibly affect the pay level of individual employees, Li & Fung Trading conducted a company-wide review and assessment of the staff's performance and pay, the findings of which were to be enforced with effect from January 1996.

(2) *Profit sharing/incentive scheme*. Li & Fung Trading had already been implementing an incentive scheme for profit sharing in the past few years. This scheme was based on the employee's performance and con-tribution to the company's profits. It was to be extended to Dodwell's staff as well.

(3) *Retirement benefits*. After considering various comparable schemes, the probability of growing employees' savings and the global trend, Li & Fung Trading decided to change Dodwell's former retirement scheme into one of fixed contribution so that all Dodwell staff would join Li & Fung Trading's provident fund scheme. However, the retirement benefits of all Dodwell staff accrued by the end of December 1995 were to remain intact.

(4) *Working hours and other fringe benefits.* To align with Dodwell's original practice, Li & Fung Trading implemented the five-day week system. To meet customers' expectations and maintain a consistent level of service, the company enforced a system for the staff to work or keep in touch with customers on weekends should the need arises.

Li & Fung Trading was genuinely concerned about employees' interests after the merger. Therefore, all arrangements were put in place to set everybody's mind at ease. The incentive scheme that pegged individual pay to the department's profit level was especially attractive to Dodwell's staff, who were worried and uncertain about the merger. The staff in general also identified with Li & Fung Trading's business philosophies and strategies. The experienced managers of Dodwell all chose to remain after the merger. Their experiences in new products, that is, those never handled by Li & Fung before, became a valuable asset for it enabled the company to broaden its product range, especially with regard to hard goods, thus giving new momentum to the company's development. After the merger, Li & Fung Trading's workforce more than doubled. The pool of human resources was enriched substantially by the joining of a group of non-Chinese managers from different parts of the world, who also helped reinforce the international aspect of the company.

After taking over Dodwell's overseas sourcing offices and customers, Li & Fung Trading substantially enlarged the coverage of its supply-chain management network and augmented its core competencies almost overnight. For a multinational trading firm like Li & Fung, the client base is its very foundation. The client base encompasses the numbers and types of clients, their product portfolios, and their markets. In the past, Li & Fung's clientele was largely in the U.S. and, to a far lesser extent, Europe. The acquisition of Dodwell boosted the dimensions of its client base considerably. Apart from bringing to Li & Fung Trading a considerable number of major European clients, Dodwell's presence in South Asia, Europe, the Mediterranean region, and Latin America, also substantially enlarged Li & Fung Trading's network of suppliers worldwide. In Li & Fung Trading's assessment, after acquiring Dodwell's, the distribution of its clients and products became more even. By location, the U.S. now accounted for 64% of its clientele, compared to 84% previously, while Europe accounted for 31%, up from 13%. Clients in other locations also increased from 3% to 5%. By product, the percentage of U.S.

textile clients dropped from 68% to 48% after the merger, while those in other countries rose from 10% to 30%. The percentage of hard goods remained unchanged at 22%.

Prior to the acquisition, Li & Fung had contacted Dodwell's accounts in Europe to understand their sourcing needs. It was found that the retail environment in Europe was lagging behind that of the U.S. by ten to fifteen years. While traditional department stores were shrinking in numbers, regional shopping malls were on the increase while bargain outlets were also mushrooming. With the change in the retail model, clients learned more about supply chain management and began to use the "one-stop shop" sourcing and fast production services offered by Li & Fung Trading. "When Dodwell's clients realized that Li & Fung's sourcing system could create more value for them," said William Fung, "they did not try to get in the way of the merger."

In addition to market development, the offices located in the neighborhood of Dodwell's markets need to be mentioned. Dodwell had set up branch offices in places like Istanbul (Turkey) and Porto (Portugal). Because of their proximity to major European markets, using them as sourcing and production bases would have the advantages of savings in transportation time, shortening the product and purchase cycles, as well as making it easier to satisfy urgent replenishment requests. Clients in Europe could turn to these offices for quick orders. Previously, if a client wanted to have his products made in China, he had to place his orders six to eight months in advance. Now he would rather pay Li & Fung Trading 20–30% more to have them made in Turkey in order to achieve faster turnover.

William explained, "Clients were beginning to see that the production cost covers not only what is charged by the manufacturer and Li & Fung for managing the production process, but also other costs such as those incurred for buying the wrong products, choosing the wrong type of products, overstocking outdated products, and running out of stock. Clients prefer most of all our kind of replenishment service. As soon as they have sold five pieces of their product, we will order five more for them from the manufacturer. This kind of replenishment service is possible only if the place of production and the client's market are near to each other. We have been offering this kind of service, for instance, to The Limited Group. By working closely with their various departments, we can effectively minimize production time for them. Our competency in this regard has made us the pioneer in the Orient. By cooperating with us, The Limited has drastically reduced its product cycle from five months to forty-five days, the biggest achievement for us since I joined Li & Fung."[17]

The contribution of these quick-response sourcing bases rose from 5% in 1995 to 11% in 1998, demonstrating the market's keen demand for such service. It can be seen that the acquisition of Dodwell to grow its client base was the main reason why Li & Fung Trading could achieve the primary goal of its second three-year plan by doubling its turnover within three years.

By mid-1996, Li & Fung Trading's merger with Dodwell was finally completed after a year's intense efforts and the upshot of the acquisition had gradually become apparent. During this period, Li & Fung's global sourcing network was enlarged to cover South Asia, Europe, the Mediterranean, Latin America, and countries like Egypt, Tunisia, Mexico, the United Arab Emirates, and Nepal. By the end of 1998, this network had spread to twenty-nine countries or regions with forty-five offices, and a supplier base of over 7,000.

Prior to the acquisition, Li & Fung Trading had estimated that 20–30% of Dodwell's clients would possibly be lost but none of them left during the merger. In 1998, Li & Fung Trading had 420 major accounts in the U.S. and Europe, most of them being large retail chains, including The Limited, Warner Brothers, John Lewis Partnership, and El Corte Ingles of Spain. In 1996, the first fiscal year when Dodwell's turnover was taken into full account, Li & Fung Trading's total turnover soared by 35.8% to HK$12.514 billion, to which Dodwell contributed 41%. Operating profit before extraordinary items was HK$326 million, up by 26.2% whereas profit attributed to shareholders was HK$300 million, up by 33.3%. However, the company's profit margin narrowed from 3.3% to 2.4% as a result of the acquisition.

On July 1, 1997, Hong Kong's reunification with China took place smoothly. Unfortunately, in the latter half of 1997, a widespread financial crisis hit East

---

[17] Harvard Business Case Studies, "Li & Fung: Beyond 'Filling in the Mosaic,'" as quoted in Li & Fung Research Center (2003), p. 123.

Asia after a number of Southeast Asian countries like Thailand, Malaysia, and Indonesia devaluated their currencies. The Hong Kong economy also suffered heavily as a result. The impact on Li & Fung Trading was such that between the end of 1997 and 1998, some of its exports could not be shipped on time. The reduction in operating expenses in Korea, Thailand, and Indonesia, however, partly offset the company's loss in profits. During 1997, Li & Fung Trading's business growth began to slow down with total turnover increasing by only 6.6% to HK$13.345 billion. After-tax profit still increased strongly by 25% to HK$375 million, though. Overall, the company's profit margin improved by 2.81%.

After the regional financial debacle in 1997, Li & Fung's two major markets—the U.S. and Europe—saw impressive economic growth, resulting in strong demands for consumer goods. U.S. retailers were increasingly reliant on supply chain management in sourcing. With an extensive and flexible global network, Li & Fung Trading was apt to satisfy clients' quick-response needs and attain satisfactory business growth. In 1998, the company's turnover and after-tax profit reached HK$14.313 billion and HK$455 million, respectively, up by 7.2% and 21.3%, respectively, from a year ago. Compared to 1995, the corresponding increases were 55.4% and 102.2%, respectively (Exhibit 6.2).

In terms of geographical location, Li & Fung Trading's export markets were also becoming more evenly distributed. The U.S. now accounted for 67.5% of turnover, instead of 84.4% previously; Europe's share increased from 12.6% to 28.6%. Even the Asia Pacific region grew in importance, accounting for 3.3–4%, up from 2.1% in the past. Indeed, Li & Fung's effort in market diversification was beginning to see progress (Exhibit 6.3). By the end of

Exhibit 6.2   Li & Fung Trading's business performance (HK$ million), 1993–1998

Year	1993	1994	1995	1996	1997	1998
Turnover	4,943	6,125	9,213	12,514	13,346	14,313
Exports	4,905	6,089	9,186	12,500	13,331	14,309
(Growth, %)	(24.1)	(24.1)	(50.9)	(36.1)	(6.6)	(7.3)
Other income	38	36	27	14	15	4
Operating profit	193	216	258	326	413	464
After-tax profit	198	553	225	300	375	455
Profit margin (%)	3.67	3.33	2.45	2.40	2.81	3.18

Source: Li & Fung (Trading) Limited Annual Reports, 1992–1998.

Exhibit 6.3 Li & Fung Trading's market turnover (HK$ million), 1994–1998

Year	1994	1995	1996	1997	1998
Total	6,125.5 (100%)	9,213.2 (100%)	12,513.8 (100%)	13,345.7 (100%)	14,312.6 (100%)
United States	5,167.7 (84.4%)	6,269.5 (68.1%)	7,977.2 (63.7%)	8,491.4 (63.6%)	9,664.9 (67.5%)
European Union	768.9 (12.6%)	2,381.2 (25.8%)	3,931.5 (31.4%)	4,040.8 (30.3%)	4,088.8 (28.6%)
Asia Pacific	129.2 (2.1%)	393.9 (4.3%)	381.3 (3.1%)	535.2 (4.0%)	471.6 (3.3%)
Other markets	59.7 (0.9%)	168.6 (1.8%)	223.8 (1.8%)	278.3 (2.1%)	87.3 (0.6%)

Source: Li & Fung (Trading) Limited Annual Reports, 1994–1998.

1998, Dodwell had already been fully integrated with Li & Fung. Its profit margin increased from 0.8% to over 3%. Li & Fung Trading's overall profit margin also rose to 3.18%, which was near the pre-merger level. By this time, the company had basically realized the goal of "filling in the mosaic" in its 1996–1998 three-year plan.

"I am very pleased that the Group's business growth has been in line with the goals of our current three-year plan," said William Fung. "Notwithstanding the economic adversities caused by the endemic financial crisis in the Asian region, we have maintained our growth momentum and, by capitalizing on our superiorities, we have continued to offer quick-response services and satisfy the keen demand from our two major markets—the U.S. and Europe."

Bridging the Cultural Gap

During the merger, the biggest challenge faced by Li & Fung Trading was the disparity in corporate culture between the two companies which engendered two different styles of operation. Given its history spanning three generations and being embedded in deep-rooted traditional Chinese thinking, Li & Fung was still very much a Chinese family firm with a unique management model. "Li & Fung is a company that cherishes Chinese traditions," said Victor Fung. "We don't easily dismiss our employees. On the contrary, we would retain those who have retired to be our advisers. Apart from that, we don't believe in ranks and grades. We treat our staff like our family."

This philosophy is demonstrated by the experience of a foreign manager of Li & Fung who recalled: "Whenever my wife comes to Hong Kong, Victor and William's mother would invite her to a *dim-sum* lunch and go shopping with her." Madam Chung Hok-mei, an accountant with Li & Fung for fifty-three years, also felt deeply about the Li & Fung's style of management. "To the bosses [Victor and William], staff relations are extremely important," she said. "They make it a rule to dine with all the staff on Chinese New Year Eve every year at the Hong Kong Convention and Exhibition Center. It was a large banquet with hundred tables. Literally everybody in the company would be invited, including the tea ladies."

Madam Chung recalled that whenever some colleagues had to work late into the night, William would ask his driver to drive them home. The company would also organize a launch picnic for the staff after completing a major project. She remained an employee of the company till the ripe old age of over seventy. When she tendered her resignation in 1995, William still tried to retain her and was interested to know why she was leaving.

"After three generations," said William Fung, "Li & Fung has already been deeply entrenched in Chinese values. We expect our employees to be loyal and reliable, and in return for their industry and performance they are duly rewarded. The reward for the managers is dished out on the basis of a generous profit-sharing mechanism whereby they receive bonuses that reflect the performance of their respective offices or departments. Understandably, industries like garments are susceptible to market conditions. Managers who are vying for stable incomes would feel uneasy about this merit-based departmental incentive scheme. We don't dismiss our staff merely because their department's profit drops in any given year; we understand all too well that market fluctuations can affect their profit performance in the short term. We were brought up to be loyal and reliable. If our staff fails to perform due to external adversities, we will always try our best to retain them or transfer them to other positions in the firm."

The Fung brothers have always been proud of their Chinese heritage but they also realize that appropriate adjustment requires taking into consideration the cultural characteristics of the countries where Li & Fung operates. "We are a traditional Chinese firm based in Hong Kong," said William Fung, "but we don't preach blindly to our Thai employees, for instance, the way things are done in Hong Kong; neither do we subscribe to the way American corporations manage their overseas branches. Instead, we allow our overseas offices to develop their own management model that fits local circumstances. Of course, core areas like remuneration and incentive schemes will be centrally managed."

Since its first public listing in 1973, Li & Fung had come a long way in its corporate development but it never consciously discarded its inherent characteristics as a traditional Chinese firm, despite the fact that an American-style management system had already been in place. Dodwell, on the other hand, was a traditional British firm under the management of a group of foreigners from abroad. Naturally these senior managers were not attuned to the operation system followed by the Chinese family firm. They had their own life-styles and expectations to remuneration that were fundamentally different to the standards adopted by Li & Fung Trading. Beyond this, the internal communication and management of the two companies also differed. At meetings, foreign managers were usually outspoken whereas their colleagues from Li & Fung Trading would seldom confront them and would usually go along with the majority view. Under these circumstances, finding a way to blend the two different corporate cultures so that the staff could work happily together under the same roof was a critical issue.

For that purpose, after the merger, Li & Fung initiated a monthly operational meeting so that the managers from all over the world could regularly come together and discuss the company's strategies. It could also facilitate face-to-face interaction between senior managers of different localities through which a transnational corporate culture could be nurtured and built. In the presence of non-Chinese staff, Victor and William would conduct the meetings in English to ensure better communication with the senior managers, as well as product and country managers. The company would also hold two meetings each year to consider its global strategy for meeting future challenges. "We would make sure that all the general managers have the chance to speak their minds," said Victor. "The final decision would of course rest with William but we must ensure that this decision is correct. By encouraging our managers to voice their views, we have come a long way from the traditional top-down approach followed by the Chinese family firm."[18]

---

[18] Li & Feng Research Center (2003), p. 125.

The acquisition of Dodwell also had farreaching but positive ramifications for Li & Fung Trading's corporate culture. For instance, Dodwell's managers were used to being stationed overseas and would readily accept the instruction to be relocated should the need arise. Managers from Hong Kong, on the other hand, were usually more reluctant to work overseas on a permanent basis. With the influx of Dodwell's managers, internal communication also assumed a different character. They found that their Chinese colleagues were emulating them by speaking out more frequently at meetings than before.

In December 1995, five months after acquiring Dodwell, Victor Fung was honored the Businessman of the Year Award, jointly organized by DHL and South China Morning Post, an award given out since 1990 to give recognition to outstanding business leaders. The same award was given to veteran banker Sir. Lee Quo-wai, the chairman of Hang Seng Bank, the previous year. At the award presentation ceremony, Victor cited the acquisition of IBS that later became Dodwell again as his most notable achievement. He admitted that this acquisition had given him immense satisfaction because it enabled his company to grow into a multinational trading group. The acquisition of IBS can be considered a major milestone for Li & Fung in the 1990s. By this move, Li & Fung had both conquered its chief rival in Hong Kong and laid the foundation for becoming the topmost trading group in Hong Kong.

To commemorate its 90th anniversary in 1996, Li & Fung spent HK$10 million to sponsor the annual fireworks display held during the Chinese New Year. The theme for the 1996 event was to extol Hong Kong's leading status in international trade. On February 20, 1996, the second day of the Chinese New Year, Li & Fung held a display of fireworks party for the staff and their families at the outdoor car park on the roof of Ocean Terminal that could accommodate 5,000 people. As may be noted, Hong Kong's Chinese New Year fireworks display dated back to 1982. The first two years were sponsored by the Jardine Matheson Group to commemorate its 150th anniversary. The theme for each year was different, depending on the sponsor. For example, Bank of China (Hong Kong) was the sponsor in 1994 after becoming the third note-issuing bank in Hong Kong. Li & Fung was given the opportunity to sponsor the 1996 event after the Dodwell acquisition, which marked its distinguished status as Hong Kong's leading trading group.

Chapter 7

Further Acquisitions to Widen the Net

"These acquisitions will significantly broaden our customer base in both of our key markets, the U.S., and Europe. The addition of Swire & Maclaine and Camberley is a further step in cementing our position as one of the world's leading sourcing and supply chain management companies."

—Victor Fung

"The rich array of resources in Swire & Maclaine and Camberley and the skills and experience of their 500-odd staff ideally complement our current business. At the same time, I believe that these companies will benefit from the integration with Li & Fung's management systems and technology support. The combined Group will also derive considerable benefits from economies of scale."

—William Fung

The Acquisition of Swire & Maclaine and Camberley

In 1998, Li & Fung Trading formulated a third three-year (1999–2001) plan aimed at doubling its profit and boosting its turnover and profit margin by 50% and 1%, respectively. In the meantime, the company continued to seek acquisition opportunities to expand its global sourcing network in order to maintain its foremost position in the increasingly competitive trade environment. The most important acquisitions in this period were Swire & Maclaine and Camberley, both under the Swire Group.

The Swire Group was not only one of Hong Kong's most prominent British trading firms but also ranked among the "Big Four," together with Jardine Matheson, Hutchison Whampoa, and Wheelock Marden. Of these four British firms, Swire was known for its pragmatism and balanced approach, though politically it was not nearly as powerful as Jardine Matheson; and, in terms of growth strategy, it was less aggressive than Hutchison Whampoa. Formerly known as Butterfield & Swire Company, the Swire Group was founded in Shanghai in 1866 by John Samuel Swire, a textiles merchant from Yorkshire, England. After establishing its foothold in China, the Swire Group had once monopolized navigation along the Chinese coast and the Yangzi River.[1] The Swire Group arrived in Hong Kong in 1870. At first, it was an agent for Blue Funnel Line, a steamship company, while also engaging in the trading of sundry goods. In 1881 and 1900, it set up Taikoo Sugar Refinery and Taikoo Dockyards, both in Hong Kong. Its business scope grew gradually to include navigation, dockyards, sugar refinery, paint manufacturing, and insurance; and it soon became a leading British firm in Hong Kong.

In the 1950s, Swire withdrew from the mainland of China and reestablished its business in the Far East, with Hong Kong as its base. It quickly emerged as a diversified conglomerate by building up its business scope that ranged from navigation and civil aviation, to real estate and other areas by acquiring Cathay Pacific Airways Limited, forming Hong Kong Aircraft Engineering Company Limited (HAECO) and setting up Swire Properties Limited. The Group also invested in Hong Kong's manufacturing industries—sugar

---

[1] Zhang, Chen, and Yao (1991), p. 87.

Li & Fung providing "one-stop shop" services to customers.

Li & Fung's professionally designed showroom demonstrates its sensitivity to market trends.

Independent showroom tailored to customers' specific needs and to facilitate business negotiation.

Making preparations before meeting with clients.

The offices of Li & Fung Trading were originally intended to be differentiated by various colors, but the concept didn't materialize due to its rapid development.

Discussing the selection of color schemes to be used for different product groups.

The start of production—the supply of raw material

packaging, beverages, construction materials, fiber glass, paints, and industrial chemicals. In 1969, Swire Industries Limited was set up to oversee the Group's manufacturing activities.

In the mid-1970s, with public-listed company Swire Pacific Limited as its flagship, the Swire Group divided its businesses into four main areas: real estate, aviation and hotels, industries, and marine services. Swire Pacific's real-estate division was operated mainly by Swire Properties Limited; the aviation and hotels division was in charge of companies like Cathay Pacific Airways, HAECO, and Hong Kong Air Cargo Terminals Limited (HACTL); the industries division managed subsidiaries like Taikoo Sugar Limited, Swire Bottlers, Swire & Maclaine, and also Camberley that was set up later; and the marine services division was in charge of joint ventures like United Dockyards and Modern Terminals.[2]

Swire & Maclaine Limited was founded in 1946 with its headquarters in Hong Kong as a trading firm that sourced high-volume and labor-intensive consumer goods. Its business nature closely resembled that of Li & Fung Trading; it dealt in apparel sourcing, which accounted for 65% of its total turnover. The remainder of its products consisted of durable goods like toys, household utensils, gift and premium items, cookery, and table wares. In terms of its market, the U.S. accounted for 80% of its turnover whereas Europe, Canada, and Japan constituted the remaining 20%. Its major customers were mostly retail chains. As well, Swire & Maclaine had eleven branch offices in Asia and one service center in the U.S. It also had eleven quality control centers for overseeing thirty-one sourcing locations. With a workforce of more than 400, it was the third-largest export firm after Li & Fung Trading and Dodwell. However, since the 1990s, its performance had not been remarkable as it experienced persistent decline in its turnover and profit. In 1998, its total turnover and after-tax profit was HK$2,356 million and HK$12.7 million, respectively.

Camberley Enterprises Limited was established in 1979 by the Honorable Lydia Dunn (later known as the Baroness Dunn), then Senior Member of Hong Kong's Executive and Legislative Councils. A garments company with

---

[2] Feng (1996), p. 181.

165 employees, it designed, manufactured, and sourced high-end apparel, ladies' sportswear, fashion wear, and household goods. Its accounts included retailers in the U.K., the U.S., and Japan, as well as fashion brands and designer collections. The U.K. accounted for 70% of its turnover, the U.S. 27%, and Japan and others the remaining 3%. Camberley had a smaller client base than Swire & Maclaine. But one of its major clients was Laura Ashley, a fashion and home-furnishing brand in the U.K. Camberly was also characterized by its operation as a so-called "virtual manufacturer." It used its own facility for designing and making prototypes for clients. It would then purchase the fabrics and outsource the production to factories in Shenzhen. The whole process was carried out and managed under a system that was even more intricate than Li & Fung Trading's supply chain management. Camberley prospered during Lydia Dunn's days but after her retirement to the U.K. in 1996, her successor was not too equally keen on its business. In 1998, it posted a total turnover of HK$495 million and an after-tax profit of HK$35 million.

After having fully integrated Dodwell with its operational structure, Li & Fung Trading sought more acquisition opportunities in 1999. Sensing that Swire Pacific was losing interest in its export-trading business, Victor and William decided on a more aggressive approach by targeting Swire & Maclaine and Camberley. Incidentally, Swire Pacific was devoting its attention to strengthening its core businesses like aviation and real estate while scaling down by parting with non-core areas such as sourcing. As a result, negotiations between the two sides proceeded smoothly. On December 29, 1999, Li & Fung Limited and Swire Pacific Limited reached a sale-and-purchase agreement, with the former acquiring from the latter its two subsidiaries, Swire & Maclaine and Camberley, for a total cash consideration of HK$450 million. The P/E ratio was approximately 9.4. This agreement was subject to the combined total net assets and combined operating assets (that is, current assets minus current liabilities) of Swire & Maclaine and Camberley, being not less than HK$71 million and HK$17.5 million, respectively. This acquisition was to be completed in or before April 2000 and Li & Fung was to be funded from internal cash reserves.

"These acquisitions will significantly broaden our customer base in both of our key markets, the U.S., and Europe." said Victor Fung. "The addition of Swire & Maclaine and Camberley is a further step in establishing our position as one of the world's leading sourcing and supply chain management companies."

"The rich array of resources in Swire & Maclaine and Camberley and the skills and experience of their over 500 staff ideally complement our current business," said William Fung. William continued, "At the same time, I believe that these companies will benefit from the integration with Li & Fung's management systems and technology support. The combined Group will also achieve considerable benefits from economies of scale."[3]

It was estimated that based on their respective financial results in 1999, Li & Fung Trading's turnover would increase to HK$17.2 billion upon acquiring Swire & Maclaine and Camberley. William was confident that after these acquisitions, Li & Fung's turnover would grow 50% by 2001 and that the goal of doubling profit would be achieved. However, some people held a different view, questioning the wisdom of acquiring Swire & Maclaine whose sourcing network overlapped that of Li & Fung. To them, it was doubtful whether the acquisition could really augment Li & Fung's existing network. William's response was that the chance to acquire a suitable target was not something that popped up every day. Li & Fung was rich in financial resources but was in need of people; Swire & Maclaine had a superb management structure and the quality of its 400 employees was remarkable—all these factors were favorable to business development. Additionally, he pointed out that Swire Pacific was one of the best-managed companies in Hong Kong and that the lackluster performance of Swire & Maclaine in recent years was due mainly to its less aggressive approach. After the acquisition, Li & Fung Trading reformed its operation model and improved its operational efficiency and profit, with a view to boosting its profit margin from 0.7% to 3% in three years.

Regarding these acquisitions, a research report produced by Credit Lyonnais Securities Asia (CLSA) commented that the two subsidiaries had certainly been sold at a discount by Swire Pacific because as the second-largest export sourcing company in Hong Kong, Swire & Maclaine had always been Li & Fung's major rival. In addition, the purchase price paid by Li & Fung was

---

[3] Li & Fung Limited's press release, "Li & Fung to acquire Swire & Maclaine and Camberley," December 29, 1999.

based on the two subsidiaries' profits in 1998, i.e., immediately after the collapse of the Asian financial markets in 1997. The CLSA report also suggested that the acquisitions would not only reinforce Li & Fung Trading's business but also ensure the company's leadership in Hong Kong's consumer-goods export.[4]

The acquisition also allowed Li & Fung Trading to make use of Camberley's "virtual-manufacturing" model to develop its own fashion-design capabilities. Camberley's operation model differed quite significantly from Li & Fung's. Under "virtual manufacturing," Camberley was more than just a supplying agent; it was both a designer of ladies' fashion wear and accessories and a direct supplier at the same time. Its clientele included European and American high-fashion brands and its markets were mainly the U.K. and the U.S. Moreover, about 20% of Camberley's workforce was responsible for sales. The remaining 80% was engaged in support functions like product design, prototype making, production outsourcing, as well as quality control and assurance. They offered customized services to clients and prepared reports on fashion trends every spring and autumn with forecasts for the coming year. They also undertook product-design projects by designing and improving client's products, as well as managing the sourcing of fabrics and materials in order to ensure efficient cost control and higher profit margins for clients. Although Camberley did not run any factory, it had very close business relationship with manufacturers and, in fact, managed the whole production process.

Concerning Camberley's production, it was anchored in four different locations in Shenzhen and Guangdong, and one location each in Jiangsu, Zhijiang, and Sichuan. It worked with just a handful of factories, many of which had served it for over ten years—the result of which was a high degree of mutual understanding between them. Throughout the whole production process, Camberley's technicians and quality-control officers were stationed in the factories to manage and monitor every aspect of the production, as well as to ensure effective risk management.

"The Camberley's mode of operation was essentially what Li & Fung aspired to, that is, a genuine product supplier, instead of merely a supplying agent. Camberley was managing and enhancing the whole apparel supply

---

[4] *Oriental Daily News*, Hong Kong, January 6, 2000, p. B145.

chain. Vis-à-vis the production model of the traditional enterprise, "virtual manufacturing" emphasized meeting customers' needs and truly implementing the customer-oriented concept. The way Camberley produced apparels was a manifestation of this difference."[5] Through this acquisition, Li & Fung Trading inherited Camberley's unique strengths, which enabled it to move upstream in the supply chain and serve clients with a wider service portfolio.

In the three decades—from the 1970s to 1990s—the British firms (e.g., Dodwell and Swire & Maclaine) and the Chinese firm (e.g., Li & Fung Trading) had always been at the forefront of Hong Kong's export scene. By acquiring its two largest competitors and integrating their businesses under the same roof, Li & Fung Trading essentially brought an end to Britain's dominance in Hong Kong's external trade.

The Acquisition of Colby—"The Other Giant under the Same Roof"

In 2000, Li & Fung Trading moved on to make a new acquisition. This time the target was a consumer-goods trading firm that enjoyed as much reputation as itself—Colby Group Holdings Limited (Colby).

Colby was founded in 1975 by a brilliant Jewish businessman, Allan Zemen. Having started as a merchandiser in Canada, Zemen's business had extended to various parts of Europe and America. He came to Hong Kong in the 1970s and turned Lan Kwai Fong in the central district of Hong Kong, of which he owned over 80%, into a world-famous entertainment attraction with European flavors, boasting of thirteen restaurants, bars, and clubs. In fact, Zemen is venerated as "The father of Lan Kwai Fong." It has been estimated that his California Tower in Lan Kwai Fong is worth over HK$500 million.

Since its establishment more than twenty years ago, Colby had been a major rival of Li & Fung Trading, with more or less equal reputation. The two had been dubbed "two giants under one roof."[6] Colby's main business

---

[5] Li & Fung Research Center (2003), p. 98.
[6] *Morgan Stanley Dean Witter*, November 10, 2000.

was in the sourcing of apparels and sundry goods for retailers. It had thirty-five offices worldwide with a total workforce of 600. Its sourcing network embraced fifty-five countries in Asia, Central America, Africa, Europe, North America, the Middle East, the Pacific, and the Caribbean regions. With a supplier base of some 4,200, its sourcing list covered female and male apparels, children's wear, fashion accessories, household goods (including electrical and electronic products), premium items, shoes, traveling goods, handbags, and household utensils. Textiles accounted for 80% of its turnover while sundry items the remaining 20%. This product mix closely resembled that of Li & Fung Trading before its spate of acquisitions.

Colby's clients were mostly famous department stores in Europe and America, such as Fred Meyer, Belk Stores, Cato and Wet Seal, as well as retail chains, mail-order firms, importers of well-known brands, and other retailers. Kohl's, its largest account, is a major department store with 286 shops all over the U.S. and accounted for one-third of Colby's sales. Colby had sole agency agreements with 95% of its clients—the U.S. accounted for 83% of Colby's turnover, whereas South America, Australia, Europe, and Canada the remaining 17% (Exhibit 7.1).

Exhibit 7.1 Business comparison between Li & Fung Trading and Colby, 1999

	Li & Fung Trading	**Colby**
Number of offices	48	35
Product mix		
Hard goods	20%	20%
Soft goods	80%	80%
Client distribution		
the U.S.	68%	83%
Europe	28%	—
South America & others	4%	17%
Major clients	Walt Disney, the Limited, Gymboree, Toys "R" Us, Abercrombie, Standard Fireworks, Tesco, American Eagle & Outfitters, Goody's Family Clothing, Avon Products	Kohl's, Fred Meyer, Belk Stores, Cato, Wet Seal, Graffiti, Boutique Jacob
Turnover	HK$16.298 billion	HK$3.52 billion
Key operating ratios		
Gross margin	3.6%	2.0%
Net margin	3.5%	2.0%

Source: Li & Fung (Trading) Limited.

Colby made use of its global network to provide a wide range of sourcing services to its clients, including on-the-spot quality control, plant assessment, inspection for compliance, offering recommendations for product development, and assisting clients to investigate suppliers' financial position. Its income was derived mainly from sourcing commissions while export sales and the trading of apparel export quotas also generated some income. Colby's turnover growth was quite impressive before it was acquired. In 1999, its total turnover and after-tax profit were HK$3.52 billion and HK$68.1 million, respectively, growing by 10.3% and 17.8%, respectively, from 1998. In the first half of 2000, its turnover reached HK$1.9 billion, up by 64% from the corresponding period the previous year. The forecasts were that its total turnover and profit for the full year would climb to HK$5.9 billion and HK$130 million, up by 69% and 74%, respectively. However, owing to sole-agency agreements with its clients, Colby's profit margin was just about 2%, lower than Li & Fung's.

In April 2000, Colby attempted to go public on the Growth Enterprises Market (GEM) board of the Hong Kong Stock Exchange under the name of Colby Net at the offer price of HK$2.68–3.88 a share, representing a P/E ratio of 90. It aimed to raise some HK$2.7 billion. However, this attempt was aborted due to the burst of the dotcom bubble in the U.S. Unperturbed, Colby made a second attempt in May with the offer price of HK$1.40–1.80 a share. It failed again because investors' interest in dotcom stocks was already watered down by the wild fluctuations in the NAZDAQ index. According to Allan Zemen, the repeated failures were mainly due to the global adjustment of technology stocks and Colby was unwilling to lower its offer price to HK$1.12 a share. The IPO was, therefore, postponed indefinitely. It was at this time that Zemen and his senior management started thinking of selling Colby.

Zemen admitted that it was he who first approached Li & Fung Trading. After the sale, he once admitted before the media: "The decision to sell a business founded by myself is definitely a difficult one." He also asserted that the idea came up during Colby's applications to go public. "Once we had decided to go public," intimated Zemen, "we started approaching various banks and investors to promote our company. Each and every banker and investor we spoke to would invariably compare us with Li & Fung and ask how we could surpass them...For twenty-odd years, we had been on good terms with Li & Fung but it only occurs to us now that the synergy to arise from our merger will benefit us both." Zemen, therefore, made the biggest decision in his life by selling Colby to Li & Fung in return for an amount of cash and some Li & Fung Limited shares. The sale signified Zemen's determination to bow out from the sourcing scene and devote attention wholeheartedly to his entertainment and real-estate businesses. His cofounder, Bruce Rockowitz, joined Li & Fung Trading's management and continued with the trading business.

On November 9, 2000, Li & Fung Limited announced that it had signed a sale-and-purchase agreement with Colby Group Holdings Limited to acquire from Allen Zemen, its chairman, and Bruce Rockowitz, its CEO, 100% of Colby's shares. The total consideration was approximately HK$2.2 billion, which consisted of a payment of HK$247.5 million in cash and an issue of 113.2 million new Li & Fung shares (equivalent to 3.95% of the enlarged share capital) at HK$17.25 each. The issue price represented a premium of 14% to the closing price on November 8, 2000 at HK$15.15. Under the agreement, Allen Zemen was allowed to sell 50% of his Li & Fung Limited's shares only half a year later, and the remaining 50% after one year, whereas Bruce Rockowitz could do so in three years—one-sixth every six months. At any rate, Zemen indicated that he would treat his Li & Fung shares as a long-term investment. Rockowitz also said that he was bullish about the prospects of the merger and would take a long position regarding the Li & Fung shares.[7]

The sale price of Colby was substantially lower than the valuation of over HK$5.6 billion at the beginning of 2000 when the company was trying to go public. On this, Zemen explained that the prevailing market environment was more realistic than before and because he and Bruce were both optimistic about the merger, they would continue to hold their Li & Fung shares. William Fung felt that the consideration was reasonable and had taken into account Colby's commitments. Under the sale-and-purchase agreement, the sellers guaranteed that by the end of 2000, Colby's annual profit would not fall short

---

[7] In 2005, through Goldman Sachs, Allen Zemen and Bruce Rockowitz sold all their Li & Fung Limited shares at HK$17.25 a share to institutional investors.

ERRATA

100 Years of Li & Fung:
Rise from family business to multinational
ISBN-13: 978-981-265-966-8
ISBN-10: 981-265-966-8

1. In chapter 7, Allan Zemen or Allen Zemen should be spelt as Allan Zeman.

2. In footnote 7 on page 142, it was mentioned that both Allan Zeman and Bruce Rockowitz sold all their Li & Fung Limited shares, according to *The Standard*, September 28, 2005. However, the newspaper amended this statement the following day. Only Allan Zeman sold all his shares.

(Updated: January 31, 2007)

of HK$134.5 million or else they would have to make up for the difference. William believed that this profit target was attainable because Colby's profit in the first eight months of the year had already reached HK$66 million.

At an interview, Frank Leong, CFO of Li & Fung Limited, who took part in the acquisition plan, thought that it was an easy decision to make:

"Allan [Zeman] wanted to pursue his other business, like entertainment, so they were looking to sell, but who could afford to buy such a big company? So they approached us with a possibility of merging with them. The deal was cut such that they would undertake to deliver a certain amount of net tangible assets (NTA). That is, when they gave us the balance sheet at the end of December, they had to top up any shortfall of the agreed NTA by cash. We believed that there was more cash on the balance sheet than the agreed NTA. We diluted our capital by about 4% and increased profit by 15%. It was a good earnings-per-share enhancing deal."[8]

According to the evaluation report of Colby's auditors, as at August 31, 2000, Colby's audited net assets were worth HK$178.7 million, which meant that Colby's goodwill was valued at HK$2.0213 billion. Li & Fung Trading indicated that the substantial goodwill arising from the acquisition would be deducted from the contributed surplus. William Fung explained that the proportion between cash and new shares in the consideration was determined on the advice of financial advisers. The premium arising from the new shares would be approximately HK$1.9497 billion, which was basically equivalent to that from the goodwill.

For Li & Fung Trading, this acquisition enabled it to enter a new market realm and become a supplier with a more comprehensive product range. Upon merging with Colby, its global sourcing offices would increase by 23%, from forty-eight to fifty-nine, and its staff force would increase to 4,500 (of whom 1,200 were based in Hong Kong). In other words, it would be the world's largest sourcing group. The acquisition of Colby, its longstanding rival, clearly had immeasurable strategic value for Li & Fung Trading, particularly when 89% of the consideration was to be covered by a premium of newly issued shares and the P/E ratio was only 16.35 times. It would also

---

[8] *Finance Asia*, February 2001, p. 10.

result in a significant drop in the P/E ratio of Li & Fung Limited's shares, which then stood at 55. The synergy to arise from this merger would be considerable for Li & Fung Trading. It is worth noting that Colby operated an extensive sourcing network worldwide, especially in the Chinese mainland and the Caribbean (including Jamaica and the Dominican Republic) and its client base did not overlap Li & Fung's. Besides, Li & Fung focused on private labels whereas Colby's accounts were mostly in department stores. Thus, apart from the acquisition of Colby enabling Li & Fung to acquire these accounts, it would be able to penetrate a market segment that was new to it.

Following the integration of Colby and Li & Fung Trading's structure, William Fung estimated that the enlarged group's turnover and net profit could increase by 22% and 13%, respectively. He said that the two companies' sourcing networks would be reorganized, with a view to merge the operational and functional departments so as to attain higher efficiency. He also disclosed that Li & Fung Trading's cash reserves amounted to HK$2.5 billion, only 10% of which was required for the Colby acquisition, and that the remaining HK$2.2–2.3 billion would be sufficient to meet with any subsequent acquisition and business development needs.

Toward the end of the 1990s, the U.S. economy showed signs of weakening after nearly a decade of prosperity, which created much pressure for Li & Fung Trading since it relied heavily on the U.S. market. With the U.S. economic slowdown, Colby became Li & Fung Trading's main driver for growth for the simple reason that five of Colby's clients accounted for 70% of its turnover and its largest client—Kohl's was the fastest-growing retail group in the U.S. and Colby handled 20% of Kohl's sourcing needs. According to a securities analyst report in Boston, Kohl's growth alone could ensure that Colby would double its turnover in three to four years. It should be noted, however, that Colby's profit margin was just about 2%, which means that this acquisition would lower Li & Fung Trading's profit margin from 2.8% to 2.5%.

The acquisition also carried with it another problem. The two companies had quite similar geographical coverage. U.S. clients made up a large part of their client base. The logical question was: would the merged entity become even more susceptible to the ups and downs of the U.S. economy? On this, Frank Leong had this to say: "At the moment, there are investors who worried about us because of the slowdown in the U.S. market. But we are quite comfortable. During the tough times, people will consolidate their sources more and they will deal with less suppliers and we have a better chance of producing more for the same customers. In some cases, they may have a reduction in their business overall but may buy more from us. A Hong Kong bank's analyst actually did a study on the Li & Fung group's growth patterns and found that there was no correlating relationship. In some cases, when the market goes down, our growth went up."[9] William Fung also pointed out that the more difficult the economic environment, the larger the number of new clients who would come to Li & Fung Trading for its services.

Strategic Alliances with European and Japanese Enterprises

One key goal in Li & Fung Trading's "Filling the Mosaic" three-year (1996–1998) plan was to attain a bigger presence in the European and Japanese markets.

In July 1996, the company announced that it had formed a strategic alliance with the largest enterprise in Italy, the Agnelli Group. The Agnelli family had been in the European business scene for over a century and was the founder of Fiat, the famous Italian car brand. Fiat's turnover and net income in 1995 were US$50 billion and US$1.45 billion, respectively. The Agnelli Group's investments in Europe is highly diversified, covering retailing, packaging, foodstuff, holiday resorts, sports, and construction materials.

Under this alliance, the Li & Fung Group sold, through Li & Fung (1937) Limited (jointly owned by Victor and William), 30 million Li & Fung (1937) Limited's shares, which represented 4.8% of Li & Fung Limited's issued shares, to Exor Group S.A. (owned by the Agnelli family), at HK$7 a share. In return, Exor agreed to go along with Li & Fung (1937) on all voting matters. Exor was an international investment company under the Agnelli family with a presence in America, Europe, and Asia. Accounting for less than 10% of the Exor group's net worth, Exor (Asia) was headquartered in Hong Kong. In 1995, its total assets and net income were US$2.4 billion and US$189 million, respectively.

---

[9] *Finance Asia*, February 2001, p. 10.

"We are very pleased to have secured a long-term alliance with one of the leading business families in Europe," said Victor Fung. "We will be seeking to expand Li & Fung's customer base in Europe with the support of this alliance."

"Exor is delighted to establish a strategic relationship with Li & Fung," said Caleazzo Scarampi, President of Exor Asia in Hong Kong. "Li & Fung is a long-term investment and a very suitable partner for us in this region. We value its management expertise, global outlook and success in sourcing consumer goods from Asia to serve markets in Europe and the U.S."[10]

Li & Fung Trading and the Agnelli group had a good cooperative relationship. Unfortunately, the financial crisis that swept Asia in 1997 dealt a serious blow to the regional economy. Having suffered heavy losses in its investments in Asia, Exor eventually decided to retreat from Hong Kong and Asia altogether. In January 1999, Exor sold all its 30.8 million Li & Fung Limited shares at HK$14.6 a share in the market through Goldman Sachs, which represented a total cash income of HK$449.7 million. Exor's investment in Li & Fung Limited gave rise to a profit of HK$220 million. The market analysts' view on Exor's move was that it had stemmed more from the need to cash in than a negative position on Li & Fung Trading's prospects.

Li & Fung Trading did not really make any headway in penetrating the Japanese market during its three-year (1996–1998) plan as it had hoped to. In the company's analysis, the main reason was that the time was not yet ripe. Japanese retailers in general still held the view that consumers in their country preferred the more expensive local products. Moreover, these retailers could not savor the idea of purchasing directly from overseas trading houses and manufacturers, and would rather continue to buy from Japanese importers and wholesalers. Certain business practices in Japan also differed from Li & Fung Trading's practices; for instance, one could point to the difference regarding payment terms. Li & Fung Trading, therefore, did not believe that it was ready to enter this market.

As early as 1997, Li & Fung Trading was eyeing the Japanese and Southeast Asian markets. William Fung had publicly said that these markets made

---

[10] Li & Fung Limited's press release, July 18, 1996.

up less than 5% of Li & Fung Trading's revenues and Japan was next only to Europe and the U.S., in terms of exports. He thought that Japan had great potential for imports as its living standards were high, its population was aging, and its trade practices were immensely complex. To prepare itself to penetrate the Japanese market, Li & Fung Trading set up a working group to conduct a feasibility study on acquiring a sourcing company in Japan, with a view to raising the revenue contribution from this market to over 10%. William also disclosed that his company could make use of about HK$450 million from its cash reserves for acquisitions and was in negotiation with three or four companies for that purpose.

In August 2000, there was talk that Li & Fung Trading was actively seeking to enter the Japanese market through acquisitions, with one of its possible targets being William E. Conner, a trading firm engaged in sourcing in Japan on behalf of overseas clients and headquartered in Hong Kong. After an extraordinary general meeting in December, William explicitly indicated that after acquiring Colby, Li & Fung Trading had reserved HK$2–2.5 billion for further M&A, and was now in the process of identifying sourcing firms to develop the Japanese market. Further to this explicit intention, on October 31, 2001, Li & Fung Trading announced that it had signed a memorandum of understanding (MOU) with Nichimen Corporation, a well-known Japanese trading firm, in connection with a possible business alliance to jointly develop the Japanese market. Under this MOU, Li & Fung Trading and Nichimen were to cooperate with each other in sourcing for Japanese clients, marketing, and distributing apparel and high-end household goods. They would also develop, manage, and operate a management and operation system specifically for the Japanese market. Li & Fung Trading would become Nichimen's sourcing agent while Nichimen would focus on client relations, marketing, logistics, and the distribution system and network.

The two companies also entered into an agreement for cross-shareholding, allowing Li & Fung to issue 4.6 million new shares at HK$7.3974 a share to Nichimen—representing approximately 0.16% of its issued shares, and also to purchase 4 million existing outstanding shares of Nichimen at 134 Japanese Yen a share, which was roughly equivalent to 1% of Nichimen's issued shares. The value of the shares involved would amount to approximately US$4.4 million for each party. It is to be noted that established in 1892, Nichimen Corporation is one of Japan's leading general trading companies engaged in a diverse range of activities, including trading, financing, and investment. Its trading business covers products like textiles, plastics, chemicals, energy, foodstuffs, condominium units, forest products, general merchandize, machinery, and metals. Its turnover at the end of March 31, 2001 totaled US$19.5 billion, of which US$500 million came from its retail accounts, including Muji, Fast Retailing, and Uniquo. In recent years, Nichimen has tended to focus on developing its textile and apparel businesses in Japan.

The strategic alliance between Li & Fung Trading and Nichimen signified their common desire to open up new markets by capitalizing on each other's advantages. Given that Nichimen had only a small sourcing network concentrated mainly in the Chinese mainland, the alliance would allow it to make use of Li & Fung Trading's global sourcing network to supply more competitive products to its accounts. Under this alliance, Li & Fung Trading would assume the role of "comprador" for Nichimen. In accordance with Nichimen's designs and specifications, it would source the best supplies from its global network. Nichimen, on the other hand, would focus on client relations and financing matters. Through this alliance, Li & Fung Trading was seeking to develop the Japanese market for apparel and home-furnishing items.

Commenting on this alliance, William Fung opined, "We are glad to be working on this business alliance with Nichimen. We believe the synergy that results will be mutually rewarding. The cross-shareholding arrangement is a customary practice in dealing with Japanese customers and an indication of both sides' sincerity and commitment to this alliance."[11]

According to an analysis undertaken by J.P. Morgan Chase, if Li & Fung Trading were to source for Nichimen in 2003 merchandize valued at US$100–150 million at a margin of 2.5%, its profit for that year would increase by 3–4%. Should Li & Fung's initial investment be taken into account, however, the contribution to its short-term profit would be insignificant.[12] Given that the Asia Pacific market accounted for only 2.4% of Li & Fung Trading's business, the alliance should help the company break into the traditionally xenophobic Japanese market in the longer term, thus reduc-

---

[11] Li & Fung Limited's press release, October 31, 2001.
[12] *Ming Pao*, November 2, 2001, p. B5.

ing its reliance on the U.S. and Europe and ensuring better market-risk management. However, some analysts observed that Nichimen's turnover had been on the decline, falling from US$30 million in 1997 to US$19.5 million in 2001; and within this period, losses were incurred in two years. They, therefore, remained doubtful whether the expected synergy would materialize from the alliance.[13]

Li & Fung Trading's three-year (1999–2001) plan was marked by a spate of M&A, notably Swire & Maclaine, Camberley, and Colby, as well as the strategic alliance with Nichimen. During this period, Li & Fung's global network was further enlarged to include sixty-eight offices in forty countries or regions worldwide and seventeen offices in China. With that powerful sourcing network and a total workforce of 5,000, it was among the world's largest sourcing groups (Exhibit 7.2). At a press conference held to announce the company's annual results in 2001, William Fung was asked about the implementation of the three-year plan. He replied: "We did not factor the formulation of that plan in the acquisition of Colby; it certainly was not something we could predict. Although we have not been able to achieve some of our targets due to this acquisition, we still consider it as a rare opportunity we should not miss."[14]

The U.S. retail sector was thriving while the European Union was also emerging from economic doldrums during those years. The birth of the Euro had resulted in substantially greater price transparency and more intense price competition. European retailers were compelled to improve their operational efficiency and fortify themselves. Li & Fung Trading was able to benefit from the new business opportunities that emerged by winning more sizable accounts. Its turnovers in 1999 and 2000 were HK$16.298 billion and HK$24.992 billion, respectively, up by 134.9% and 53.3% respectively year-on-year. Its after-tax profit for these two years were HK$577 million and HK$860 million respectively, up by 26.8% and 49.0% respectively. More

---

[13] After four years, the alliance between Li & Fung Trading and Nichimen did not work out as successfully as expected. Several inhibiting factors were at work—an important one of which was the language barrier that had to be overcome before anyone could really enter the Japanese market.

[14] Li & Fung Research Center (2003), p. 136.

Exhibit 7.2   Distribution of Li & Fung Group's subsidiaries and joint ventures, 2002

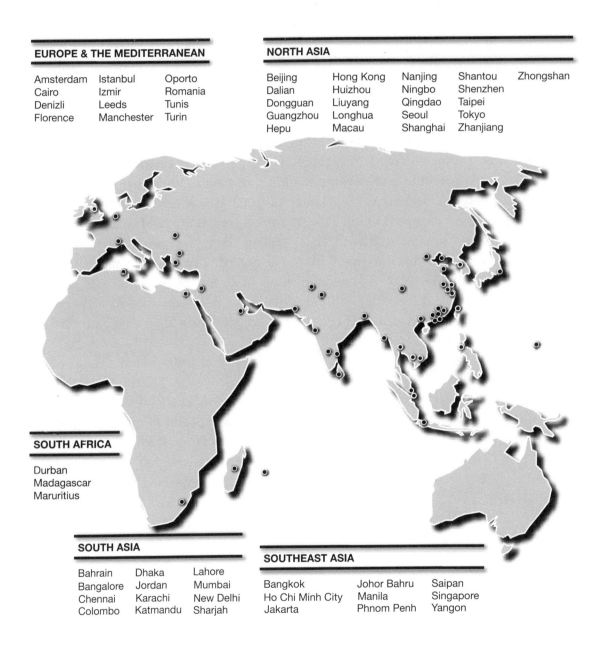

EUROPE & THE MEDITERRANEAN

Amsterdam	Istanbul	Oporto
Cairo	Izmir	Romania
Denizli	Leeds	Tunis
Florence	Manchester	Turin

NORTH ASIA

Beijing	Hong Kong	Nanjing	Shantou	Zhongshan
Dalian	Huizhou	Ningbo	Shenzhen	
Dongguan	Liuyang	Qingdao	Taipei	
Guangzhou	Longhua	Seoul	Tokyo	
Hepu	Macau	Shanghai	Zhanjiang	

SOUTH AFRICA

Durban
Madagascar
Maruritius

SOUTH ASIA

Bahrain	Dhaka	Lahore
Bangalore	Jordan	Mumbai
Chennai	Karachi	New Delhi
Colombo	Katmandu	Sharjah

SOUTHEAST ASIA

Bangkok	Johor Bahru	Saipan
Ho Chi Minh City	Manila	Singapore
Jakarta	Phnom Penh	Yangon

THE AMERICAS

Boston
Dominican Republic
Florida
Guadalajara
Guatemala
Honduras
New York
Nicaragua

Source: Li & Fung Limited Annual Report 2002.

importantly, the company saw a striking change in its trade portfolio with considerable increase in the sales of durable goods, thus giving a higher gross margin than apparel and helping it to achieve the goal of increasing its profit margin.

The terrorist attacks on September 11, 2001 plunged the U.S. economy into a state of recession after a ten-year boom. For Li & Fung Trading, it was a difficult year but, after merging successfully with Colby, it still recorded an increase of 31.8% in turnover to HK$32.941 billion. The increase would have been just 5%, if Colby's contribution had been excluded. After-tax profit for the year was HK$951 million, up by 6.5%. However, after fully providing for its HK$169 million investment in StudioDirect, its Internet-based company in the U.S., its after-tax profit should be HK$782 million, down by 12.4%. By 2001, in terms of contribution to revenue by market, North America accounted for 75%, Europe 21%, the Southern Hemisphere 3%, and East Asia 1%. In terms of product, the weight of textiles decreased from 78% in 2000 to 72% in 2001, while hard goods increased from 22% to 28% during the same period.

In 2001, Li & Fung celebrated its 95th anniversary by hosting a reception at the Hong Kong Convention and Exhibition Center on November 30, with Professor Paul Krugman of Princeton University as the special guest speaker for the Li & Fung Lecture on Commerce and Industry organized by the Chinese University of Hong Kong. The reception was attended by Hong Kong's celebrities, including senior government officials like Tung Chee-hua, Chief Executive of Hong Kong Special Administrative Region; Donald Tsang, Chief Secretary; and Anthony Leung, Financial Secretary. At his welcoming speech, Victor Fung, the Group Chairman said: "Li & Fung's development reflects how the entrepreneurial spirit can successfully drive economic growth and I feel proud of it. Economic globalization and China's accession to the WTO are expected to give rise to new challenges and opportunities. Given Hong Kong's strengths in traditional trade and the opening of the Chinese market to the world that has already started, Hong Kong should be able to benefit, especially from promoting economic integration in the mainland and from adding value to the mainland's export sector, particularly in the Pearl River Delta."[15]

---

[15] *Li & Fung Retailing Group Newsletter*, January 2002.

Chapter 8

Birth of the Third Pillar — Distribution in Asia

"These acquisitions will significantly broaden our customer base in our key markets, the US and Europe. The addition of Swire & Maclaine and Camberley is a further step in reinforcing our position as one of the world's leading sourcing and supply chain management companies."

—Victor Fung

Acquisition of Inchcape Marketing Asia Pacific

The Inchcape Group was at the heyday of its success in the 1990s. Its share price was climbing and at one point it was one of the top four British firms public-listed in Hong Kong. Unfortunately, the good times did not last. After a spate of blunders committed by its management in mergers and acquisitions, Inchcape sustained heavy losses and ran into serious financial troubles. It then entered a period of instability. There were frequent shuffles at its top management, which inevitably affected the consistency of its policies and strategies. Inchcape's business worldwide was languishing and its share price kept falling. The 1997 Asian financial crisis was the snapping point that shattered what remained of its illusion about the region's business prospects. Consequently, it decided to scale down its operations by focusing only on its core business in the region—car distribution. Its non-core businesses, including marketing services, in Asia were to be sold off one by one.

While Inchcape was bowing out from the regional marketing scene, Li & Fung was attracted by Inchcape's marketing capabilities which, it believed, would create considerable synergy with its own business. In November 1998, through their jointly owned company, Li & Fung (1937) Limited, Victor and William lined up four other investors, namely, Prudential Asset Management Asia Limited, Advent International Corporation, AEA Investors Inc., and CVC Capital Partners Limited, to set up Li & Fung (Distribution) Limited as the platform for entering the marketing business. This new company was 67%-owned by Li & Fung (1937) Limited. In those days, the most powerful distributor with the broadest market network in the Asia Pacific region was none other than Inchcape's marketing division, which eventually became Li & Fung's target for acquisition.

On January 8, 1999, Li & Fung Distribution announced that it had reached two sale-and-purchase agreements with the Inchcape Group. The first one was a "call and put options" agreement made with Inchcape Overseas Investment B.V., a wholly-owned subsidiary of the Inchcape Group, to acquire 63.3% of its Singapore-listed subsidiary, Inchcape Marketing Services Limited (IMS) at S$0.85 a share, involving a capital expenditure of about S$88 million (HK$407 million). Upon the completion of this acquisition, Li & Fung Distribution would offer to buy out the remaining IMS shares from the minority shareholders, which meant that the total consideration for the acquisition could amount to S$139 million (HK$643 million). It was also stated in Li & Fung Distribution's announcement that the acquisition was subject to confirmation after the release of the 1998 results of Inchcape's business in the Asia Pacific. If no agreement was reached before March 22, 1999, the sale-and-purchase agreement would be declared void or postponed. The second agreement was made to acquire Inchcape Marketing Asia Pacific (IMAP), a privately-owned business of Inchcape's, which was the sole agent for a number of multinationals in distributing consumer goods and industrial products in Asia, and a logistics service provider. The consideration for the acquisition was £60.4 million (S$163 million).

The two acquisitions involved a total consideration of S$251 million (HK$1.162 billion). IMAP's operating profit and net assets were £3.7 million (around HK$46.23 million) and £219.3 million (around HK$2.74 billion), respectively. Of the net assets, £33.4 million (around HK$413 million) was in cash and held by IMS. Should the acquisition proceed as planned, it would be completed in mid-1999. By May 1999, Li & Fung Distribution was already holding 92.38% of IMS's share and going through the legal process to privatize IMS. The acquisition was completed without a hitch. As disclosed by Victor Fung, the total consideration for acquiring both IMS and IMAP was US$230 million (HK$1.794 billion), equivalent to two-thirds of the net assets of the two entities or a P/E ratio of 7. The whole acquisition exercise was quite complicated but easy on the pocket.

Philip Cushing, the CEO of the Inchcape Group commented that this transaction was in the interests of Inchcape shareholders and had taken into full account the trade environment in Asia that had yet to recover and other major uncertainties. On this acquisition, Victor Fung said: "The Inchcape Group has already established in the Asia Pacific region a marketing distribution network with great potential for growth in the long term. We are ready to further expand the businesses we have acquired as soon as the regional economy is revived and resumes its growth momentum in the foreseeable future."

For Li & Fung Distribution, the primary objective for acquiring IMAP and IMS was to establish a presence in the Asia Pacific market and create the "third pillar" for the Li & Fung Group. To Victor, the U.S. market was Li & Fung's "first pillar." The acquisition of Dodwell (IBS) gave it the "second pillar," that is, the European market. The acquisition of IMS and IMAP represented the birth of the "third pillar"—the Asian market. Li & Fung was hoping to leverage Inchcape's broad-based distribution network and to capitalize on its own advantages in the Pan-Asian region to further its development in Asia, particularly in China.

Upon acquiring IMAP, Li & Fung Distribution immediately assumed control of all the assets and business operations of IMS and IMAP, such as the JDH Center at On Ping Street, Shatin. On June 14, 1999, a simple but formal renaming and flag-hoisting ceremony was held at the rooftop of that building, which was officially renamed LiFung Center and which became the headquarters of Li & Fung Distribution. This ceremony signified Li & Fung Distribution's successful acquisition of Inchcape's marketing, distribution, retailing, industrial, and subcontracting businesses in the Asia Pacific. In view of its well-established image and reputation in Hong Kong, Taiwan, and the Chinese mainland, the JDH brand would be retained for consumer goods and medical products. Except for a few senior managers who left for personal reasons, the original management team remained. These included Jeremy Hobbins, former CEO of IMS, who became the managing director of Li & Fung Distribution. The transition took place smoothly.

Li & Fung Distribution was operating some forty distribution centers in nine countries or regions in the Asia Pacific, including Hong Kong, the Chinese mainland, Taiwan, Thailand, Malaysia, Singapore, Indonesia, the Philippines, and Brunei. Equipped with advanced corporate resource management systems and IT infrastructure, these centers employed a total staff force of 6,000, including 1,800 marketing experts and professionals who served over 300 multinationals worldwide and distribute products to 20,000 accounts in the region. In addition, Li & Fung Distribution also owned a number of factories in Thailand, Malaysia, Indonesia, and China that manufactured foodstuffs, household utensils, and medical equipment for clients on contract basis (Exhibit 8.1).

Li & Fung Distribution Group's core business was to offer "one-stop shop" distribution agency services for American and European products in the Asia Pacific, comprising production, brand building, retail outlet management, and logistics. It aimed to promote the concept of supply chain management in the Pan-Asian region and to provide comprehensive services, especially midstream supply chain management. According to Li & Fung Research Center, Li & Fung Distribution was characterized by four striking features:

- It was client-oriented;
- It had an extensive network in the Pan-Asian region:
- It was equipped with state-of-art IT systems; and
- It was also experienced in supply chain management.

Exhibit 8.1 Li & Fung Distribution's business network

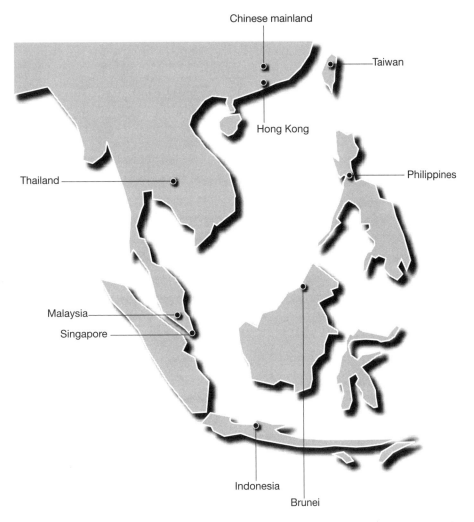

Source: Li & Fung Research Center (2003). *Supply Chain Management—The Practical Experience of the Li & Fung Group*, p. 261.

From Li & Fung Distribution to IDS—Restructuring and Public Listing

Having acquired Inchcape's marketing business in the Asia Pacific, Li & Fung Distribution became a leading distributor in both Hong Kong and the region. It was headquartered at LiFung Center in Shatin and headed by Victor Fung, who doubled as board chairman and CEO, reflecting how much the company meant to him.

Soon after the acquisitions, Li & Fung Distribution's management embarked on corporate restructuring. Three mainstreams were identified as its core businesses—marketing, manufacturing, and logistics. In September 1999, it came up with its first three-year (1999–2001) plan, with three initiatives as the theme for this period. First, it was to build up a strong management team and powerful logistics infrastructure in the Pan-Asian region, with a view to transforming its logistics operation from a backroom supporting service into a frontline service under IDS Logistics. Second, it was to construct an integrated regional IT platform that could enhance the transparency of information. It did that by initially replacing the various existing systems with a common system. In 1999, it adopted SSAWMSEXceed—a warehouse management software that was fully interfaced to PeopleSoft EnterpriseOne, the software used for distribution and financial management. The third initiative was to reform the company's management structure. Under the Inchcape Group, IMAP's management structure was country/region-based. The country manager was in charge of everything in his country or region. Li & Fung Distribution dispensed with this old practice by establishing a core business-based management structure. All the operation units within the region were linked up to reinforce the capabilities of respective core businesses so that they could undertake projects on a regional basis.

In August 2001, Li & Fung Distribution launched its second three-year (2002–2004) plan. It aimed at improving the company's business performance and internal controls, paving the way for going public by the end of 2004. With the success attained in implementing the three main initiatives in the first three-year plan, Li & Fung Distribution was set to profit from the growth potential of distribution and logistics by positioning its logistics business as the core element for raising the efficiency and added value of the supply chain, and as the crucial link between its marketing and manufacturing businesses, thus creating an end-to-end value chain.

In May 2003, Li & Fung Distribution streamlined its management structure by separating the management teams for its three core businesses from its other businesses, such as the distribution of fashion wear and industrial products, and by grouping the three core businesses under the IDS brand. On November 5, 2003, the company started using the name "Integrated Distribution Services (IDS) Group" officially in internal communications. In February, the "IDS" brand was introduced to clients, business partners, and other external parties.

After the restructuring, the IDS Group has become a supplier of integrated distribution services in Asia with three core business streams—IDS Marketing, IDS Manufacturing, and IDS Logistics. It serves mainly brand owners of consumer and healthcare products who wish to enter the Asian market (Exhibit 8.2). By the end of 2004, the IDS Group had over 4,300 employees, of whom IDS Marketing accounted for 1,700, IDS Manufacturing 900, and IDS Logistics 1,600.

The IDS Group's core business is IDS Marketing (formerly JDH Marketing Limited under the Inchcape Group). A leading distributor of consumer products in the Pan-Asian region, the IDS Group has over 150 years' experience and a sprawling distribution network. Its subsidiary, JDH (Hong Kong) Limited (formerly John D. Hutchison & Co. established in 1860), has enjoyed good reputation and a track record in distributing consumer products in the Asian region. IDS distributes mainly fast-moving consumer and healthcare products, with its services ranging from distribution and marketing to credit and cash management, logistics, inventory management, and other value-added services.[1] It distributes various types of consumer and healthcare products for over 220 American and European brands through its offices in Hong Kong, the Chinese mainland, Thailand, Malaysia, Singapore, the Philippines, Indonesia, and Brunei. In addition, through its 80%-owned subsidiary, Slumberland Asia Pacific Limited, it markets, distributes, and manufactures branded mattresses and related products in eleven countries or regions in Asia. During the second three-year plan period, IDS Marketing's contribution to the IDS Group's total revenue was in the range of 63.3% and 71.9% (Exhibit 8.3).

The Hong Kong market accounts for the largest share of IDS Marketing's revenue whereas the China market demonstrates the greatest potential for growth. In the Inchcape days, IDS already had a sizeable operation in China, covering areas like sourcing, food processing, and logistics. It had trading

---

[1] *IDS Group Limited Global IPO Prospectus*, November 24, 2004, p. 74.

Exhibit 8.2 IDS Group's organizational structure

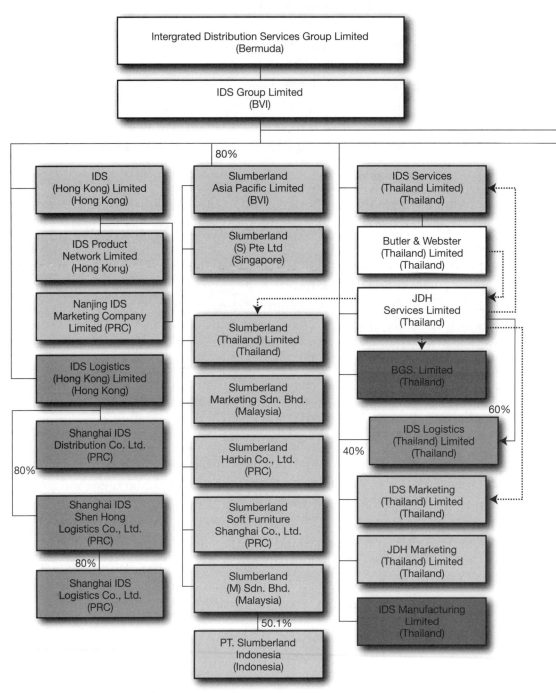

Source: IDS Group Limited Annual Report 2004.

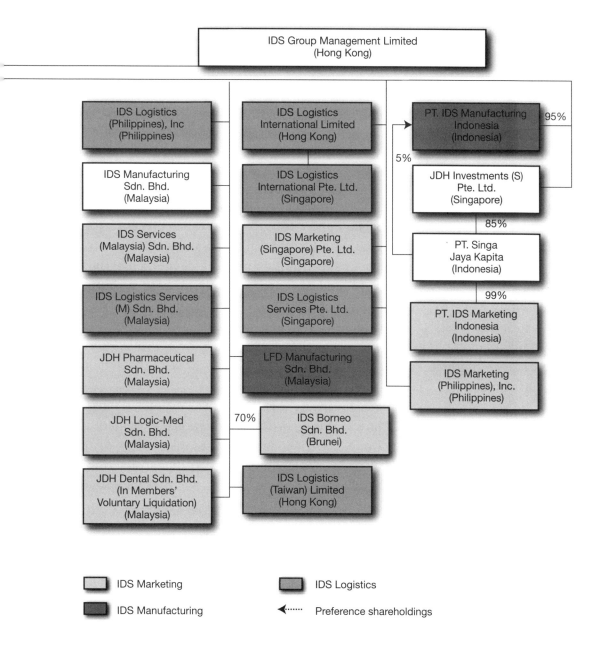

IDS Group Management Limited
(Hong Kong)

IDS Logistics
(Philippines), Inc
(Philippines)

IDS Logistics
International Limited
(Hong Kong)

PT. IDS Manufacturing
Indonesia
(Indonesia)   95%

5%

IDS Manufacturing
Sdn. Bhd.
(Malaysia)

IDS Logistics
International Pte. Ltd.
(Singapore)

JDH Investments (S)
Pte. Ltd.
(Singapore)

IDS Services
(Malaysia) Sdn. Bhd.
(Malaysia)

IDS Marketing
(Singapore) Pte. Ltd.
(Singapore)

85%

PT. Singa
Jaya Kapita
(Indonesia)

IDS Logistics Services
(M) Sdn. Bhd.
(Malaysia)

IDS Logistics
Services Pte. Ltd.
(Singapore)

99%

PT. IDS Marketing
Indonesia
(Indonesia)

JDH Pharmaceutical
Sdn. Bhd.
(Malaysia)

LFD Manufacturing
Sdn. Bhd.
(Malaysia)

IDS Marketing
(Philippines), Inc.
(Philippines)

JDH Logic-Med
Sdn. Bhd.
(Malaysia)

70%   IDS Borneo
Sdn. Bhd.
(Brunei)

JDH Dental Sdn. Bhd.
(In Members'
Voluntary Liquidation)
(Malaysia)

IDS Logistics
(Taiwan) Limited
(Hong Kong)

◻ IDS Marketing   ◻ IDS Logistics

◼ IDS Manufacturing   ◀┈┈ Preference shareholdings

Exhibit 8.3 Performance of the IDS Group's three core businesses (US$ '000), 2001–2004

Revenue	2001	2002	2003	Jan 1 – Jun 30, 2004
IDS Marketing	335,792 (71.9%)	324,382 (68.2%)	424,070 (70.2%)	174,567 (63.3%)
IDS Manufacturing	82,452 (17.7%)	82,375 (17.3%)	101,414 (16.8%)	60,179 (21.8%)
IDS Logistics	48,673 (10.4%)	69,203 (14.5%)	78,764 (13.0%)	40,875 (14.8%)
Total	466,917 (100%)	475,960 (100%)	604,248 (100%)	275,621 (100%)

Source: IDS Group Limited Global IPO Prospectus, November 24, 2004.

branches in places like Shanghai and Nanjing. IDS's China business is based in Nanjing with subsidiaries in nine different cities, including Shenzhen, Zhuhai, Guangzhou, Shanghai, Beijing, and Chengdu. It also has offices in forty cities like Zhongshan, Dongguan and Shantou in Guangdong, Hangzhou in Zhejiang, and Suzhou in Jiangsu. Its distribution network covers some seventy major cities. The well-known brand of powdered milk, Abbott, is shipped from Hong Kong to Nanjing and then distributed through IDS's network of over hundred wholesalers to retail chains and hospitals in China. In April 2004, IDS Marketing became one of the first companies to be approved under the Closer Economic Partnership Arrangement (CEPA) to set up a wholly-owned company in China.

IDS Marketing's healthcare business was formerly Watson's Pharmaceutical Limited. It is the distribution agent for multinational pharmaceutical manufacturers in Hong Kong, the U.S., and the U.K., as well as dental equipment suppliers, medical equipment manufacturers, diagnostic equipment suppliers, and manufacturers of generic drugs. Its markets include Hong Kong, the Chinese mainland, Singapore, Malaysia, Thailand, Brunei, and Indonesia. IDS Marketing's largest market is Hong Kong where IDS is one of the leading distributors of pharmaceuticals with the best-equipped pharmaceutical warehouse and distribution system. Its warehouse occupies a gross area of 50,000 square feet. Up to 95% of its orders can be delivered within twenty-four hours and up to 99% can be delivered within forty-eight hours. Its points of sale include Hong Kong's public and private hospitals, drugstores, optical shops, retail chains, department stores, supermarkets and over 10,000 physicians and pharmacists. In 2000, IDS Marketing (Healthcare) was accredited with ISO 9001 and ISO 9002 certifications, making it the first healthcare distributor to be so accredited. IDS Marketing's agency fee used to be as high as 12% but it has fallen sharply to around 4% in recent years, owing to mergers in the pharmaceutical industry which have in turn diminished the role of distributors.

Another core business of the IDS Group is IDS Manufacturing, previously known as JDH Manufacturing—a company with over forty years of experience in making foodstuffs, pharmaceuticals, personal care products, and home care products. At one point, it was manufacturing 3,000 brands of products for some 900 multinationals. After restructuring, it manufactures over 100 brands of products for more than forty accounts. The major products are food and beverages, pharmaceuticals, personal care products, and home care products. IDS Manufacturing runs a number of large factories in Thailand, Malaysia, and Indonesia, respectively, with 118 production lines and an annual output of 189,500 tons. During the second three-year plan period, IDS Manufacturing's contribution to the IDS Group's total turnover ranged from 16.8% to 21.8%.

IDS's factory in Pathumthani, Thailand, was commissioned in 1962. It has fifty-six production lines and an annual capacity of 62,000 tons. It manufactures cosmetics, home care items, aerosols, and pharmaceuticals—80% of which is for the local market, whereas the remaining 20% is exported to Malaysia, Singapore, Vietnam, Taiwan, Myanmar, and Hong Kong. IDS's factory in Kuala Lumpur, Malaysia, occupies an area of 16,700 square meters, with thirty-nine production lines specializing in beverages, foodstuffs, as well as personal care and healthcare products. Its certifications include GMP, ISO 9002, HACCP, and Halal. IDS's factory in Jakarta, Indonesia, is 6,000 square meters in area and making mainly personal care and home care products.

The IDS Group's third core business is IDS Logistics, a spin-off of IDS Logistics under JDH Marketing. IDS Logistics is a Pan-Asian logistics company with its regional headquarters in Singapore. Its geographical coverage stretches from Hong Kong, the Chinese mainland, and Taiwan, to Singapore, Thailand, Malaysia, and the Philippines. The company offers comprehensive logistics solutions to over 100 local, regional, and multinational accounts, specializing in the logistics of fast-moving consumer goods, healthcare products, apparel and footwear, industrial, and electronic products, as well as the retail sector. Its services are highly diversified, encompassing regional hub, cross-docking, bonded warehousing and other value-added services, such as reverse logistics, packaging, and labeling. In the second three-year plan period, IDS Logistics' contribution to the IDS Group's total revenue was between 10.4% and 14.8%.

IDS Logistics has forty-two distribution centers and depots with a gross floor area of 348,200 square meters and a total capacity of over 295,000 pallet spaces. Most of the distribution centers and depots are installed with the Automated Storage and Retrieval System (ASRS). The one in Singapore is a 14,300-square feet facility that is fully air-conditioned, with a capacity of 44,000 pallet spaces and operates on ASRS. Commissioned in 2001, it is the largest bonded facility in Singapore, as well as one of Asia's largest distribution centers.

In Hong Kong, IDS Logistics has already set up a wholly-owned distribution center in 1980. It operates a 600,000-square feet warehousing facility at LiFung Center that provides temperature-controlled and ambient storage with 20,000 pallet spaces and a truck fleet of thirty-eight. All the logistics are managed by a real-time inventory and warehouse management system. Through its distribution center at LiFung Center, IDS Logistics distributes fast-moving consumer products to over 5,000 wholesale outlets all over Hong Kong. On top of that, its pharmaceutical logistics segment supplies to some 7,500 retail outlets in Hong Kong.

Since the late 1980s, IDS Logistics has been operating in the Chinese mainland. Headquartered in Shanghai, it has set up distribution centers in several major Chinese cities such as Guangzhou, Changchun, Qingdao, Wuhan, Zhangzhou, Chengdu, Xian, and Urumchi. It has a very extensive service network in the mainland that covers more than 250 cities. IDS Logistics also owns a number of companies and joint ventures in China, including the wholly-owned Shanghai IDS Distribution Company Limited, the 80%-owned Shanghai IDS Shen Hong Logistics Company Limited, and the 50%-owned Shanghai Land Ocean IDS Logistics Company Limited. Established in 1987, Shanghai Land Ocean IDS Logistics Company Limited has two container terminals in Songhu, Shanghai, warehousing facilities with a gross area of 50,000 square meters, and a truck fleet of 2,500. This company is based in Shanghai with sub-offices in places like Ningbo, Nanjing, Hangzhou, and

Suzhou. Taking advantage of the network built up by Shanghai IDS Distribution, Shanghai Land Ocean IDS Logistics provides "one-stop" logistics services that ensure the expeditious distribution of goods to all parts of China.

In 2003, the IDS Group generated total revenue of HK$4.616 billion, up by 27% year-on-year. Its operating and after-tax profits were HK$102 million and HK$71.32 million, respectively, up by 135% and 167% year-on-year respectively. In the first half of 2004, the IDS Group's revenue, operating and after-tax profits were HK$2.101 billion, HK$55.96 million, and HK$54.89 million, respectively. Despite a slight drop in revenue, it's operating and after-tax profits increased by 211% and 469%, respectively. To Li & Fung Distribution, the time is now ripe for IDS to spin-off and go public.

On November 24, 2004, the IDS Group Limited announced its global IPO plan with Hong Kong & Shanghai Banking Corporation as its global coordinator, bookrunner, lead manager, and sponsor, and PNB Paribas, Cazenove Asia, DBS Asia Capital, and Macquarie Securities as global underwriters. Through a global offering comprising a public offer and an international placing, 120 million shares, comprising 60 million new shares and 60 million sale shares, was to be offered at a face value of US$0.10. Of the offer shares, 12 million shares was to be allocated for public offer in Hong Kong, while 108 million shares was to be available to professional and institutional investors through the international placing at not more than HK$3.75. In total, these offer shares would make up 40% of the Group's enlarged share.

In its IPO prospectus, the IDS Group stated: "IDS Marketing is one of the first distribution companies to be granted an approval to set up a wholly-owned entity in the Mainland of China under CEPA in April 2004. This enables us to conduct distribution and import and export of consumer products on a nationwide basis. With over a decade of experience operating in the Mainland of China, we understand local relationships and trade practices of the market. IDS Logistics has secured the necessary licenses for providing logistics services, allowing us to establish an extensive logistics network and distribution infrastructure in the Mainland of China."[2]

---

[2] *IDS Group Limited Global IPO Prospectus*, November 24, 2004.

IDS's IPO met with overwhelming response in Hong Kong. The public offer was oversubscribed by 152.7 times, thus triggering the claw-back mechanism by which the final number of public offer shares was increased from 12 million to 60 million, whilst the final number of international placing shares was lowered from 108 million to 60 million. The price of the offer shares was fixed at HK$3.50 a share, which meant that the IPO would raise a capital sum of HK$420 million. This capital was to be used by the IDS Group in reinforcing its core businesses like logistics and marketing in Hong Kong and the Chinese mainland, as well as for mergers and acquisitions in the region to further the development of its core businesses.

On December 7, the IDS Group's shares made its debut at the main board of the Hong Kong Stock Exchange. The Hang Seng Index closed 21 points down that day, but IDS's shares was sought after by investors, rising by 31.4% to HK$4.60 at one point and closing the day at HK$4.35, up by 24.3% from its offer price. In April 2005, the IDS Group announced its 2004 annual results. Revenue was US$585 million, down slightly by 1.2% from 2003 but operating profit (excluding other expenses and income) soared 72.8% to US$13.4 million. Profit attributable to shareholders rose 26% to US$10.5 million, or 9.9% higher than the forecast in its IPO prospectus. Among the three core businesses, logistics and manufacturing stood out with robust growth. The revenue and operating profit of IDS Logistics were up by 19.7% and 85.2%, respectively, while those of IDS Manufacturing were up by 22.1% and 77.3%, respectively.

In the IDS Group's 2004 annual report, the chairman Victor Fung said: "We believe the Group now has a solid foundation on the basis of a strong Asia-wide logistics and technology infrastructure and is well positioned to redefine the traditional distribution industry, capitalizing on the strong resurgence of the Asian economy."

Exhibit 8.4 Performance of the IDS Group during its second three-year (2001–2004) plan (HK$ '000)

	2001	2002	1H2003	2H2003	1H2004
Billings	3,760,460	3,934,400	5,073,990	2,358,520	2,335,530
Revenue	3,570,071	3,635,190	4,616,150	2,162,070	2,101,270
Gross profit	888,760	1,032,310	1,116,870	537,690	590,940
Operating profit	149,120	43,450	102,160	17,980	55,960
After-tax profit	76,870	26,710	71,320	9,650	54,890

Source: IDS Group Limited Global IPO Prospectus, November 24, 2004.

IDS Logistics, a logistics company in the Pan-Asian region.

A corner of the IDS Group's office for resting and meeting with visitors.

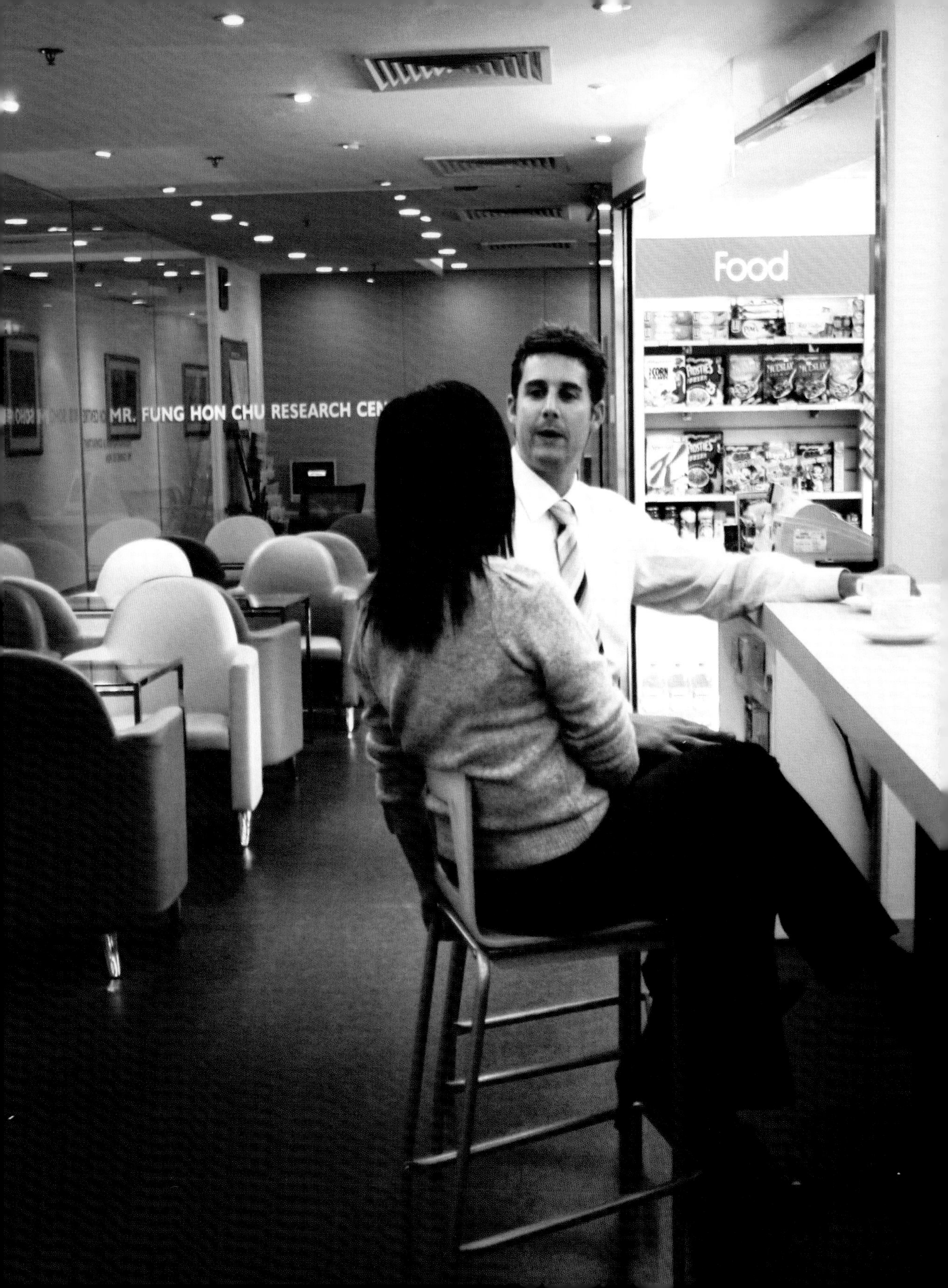
MR. FUNG HON CHU RESEARCH CEN
Food

Employees form one of the buyers of products distributed by the IDS Group.

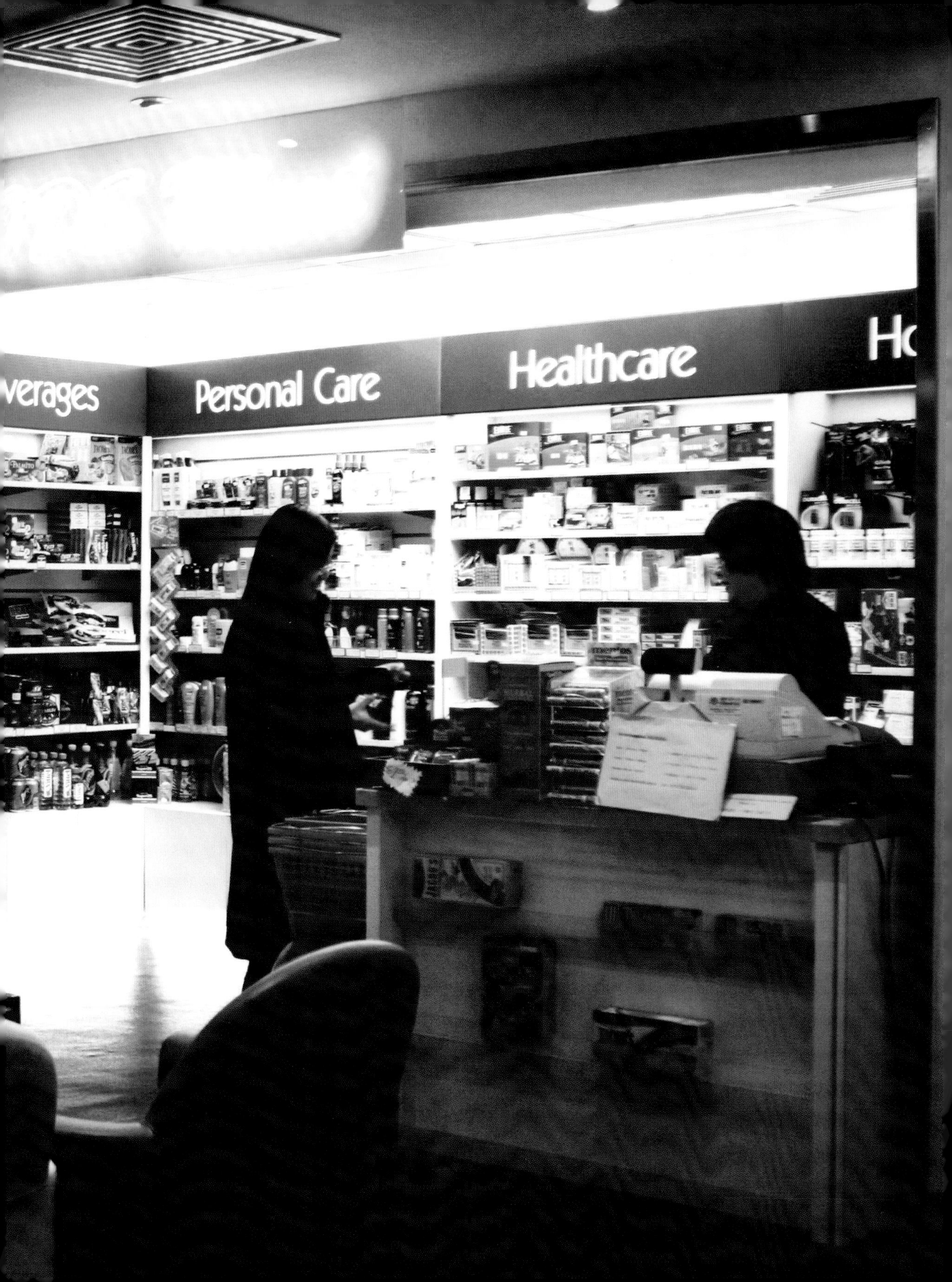
verages
Personal Care
Healthcare
Ho

A fully computerzied IDS Logistics' distribution center. Most centers are installed with the Automated Storage and Retrieval System (ASRS).

A IDS Logistics' warehouse, offering a wide range of
logistics services and solutions.

Presence in China's Logistics Sector

Since the 1980s, Li & Fung has set about increasing its presence in the Chinese mainland by investing over US$50 million directly in no less than twenty projects. Its purpose has been to develop logistics centers in China by capitalizing on its global network to attract foreign firms and multinationals and to serve them with well-equipped facilities and distribution centers. Among these investment projects, the most important ones are Panyu Trade Town and Heshan Food Town in Guangzhou.

After Deng Xiaoping's southern tour in 1992, China started implementing an even more liberal economic policy. Bullish about China's economic outlook, Li & Fung invested in a 2.2-million-square-meter project in Panyu, Guangzhou, known as Trade Town. This project was originally meant to be a science park for the manufacturing, warehousing, distribution, and assembly of products. In January 1995, Li & Fung joined Mitsubishi Corporation (Japan), LG Group (Korea), Lend Lease Group (Australia), and Manhattan Garments Group (Hong Kong) to set up LF Distribution Centers Limited with an equal share of 20% each. This joint venture aimed to develop wholesale and distribution centers in major cities along the Chinese coast that would operate on the "purchase-and-pick-up" model, which could avoid or minimize all sorts of transaction and transportation problems that were bothering manufacturers, wholesalers, and retailers alike.

Li & Fung's plan was to introduce that idea in Guangdong first before taking it to major cities like Shanghai and Wuhan, with a view to establish seven to ten similar centers in ten years. On July 21, 1995, Li & Fung announced that a joint venture, Lifung (Panyu) Trading Town Company Limited, had been set up in Panyu through LF Distribution Centers Limited with a Chinese partner, with LF Distribution Centers Limited owning 70%, and the other party owning the remaining 30%. The joint venture would invest US$100 million to construct the first wholesale and distribution center in the mainland. This facility would occupy a gross area of 759,000 square meters, including a thirty-three-story wholesale building, showrooms, and warehouses. It was to operate on the "purchase-and–pick-up" model whereby the buyer would pay for what they wanted to buy before going to the warehouse to pick up the goods.

Lifung (Panyu) Trading Town was the first cargo handling center to operate on the "purchase-and-pick-up" warehouse model in China. It aimed to resolve the two major issues faced by joint ventures and foreign enterprises in China, that is, delivery and payment. Due to the lack of direct transaction channels between foreign manufacturing firms and buyers, the former would have to go through various intermediaries before their goods could reach the latter. Because the rule at Lifung (Panyu) Trading Town was that all the goods were to be sold on cash basis and the buyer was to arrange for transportation, the buyers were mostly individual retailers and not large-scale state enterprises or department stores. In those days, harassed by the so-called "triangular debt" problem, state enterprises had difficulty settling payments. On the other hand, the credit risk in regard to individual operators was also quite formidable as there were too many of them and delivery was not feasible as they were scattered all over the mainland. By centralizing the showroom, warehouse, and office in one single facility and providing direct cargo-handling services, Lifung (Panyu) Trading Town simplified the sale procedure considerably, thus overcoming the difficulties in distribution.

"The cargo-handling center has been designed to take into account the peculiar characteristics of the Chinese market," said Victor Fung, chairman of the Li & Fung Group. "In the course of time, it is going to be integrated with the mainstream distribution channels."

According to Dickson Lo, the project director of Lifung DistriCenters Management Limited, the idea of the wholesale and distribution centers emerged three years ago. It was inspired by the product distribution center in Bologna, Italy, which was a single-layer facility encompassing both shop and warehouse. It gradually evolved into a regional distribution center with a broad network. Similar centers have become quite popular in China in recent years; hence, the idea to establish the DistriCenters. The showrooms and warehouses are leased out on flexible tenancy terms; they could also be sold to large and reputable foreign companies with factories in the mainland and the right to domestic sales.

Dickson Lo pointed out that buyers and sellers would be attracted to these centers to conduct direct transactions, thus bypassing the possible problems that could arise from payment and delivery arrangements with manufacturers, wholesalers, and retailers. This was essentially a more systematic and efficient means of distribution for foreign manufacturers and was also able to foster the development of the wholesale and distribution market for consumer goods in Southern China. He added that Panyu was chosen as the entry point because of its location in the Pearl River Delta, with a huge market for consumer products and its close proximity to Huangpu, the biggest port in Southern China, which was only a ten minute's drive from the soon-to-be-built Guangzhou-Shenzhen-Zhuhai Expressway.

The Lifung (Panyu) Trading Town project in Panyu was originally divided into four phases, with the first phase scheduled to be completed in the third quarter of 1996. In October 1997, David Allen, the managing director of Lifung DistriCenters Management Company Limited, announced that thirty-two units for the first phase were to be completed in November and that the project would be completed in 1999. The project attracted a favorable response from the market and up to 75% of the units were leased out mainly to foreign manufacturers of electrical products at US$8,000 a month per unit. He estimated that the project would generate an annual rental income of 127 thousand yuan. In 1998, the first phase of the project was fully completed with a gross area of 230,000 square meters, consisting of nine distribution blocks, 172 basic units, and one supporting services block. However, because of the then prevailing restrictions on foreign commercial enterprises, the project failed to obtain approval from the Central Government and was forced to be suspended. By then, Li & Fung had already invested nearly 1 billion yuan in the Panyu Trade Town project.

In November 2001, China became a member of the World Trade Organization. Hopes arise that she would soon open up her gigantic domestic market to the outside world and investment sentiments in the Pearl River Delta were given a boost. On the other hand, development needs led to the enlargement of the Guangzhou municipality to cover Panyu as well, effective from May 2000. To Li & Fung, these new developments present new business opportunities. Giving in to practical needs, it amended its Panyu Trade Town project to build instead a high-class integrated commercial complex with international characteristics. The new project not only retains the functions of Trade Town as a one-stop logistics center and a base for foreign enterprises, but also includes a new feature as a high-quality business complex. The original wholesale and distribution center would be developed into a large-scale logistics center to offer superior facilities and professional services to tenants at low costs.

As Li & Fung's most important investment in the Chinese mainland and as the first facility commissioned at the Panyu Trade Town, Lifung (Panyu) Trading Town has been facing three main problems. The first problem is the extent to which the Central Government was willing to allow foreign investors to enter China's services sector. Secondly, there is the transportation problem which cannot be solved without an efficient road network connecting Lifung (Panyu) Trading Town to other locations. The third major problem is whether Li & Fung is ready to increase its investment so as to launch the logistics and distribution functions of the Center. Li & Fung is in the process of studying various relevant solutions in connection with the regulations governing foreign-invested enterprises, including the application of retail and wholesale licenses from the Central Government or the application of a relevant license for Lifung (Panyu) Trading Town as a special trial project.

The other major investment made by Li & Fung in the mainland is Food Town in Heshan, Guangdong. In 1993, Li & Fung set up LF Industrial Estates Limited in partnership with companies like Li & Fung Development (China), King Fook Engineering (a subsidiary of New World Development Group), Manhattan Garments, and China-Hong Kong Photo. The joint venture would partner with Heshan Economic Development Company to set up Heshan Lifung Harbor District Development Company Limited and invest 500–600 million yuan to open a Chinese food town in Heshan, which is located in the Pearl River Delta region. Food Town would provide suitable infrastructure and supporting facilities for the food-processing industry and assist overseas investors in obtaining approval to set up factories and expediting other procedures required for commissioning.

Heshan Lifung Harbor District Development Company Limited was 70%-owned by LF Industrial Estates Limited and 30%-owned by Heshan Economic Development Company through which, the Heshan Municipal Government invested directly in the project concerned. The whole project was to be managed by Li & Fung. Under the joint-venture agreement, Food Town would occupy a gross area of 1.7 million square meters, adjacent to the Heshan Port and overlooking Xijiang. The original idea was to focus on the food industry by creating an efficient and high-quality production environment for foreign food manufacturers in a food town with modern facilities.

The whole Food Town project was to be implemented in three phases and originally scheduled for completion in 2000. Phase One included a road network, water and electricity supplies, as well as a 650,000-square-meter reclamation project. It involved an investment of 150 million yuan and was scheduled for completion in mid-1996. The registered capital for the project was HK$65 million and the remainder was to be borrowed from banks. A number of foreign food manufacturers including those from Japan, Korea, and Europe indicated interests in investing in it. In December 1995, the first trunk road to Food Town was opened and the office of Food Town also commenced operation. On December 18, the first anniversary of Heshan's status as a city, the US$15 million complex of Asia Pacific (Guangdong) Company Limited—Food Town's first occupant—was officially opened by Song Yixing, Mayor of Heshan; Victor Fung, Chairman of Li & Fung Group; and Ou Wenzhong, Managing Director of Asia Pacific (Guangdong). Asia Pacific (Guangdong) was engaged mainly in the manufacture of chocolates, biscuits, confectionaries, as well as processed meat and fish. Its production in Food Town was originally scheduled for commissioning in March 1996.

The development of Food Town proceeded smoothly at the initial stage. William Fung said publicly in 1996 that quite a number of foreign firms were in discussion with Li & Fung about leasing or buying some land in Food Town. The potential buyers were mostly from Southeast Asia whereas the potential tenants were mainly multinationals. Li & Fung intended to reserve about 10% of the land for its own use and to put on sale or lease out the remaining 90%. Unfortunately, owing to the impact of China's macroeconomic adjustment measures and the 1997 Asian financial crisis, the occupancy of Food Town was not up to expectation and the development project was subsequently put on hold.

Into the 21st century, especially after China's accession to the World Trade Organization, Li & Fung revived its interest in the Food Town project. In view of the Food Town's proximity to Xijiang and the possible water pollution that could result from large-scale industrial activities, Li & Fung has to modify the original plan. In the new plan, the northeastern part of Food Town is to be earmarked for limited small-scale food processing while various other business activities are to be introduced to bolster district investment and attract foreign investment.

Chapter 9

Restructuring and Repositioning the Retail Components

"Retail is a service industry. I am sure we can enhance our competitive edge in the market by delivering superior services to customers, capitalizing on the Group's support to achieve economies of scale, and using the promotional channels that are available through our sister companies."

—William Fung

Reorientation of Circle K's Business Model to Focus on Customers

Economic recession immediately befell Hong Kong after the 1997 regional financial crisis interest rates rose while stock and property prices plummeted. The Hang Seng Index slipped from 16,673 on August 7, 1997 to 6,600 on August 13, 1998. Property value dropped more than two-thirds in the ensuing years. Moreover, under the impact of high interest rates and the "negative equity" phenomenon pervasive amongst home-owners, investment and consumption inevitably contracted. Not surprisingly, the major economic sectors were all detrimentally affected, and the retail sector, restaurants, and tourism were not exempted. A period of deflation started in November 1998 lasted for five long years.

A direct consequence of this economic climate was that local workers' wages were either frozen or slashed, and the unemployment rate kept climbing to new heights. Local consumption shrunk and the retail sector in particular was hard hit. A number of large department stores and retail chains also went under. In fact, statistics showed that Hong Kong's overall retail spending fell from HK$211 billion in 1995 to HK$180 billion in 1999, down by 14.6%. During the same period, the retail sector's contribution to Hong Kong's GDP decreased from 19.5% to 14.6%.[1]

As expected, the business of Circle K under Li & Fung Retailing Group also suffered from the sluggish retail environment. Heavy deficits were incurred due to low consumption, loss of customers, and organizational defects. It struggled to stay afloat just like other retailers. In particular, Li & Fung Retailing made the decisive move to part with its non-core businesses, such as Fotomax and Fun Fun World, and restructured and reinforced its core businesses, i.e., Circle K and Toys "R" Us. In February 1997, Victor Fung, the chairman of Li & Fung Retailing Group, resolved to reorganize Circle K Convenience Stores (Hong Kong) Limited—the operator of Circle K stores in Hong Kong—as a wholly-owned company. In October 1998, on Victor's invitation, Richard Lap-bun Yeung became CEO of Circle K. Richard's pri-

---

[1] *Hong Kong Monthly Digest of Statistics*, 1995–1999.

mary tasks were to reform the store chain's management and, through supply chain management, drive its transformation so that it could emerge from its defensive position.

Having majored in accounting and computer science at the university, Richard has worked in many different sectors and positions. "My goal is to be a CEO," he said, "so it is important for me to widen the scope of my working experience." As a practicing accountant in the U.S., he once served as a consultant for Arthur Anderson's head office where he first came into contact with supply chain management. He later joined Havi as its vicepresident in the Far East. The Havi Group supplies food and paper products to McDonald's in the US and Asia. Richard was in charge of setting up a supply chain system for McDonald's in the whole Southeast Asian region. This project took ten years during which Richard gained deep insights into the importance of supply chain management in the modern-day business world.

Richard initiated a host of major reforms upon becoming Circle K's CEO. To prevent further loss, he closed fourteen poorly-located shops that were in deficit. Underperforming employees were dismissed. Negotiations for lower rent were held with the landlords so that more financial resources could be made available for business development. At the same time, long-term business strategies and implementation plans, which included the redecoration of Circle K shops with a new interior design, the establishment of new business standards, the delineation of Circle K's core business scope, and the setting of key targets were formulated. All these were meant to enhance the convenience store chain's efficiency, competitiveness, and profitability. At the same time, staff training was to be stepped up and a performance-based incentive scheme introduced. The prices of some of the goods were lowered to ensure "value for money." With the assistance of independent consultants, Circle K launched what it called the STF Quality Services Scheme that emphasized "speed, tidiness, and friendliness" in serving customers. Concurrently, Circle K introduced a partnership scheme to foster closer cooperation with major suppliers.

One of Circle K's key reforms was to reestablish a model for business development. The traditional retail store would usually be driven by operational convenience under which distinct brand positioning, efficient supply chain, and good management culture were absent. The management would need to shoulder all the responsibilities and would only copy from other market players. Cost efficiency, therefore, was extremely low. Circle K's reforms aimed to move from the old supply-driven business model to a demand-driven one so that customers, instead of suppliers, would influence the sales of the entire store chain. Under the new model, customers' demand would shape Circle K's strategies, shop locations, product offerings, and management culture. Pricing was expected to be based on supply and demand. Customer satisfaction being a top priority, after-sale service as well as quick response and adjustment would be improved. Cooperation with suppliers would be strengthened by means of a partnership scheme. At the same time, it would put into operation a supply chain management system to ensure better operational efficiency and cost control. As one of its senior managers admitted, Circle K was badly in need of an efficient supply chain to maintain competitiveness.

The convenience store differs from the supermarket in that the former is characterized by its higher degree of convenience and speed for shoppers. A convenience store's success or failure often depends on its location, interior design, service efficiency, and management. Circle K's new vision was "to be the preferred convenience store in Hong Kong that offers the right products at the right prices, and excels in speed, tidiness, and friendly service."

On the choice of location, Circle K prefer areas with a high pedestrian traffic, such as busy commercial districts, residential districts, locations in the vicinity of schools and bus stops, and entrances to subway stations. Its product offerings would be based on consumers' specific needs, buying habits, as well as tastes and preferences. In terms of interior design, the new Circle K store discarded the old jam-packed format and instead emphasized on tidiness, comfort, and the modern look. In accordance with customers' needs, shops in different locations would offer different special items. Those located in busy commercial districts would have a bakery section where office workers could buy breakfast or lunch. Those near schools would be stocked with more fast food, snacks, and trendy products; they would also offer redeemable trendy items and make use of idol effect to attract teenage consumers. In 2002, one Circle K store experimented with a coffee counter in an attempt to expand its product range and customer base.

In order to keep pace with market trends and cater to customers' demands, Circle K engaged a market research firm to submit a half-yearly survey report on consumers at convenience stores and supermarkets. The report covered areas such as the sales of different types of products, consumers' brand preferences, and spending per shopping, as well as information about its rivals. In collaboration with the market-research firm, Circle K organized regular forums to meet directly with consumers to collect firsthand information on their tastes and preferences and buying habits, which would form the basis for adjusting its sales strategy.

In a bid to attract more customers, Circle K rolled out a scheme called "Four Easy Areas," meaning "easy to enter and exit," "easy to choose," "easy to decide," and "easy to pay." To make it more convenient for shoppers to enter and leave, the shops would use automatic doors or simply dispense with doors. To facilitate choice and decision, the goods would be clearly classified and tidily arranged. The promotion of products in different stores would take into account the location and the major categories of customers (such as white-collar and blue-collar workers, or tourists). In the blue-collar districts, for instance, large-bottled beers and Chinese liquors would be promoted; in the white-collar districts, small-bottled beers, with brands like Carlsberg and Blue Girl, would be promoted; for shops located at the Hong Kong International Airport, the Hong Kong Convention and Exhibition Center, and Stanley district, tourist items would be displayed more prominently. Certain items in the major categories would be earmarked daily for bargain sale to attract shoppers who only wished to economize without caring too much about brands. To enable easy checkouts, Circle K invested HK$30 million in an electronic sales system to shorten the checkout time to six seconds, and ensure that the queuing time would be under no circumstance exceed one minute.

To drive repeat purchases and foster customer loyalty, Circle K introduced the STF Quality Services Scheme in its shops and set up the STF Superstar Service Grand Prize as an internal recognition. Through the Mysterious Shoppers Program conducted jointly with the Hong Kong Retail Management Association, Circle K shops would be assessed annually by a set of criteria covering two main areas—shopping environment and shopping experience. Shopping environment covered staff appearance, staff attitude and proactiveness, and store housekeeping. Shopping experience would include staff assistance and dispute-handling ability, product knowledge, cashier service, after-sales service, and team spirit. After the assessment, the company would reward those employees with outstanding performance and service manners. Circle K was recognized as a Service Industry Leader under the Mysterious Shoppers Program in 2000.

To Circle K, staff training is very important. It requires all staff from front-line workers to managers to attend training programs every six months at the Li & Fung Training Center. Situated at LiFung Center in Shatin, the training center was designed by Victor Fung, the chairman of Li & Fung Group, by modeling on Harvard University's lecture rooms. The podium in the class-room is surrounded by seats arranged in a semicircle so that the lecturer does not require an amplifier. The training program for the Circle K staff is very wide ranged. For example, in conjunction with the company's market-ing department, a series of courses on retail skills have been co-organized with the Hong Kong Vocational Training Council to boost the staff's product knowledge and ability in ensuring customer satisfaction and handling diffi-culties encountered in their daily work.

In the first quarter of 1999, Circle K introduced the Partnership Supplier Program (PSP) for the sharing of resources with suppliers of various products to minimize risk and cost, while improving the overall operational efficiency. That year, Circle K formed a category-management working group in con-junction with British American Tobacco (BAT) to study the management of tobacco categories. As one of the world's leading suppliers of tobacco, BAT supplies over 300 brands of tobacco products. Its manufacturing network comprises eighty factories in sixty-four countries and regions, and its prod-ucts are sold in some 180 markets.

In November 2001, Circle K and BAT came up with a solution known as "Project FIRST" which stood for "Forecasting Inventory & Replenishment Solution for Tomorrow." Starting from June 2002, the two parties were to hook up with each other their IT systems and inventory support systems. They would also install an electronic data interchange (EDI) system, reorga-nize the workflows of order placement and inventory delivery, and set up a system for the supplier to manage inventory. Project FIRST enabled Circle K to reduce merchandizing costs, attain a reasonable level of gross profit and savings in logistics expenses, and increase turnover.

The drastic reforms initiated by the new management succeeded in revers-ing Circle K's deficit position that had lasted fourteen years. Owing to the closedown of fourteen shops in 1998 and price reductions in the first quarter of 1999, turnover fell marginally from HK$980 million in 1998 to HK$973 million in 1999. However, total expenditure dropped by 9.6%, while gross profit and other income increased. Operating cost as a percentage of total revenue decreased from 26.6% to 24.3%. For the first time, the company posted a pre-tax profit of HK$6.6 million.

In the second quarter of 1999, Circle K started implementing two strategies, one of which was to launch innovative promotions on a monthly basis. The promoted products were mostly fun, trendy, and usable items. In 2000, for instance, customers could get a free pack of tissue paper for buying a newspaper. The pack of tissue paper contains a card with that day's lucky index, a lucky star, or a cash coupon that was worth one, two or five dollars. During the low season after the Chinese New Year in February 2001, Circle K drove sales by launching a generous cash-coupon scheme. Promotional activities like these appealed to customers and succeeded in boosting Circle K's image, as well as repeat purchases. All in all, the marketing strategies delivered impressive results with the number of customers increasing sharply. According to a market survey conducted by AC Nielsen, in August 1999, up to 79% of shoppers were aware of the Circle K brand, which had become one of the top ten most popular retail chains in Hong Kong.

Another key strategy for Circle K was to establish an integrated supply chain network for linking up all the stores with all the suppliers through the company's central distribution center. In April 1999, the supply chain management and logistics department was set up. Some time ago, the Dairy Farm International Group, its major rival, which operated the 7-Eleven convenience store chain, among others, had already engaged an expert to set up a supply chain management system for both 7-Eleven and Wellcome. The expert had been in charge of improving the supply chain management of ASDA, a major supermarket chain in the U.K.

For old-style convenience stores, the whole cycle from order placement to sale to customers required thirty-six to forty-eight hours. The lead time would be seven days while the inventory period would be twenty-one days. With supply chain management, the whole cycle would still be thirty-six to forty-eight hours but the inventory is reduced to zero, which means that the convenience store can curtail its investment in warehousing and the expenses thereof, reduce manpower and recurrent expenditure, increase cash flow, and shorten handling time. These benefits will become all the more conspicuous in cases involving several districts and a multitude of products. Circle K once regarded the strengthening and improvement of its supply chain management as the main focus of its reform initiatives. In 1999, it invested HK$20 million in an integrated supply chain network. Coordinated by the Circle K head office, orders would be centralized and delivered to individual shops, thus reducing administrative and logistical expenses, as well as ensuring more cost-effective management. The new supply chain management system was made up of four main components—customer-demand management, logistics and delivery system management, partnership-supplier management, and information system management.

To reinforce the management of the logistics and delivery system as well as information system, the new logistics setup is divided into two main parts—direct and warehouse deliveries. Direct delivery means that the supplier will deliver the products directly from the factory to the shop; warehouse delivery means that the supplier will deliver the products to Circle K's warehouse to be delivered to the shop subsequently by Circle K staff. Perishable foodstuff such as bread, milk, ice-cream and ready-to-eat items, as well as newspapers and magazines are delivered directly by the supplier to the shop. Under the direct delivery system, Circle K has set up a confirmation and clearance system that links up suppliers with Circle K's headquarters and stores. Through this electronic system, orders from the stores will be transmitted to the ordering center at the headquarters, which will then be dispatched to suppliers. This system is effective for shortening the time for placing orders, reducing manpower, and forestalling errors (Exhibit 9.1).

The warehouse delivery system is mainly responsible for handling those products that have to be stored temporarily or processed and packaged in the central logistics warehouse. All Circle K stores will place their orders with the central warehouse through the headquarters. Warehouse staff will closely monitor the inventory and when it falls to the preset level, they will place orders with the inventory planning department through the order planning system (Exhibit 9.2). For fast-moving goods, Circle K will use "flow through" or "cross-docking" logistics management. Through the close cooperation of all the companies and departments involved, the goods that arrive at the warehouse will be immediately dissembled, packaged, and distributed to the stores so that there is zero inventory.

Exhibit 9.1   Circle K's direct delivery system

Circle K's Accounting Department

6. Invoice transmitted electronically to Accounting Department

Circle K's Headquarters

Supplier

Supplier's Warehouse

2. After order placement with supplier, order confirmation is transmitted immediately to Shop

5. Shop transmits invoice to Headquarters

4. Shop checks and acknowledges receipt of goods delivered by Supplier

1. Transmits order to Headquarters

Shop

Shop

Shop

3. Supplier delivers goods directly to Shop

Source: Li & Fung Research Center (2003). *Supply Chain Management—The Practical Experience of the Li & Fung Group*, p. 340.

Exhibit 9.2   Circle K's warehouse delivery system

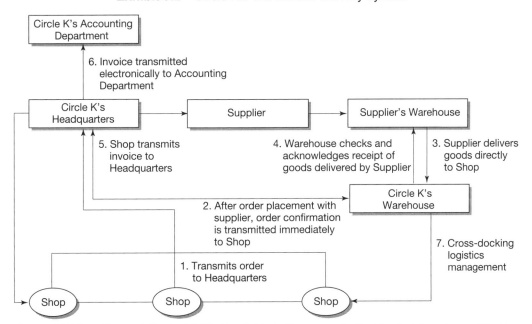

Circle K's Accounting Department

6. Invoice transmitted electronically to Accounting Department

Circle K's Headquarters

Supplier

Supplier's Warehouse

5. Shop transmits invoice to Headquarters

4. Warehouse checks and acknowledges receipt of goods delivered by Supplier

3. Supplier delivers goods directly to Shop

Circle K's Warehouse

2. After order placement with supplier, order confirmation is transmitted immediately to Shop

7. Cross-docking logistics management

1. Transmits order to Headquarters

Shop

Shop

Shop

Source: Li & Fung Research Center (2003). *Supply Chain Management—The Practical Experience of the Li & Fung Group*, p. 340.

In 1999, Circle K invested HK$30 million in setting up a third-generation electronic point-of-sale (e-POS) management system, an important tool within the supply chain. It comes with a "touch screen" design and is the fastest payment system available that can drastically reduce payment time from twelve to five seconds and ensure that customers' waiting time will not exceed fifty-nine seconds. The new system can also analyze sales data and keep track of customers' preferences, with a view to relaying the data collected to various departments to shorten the turnover cycle (from ex-warehouse to sale) to fourteen days. At an interview, Richard Yeung said: "There is fierce competition in our industry where the profit margin in general is just around 4%. Circle K's new system can result in cost savings of 2–4%, which means a lot to our profitability."

In March 2000, Circle K invested HK$32 million to form a joint venture known as Web-Logistic (Hong Kong) Limited with Web-Logistic.com (Asia Pacific) Limited, a wholly-owned subsidiary of Goodwill Communication, Inc., a Japanese Web logistics company. Web-Logistic (Asia Pacific) provides mainly one-stop online shopping delivery services (including both B2B and B2C) to e-retailers. Through this joint venture, Li & Fung hoped to draw on Web-Logistic (Asia Pacific)'s expertise to construct its own online shopping delivery and payment channels, specifically Web logistics for e-retailers of light and no-frill products such as books, DVDs, cosmetics, jewelry, and notebook computers. The joint venture also planned to assist overseas retailers to promote their products in Hong Kong. After shopping online, customers can pay and pick up their goods at Circle K. Circle K stressed that it would only offer an additional option for customers to pay and pick up their goods without entering into e-commerce because as a convenience store, it would only focus on what it did best.

After a few years' reform effort and shaping up, Circle K has discarded its defensive position. By the end of 2000, the number of Circle K stores reached 123, out of which 12% was in Hong Kong Island, 37% in Kowloon, and 50% in the New Territories. In 2000, Circle K's turnover and net profit increased to HK$1.14 billion and HK$42.1 million, respectively, up by 7% and 94% respectively year-on-year. Its total operating expenses improved to 22% of total turnover. Up to this point, Circle K had already outgrown itself and become a full-fledged business of Li & Fung Group.

Toys "R" Us—Pioneering the Asian "Boutique Store" Model

The business development of Toys "R" Us had not been impressive since its debut in Hong Kong in 1986. Li and Fung's original intention was to introduce to Hong Kong the American model of "warehouse-retail store" which worked well in the U.S. where land resources were plentiful and rental costs were low. This model failed to work in Asia, especially Hong Kong where shop space was rare and exorbitant before the 1990s. Located in large shopping malls in busy commercial districts in Hong Kong, Toys "R" Us was continually harassed by escalating rental expenses and fierce competition from new breeds of retailers, such as bargain shops and large-scale membership discount stores.

In September 1999, Li & Fung and Toys "R" Us, Inc. signed an agreement for the establishment of a new joint venture for developing Toys "R" Us's existing business in Hong Kong and Taiwan, and for penetrating the Singaporean and Malaysian markets. Under the new agreement, Li & Fung Retailing Group would be responsible for coordinating the business development of all Asian markets, except Japan and Korea, but including Hong Kong, Taiwan, Singapore, Malaysia, Thailand, and the Philippines, as well as the Chinese mainland to the south of the Yangzi River.[2] With a view to strengthening the management of Toys "R" Us, Li & Fung Retailing assumed control over its daily operations. Bruno Li, the executive director of Li & Fung Retailing, was optimistic about this development. "The new agreement has laid a good foundation for us to develop the Toys "R" Us business in Asia," he said. "With the brand awareness enjoyed by Toys "R" Us worldwide and our market experience, we believe there is immense potential for growth, provided we can seize the unlimited opportunities that will arise with the revival of the Asian economy."[3]

As Victor Fung had just been appointed the chairman of Airport Authority Hong Kong and was also in charge of the newly formed Li & Fung Distribution Group, he found it hard to spare the time for Li & Fung's retail business.

---

[2] Li & Fung Research Center (2003), p. 354.
[3] *Li & Fung Retailing Group Newsletter*, July 1999, p. 1.

The management of Li & Fung Retailing Group was, therefore, handed to William Fung. As a result of the Asian financial crisis, Hong Kong was in a state of recession and its retail sector was languishing. However, William was still quite upbeat about the future of Li & Fung's retail business. "Retail is a service industry," he said. "I am sure we can enhance our competitive edge in the market by delivering superior services to customers, capitalizing on the Group's support to achieve economies of scale and making use of the promotional channels that are available through our sister companies." Li & Fung Retailing was aware that owing to the lack of price competitiveness, brand image, and innovation, the "warehouse-retail store" model was not feasible for the Asian retail sector. Toys "R" Us's early business strategy became a subject for review in 1997. The purpose of the review was to initiate appropriate adjustment so that Toys "R" Us in Hong Kong could extricate itself from the American "warehouse-retail store" model and evolve into a "boutique store" that should be more suitable for the Asian environment.

The first initiative in that regard was to reselect the store locations in Asia to take into account the Pan-Asian market environment and adopt the right size for the stores in order to cut costs and make it more convenient for shoppers.

At the very beginning, the size of Toys "R" Us stores would range from 20,000 to 40,000 square feet. Having regard to Hong Kong's retail environment, Li & Fung Retailing came up with standard store sizes for its flagship store, regional store, and express corner. To uphold its unique image, Toys "R" Us would set up a flagship store each on Hong Kong Island and the Kowloon Peninsula. These two stores would occupy an area of 20,000–30,000 square feet each and be designed in such a way as to single out the corporate image and exhibit the whole array of Toys "R" Us products. Spacious enough for large-scale promotions and various activities for children, these stores are meant for family shopping, as well as for stimulating purchases and enriching customers' shopping experience.

The regional stores would be in sizes of 10,000–15,000 square feet and located in busy commercial districts or shopping malls in densely-populated districts. The products found in these stores are mainly hot, premium, and branded items. To meet the demand of customers in different districts, the selection of products is based on customers' preferences. The Toys "R" Us store opened in December 1998 in Kowloon Tong belongs to this type. With a gross area of around 15,000 square feet, it is located on the top floor of Festival Walk above the Kowloon Tong subway station. Its interior design accommodates a new product display concept. The shelves are lower than other stores to allow customers to have a more open view and to shop in greater comfort. The express corner would occupy an area of 2,000–5,000 square feet and would be located in department stores or shopping malls with a high concentration of shoppers. It is basically a "shop within a shop" for selling popular items to different customer segments. The second initiative taken by Li & Fung Retailing was to adjust its strategy for product positioning in order to raise the profit-per-unit shop space.

During the "warehouse-retail store" days, Toys "R" Us adopted a very indiscriminate approach with regard to the selection of products. The strategy then was to offer the widest possible variety of products. As a result, there was no clear distinction between various categories of products and a unique brand image was absent. Under the new product positioning strategy, more emphasis is placed on the establishment of brand image while maintaining a wide selection of products. After conducting an analysis of all the products available at the former large-scale stores and based on the size of the new stores, the management has prescribed the quantity of products to be made available, concentrating on branded products to be promoted and with a special focus on popular items. By so doing, the company hopes to cater to customers' demand and achieve the goal of raising its profit-per-unit shop floor area.

Toys "R" Us divides its product offerings into four categories in accordance with their respective market positioning. These include products for Babies "R" Us, toys for kids (including boys and girls), toys for "tweens," and educational toys. These four categories of products, known as "Four Pillars," are displayed in four different zones in each store.

(1) *Babies "R" Us.* This zone sells mainly infant and preschool (0–3 years old) clothing and accessories, including hard goods such as safety and feeding products, and soft goods such as infant toys and other consumables. In the past, hard goods were the most popular infant items. With the launching of Babies "R" Us, all the relevant products are sold in the same zone, which has been designed to give it a unique character and to display the goods in such a way as to attract parents and drive sales. To meet the needs of first-time parents, Toys "R" Us has come up with a list of recommended products for infants aged

0–3 years. Based on this list and their experience, the shop assistants will select suitable items for customers.

(2) *Toys for kids.* This category is also known as "core toys," targeting mainly kids aged between 4–8 years old, and includes products such as dolls, games, building sets, blocks and models, interactive toys, intelligent toys (i.e., electronic pets under the Tomy brand), and toy cars. This zone is also split into the "boys" and "girls" subzones. Toys for boys include model cars and patented toys based on cartoon or movie characters. Toys for girls include dolls, stuffed toys, and dressing sets. These products are familiar to customers, hence their sales are relatively stable. Through the introduction of trendy products for youngsters, as well as games and collectibles for adults, Toys "R" Us's strategy for this zone is to offer the widest possible range of products that attract both teenagers and adults, thus enlarging the company's customer base. In view of the growing popularity of toys imported from Japan, Toys "R" Us has also brought in popular Japanese cartoon characters like Pikachu.

(3) *Toys for "tweens."* This category is also known as "transitional toys" with the "tween" group as its target customers. This group consists of those aged between 9–14 and are somewhere between the "teen" and "teenager" stages. Though fast learners, these children are not mature enough. Products offered in the "tweens" zone include various types of electronic toys, limited-edition models, and collectible figurines. Because children in this age group usually have a certain degree of autonomy in choosing their favorites and are easily swayed by peer group pressure, they would prefer trendy items. To cater to their needs and sustain their loyalty, Toys "R" Us has a policy of keeping abreast with the trend by introducing the latest electronic toys, including electronic and computer games, as well as innovative and collectable items. This policy is supported by marketing and advertising campaigns launched by manufacturers.

(4) *Educational toys.* This category caters to the needs of children aged between 0–12 years, consisting mainly of products like Lego, writing pads, books, and electronic toys. With the rise in living standards since the mid-1990s, parents in general have been more concerned about the mental development of their children. As a result, learn-

ing toys designed to facilitate the development of children's intellect have become more popular. To capture this demand, Toys "R" Us has opened a special zone for relevant products. At the same time, detecting a growing trend among Hong Kong people to buy family games, as well as sports and outdoor toys, Toys "R" Us has created the "family fun and games" and "sports and outdoor" zones, respectively. Some parents are increasingly concerned about the negative impact that popular electronic games might have on their children and, therefore, have begun to take an interest in family games, including board games, group games, as well as masks, paper cups, confectionery, and dressing sets to be used at parties or other gatherings. These family-fun items and games involve group participation and are conducive to human interaction and the family.

Other than shop location and product positioning, Toys "R" Us also focuses on brand promotion, the launching of proprietary brands, and the building of a conspicuous market image. To further the promotion of branded products, each zone in the shop will highlight those brands that are of exceptional quality, innovative, and playable, i.e., of high toy value. As a matter of fact, products sold by Toys "R" Us have all been made by "Grade A" toy manufacturers, including international firms like Hasbro and Mattel. From 1999 onward, Toys "R" Us adopted a new sales strategy by focusing not only on internationally famous brands but also other proprietary brands. It would first ask an R&D company to work on its design specifications regarding a product's function, price, and appearance. It would then outsource the production to the suitable manufacturer(s) and then arrange for the product's design registration before launching it exclusively at Toys "R" Us stores worldwide. In 2000, it rolled out Bruin, an U.K. infant toy brand, by decorating its product shelves in a special way, and by launching a point-of-purchase advertising campaign. Marked by unique packaging and colors, as well as affordable prices, Bruin products immediately became a hit among parents and kids. After its first success in Hong Kong, the sales network of Bruin has already been extended to other Asian markets and even to the U.S.

Riding on the wave of its successful experience with Bruin, Toys "R" Us has been more proactive in launching proprietary brands with good market potential, including the Animal Alley brand of stuffed toys, the Fast Lane brand of toy cars, the Imaginarium brand of creative toys, the Jessica brand of dolls, the Pavilion brand of educational toys, the Dream Dazzlers brand of accessories for girls, the Stats brand of sports items, the You & Me brand of infant toys and accessories, as well as the Edu Science brand of products about nature. The Toys "R" Us stores in other markets have also followed suit by launching proprietary brands. Owing to their appealing designs, good quality, high level of product safety, and lower prices than other international brands, these products have found a good market. Their success has not only created a new market outside the realm of the traditional brands and enlarged the customer base for toys, but also implied more choices for consumers.

A spokesman for Toys "R" Us, said: "The introduction of proprietary brands not only gives us a stronger market influence but also enhances our reputation. Because we are in control of these brands, we can achieve better cost management to ensure price competitiveness and higher profits. Apart from these benefits, these brands also augment our product offerings and allow us to develop more strategic sales plans and provide customers more options. We are very pleased that customers have been very supportive of the entry of these proprietary brands. Going forward, we will take a two-pronged approach by promoting the sales of international brands, and at the same time, develop more proprietary brands so that we can enhance our competitive edge in the market."

On the housekeeping front, the interior design of Toys "R" Us stores has taken a fun-oriented approach instead of the previous product-oriented one. The idea is to create a pleasurable atmosphere that can better attract shoppers. The U.S.-style large-scale retail outlets are going out of style. To match its new market positioning as a "boutique store," Toys "R" Us has begun to refurbish its stores in the Asian region to create a colorful appearance and a pleasurable atmosphere that are consistent with its new image.

The company attaches a high degree of importance to the quality of its customer service. A number of measures are taken to enhance its service to customers. Shop assistants with maternal experience, for instance, are assigned to the Babies "R" Us zone to serve relevant customers. The change in business strategy has led to an obviously speedier turnover of inventories from three-folds a year to five-folds a year.

In view of the economic downturn and in order to maintain its competitiveness, Toys "R" Us decided in 2000 to revamp the outlook of its six stores in Hong Kong and to set up a new and unique service in each of them. The Toys "R" Us store at Ocean Terminal was reopened in 2000 after over HK$10 million invested in a major refurbishment project. As the flagship store of Toys "R" Us in the whole of Asia, the new Ocean Terminal store occupies an area of 48,000 square feet and is highly innovative in terms of the use of space. Divided into twelve major product zones, it offers array of over a million items. More "exclusive" toys and new product series are also added to this array to further consolidate the status of Toys "R" Us as Hong Kong's leading toy retail outlet.

The new Ocean Terminal store champions the "one-stop shopping and relaxing" model complete with a coffee shop, a barber shop for kids, a Babies "R" Us zone, and a tea corner. It also has a function room and an interest corner for hosting family activities, learning classes, new product launching, and birthday parties. The opening ceremony for the newly decorated store was officiated by Victor Fung, chairman of Li R Fung Retailing Group; Larry Sze, managing director (Asia Pacific) of Toys "R" Us; Larry Gardner, vice chief operating officer of Toys "R" Us Inc.; and a group of children. Prior to the refurbishment and reopening, the store's average customer traffic was 250,000 a month. It increased by 20% after the reopening and the new store experienced a 40% rise in profits.

On November 24, 2001, the Toys "R" Us store at Windsor House, Causeway Bay, reopened after refurbishment. The reopened store is marked by the introduction of a "Small Broadway" concept manifested in a mini-theater for kids. It also offers one-stop sales services regarding baby products in its Babies "R" Us zone.

Larry Sze, the managing director (Asia Pacific) of Toys "R" Us said: "Under the prevailing economic climate, it is important for retailers to upgrade themselves to remain competitive. For this reason, each of our stores comes with new and unique services. The Ocean Terminal store reopened earlier has a barber shop and a tea corner. The new Windsor House store features a "Small Broadway" that is essentially a performance venue for children and also a cinema for staging movie shows. It is meant to create more opportunities for children to develop their interests and also to learn and interact with each other."

With a view to serving the needs of customers more effectively, Toys "R" Us started building up its sales database in the 1990s. The data to be fed into the database include information on customers' shopping activities, as well as the sales performance of individual products. Various kinds of business analysis will then be conducted on the data, including sales analysis, individual product's profit analysis, expenditure analysis, and promotion analysis. For example, based on individual country, shop, product category, and manufacturer, sales analysis will be conducted on the sales of each product type and the sales of each shelf unit. Through an analysis of product profitability, the company will have a clear understanding of each product's profit margin, gross and net profits so that it can develop different sourcing strategies for different manufacturers and products, and adjust its advertising and promotion budgets by making reference to each product's profit margin.

Maggie Chung, the head of Business Analysis & Planning of Toys "R" Us, said: "This customer database provides a solid foundation for customer relationship management. Few companies, especially in Asia, would invest in creating such a comprehensive database. Taking advantage of various data-mining techniques, we have been able to enhance our overall competitiveness and control our costs more effectively."

Toys "R" Us cares a lot about customers' shopping experience and expectations. It is especially concerned about the ability of its shop assistants in helping customers. It expects them to be able to comprehend individual customers' specific needs and offer extra advisory services for customers to select the most suitable toys and be deeply impressed with such a shopping experience. To enhance customer service, Toys "R" Us has prescribed for its staff the "Service Guidelines ABC" that must be followed in their daily work. "A" stands for "Approach," meaning that the staff must approach customers proactively; "B" stands for "Benefits," meaning that the staff must explain the benefits of products to customers; and "C" stands for "Close the deal." By cultivating a long-term relationship with customers, Toys "R" Us aims to sustain their loyalty.

At present, Li & Fung Retailing has under its banner no less than thirty-five Toys "R" Us stores that are located mainly in Hong Kong, Taiwan, Singapore, and Malaysia. Seven of them are in Hong Kong, including the Ocean Terminal store in Tsim Sha Tsui, the New Town Plaza store in Shatin, the Windsor House store in Causeway Bay, the Cityplaza store in Taikoo Shing, the Festival Walk store in Kowloon Tong, the Maritime Square store in Tsing Yi, and the Metro City store in Tseung Kwan O. In Taiwan, there are sixteen Toy "R"

Us stores that are wholly-owned by Li & Fung Retailing. They include the Taoyuan, Hsin Hsin, Tomson, and Asiaworld stores in Taipei, as well as the Kaohsiung and the Taichung stores. In November 1999, Toys "R" Us opened a store in Asiaworld Shopping Mall, which was a new high-class commercial complex in central Taipei. Retail shops in this mall are all famous brands, such as Ikea and Esprit. Owing to its central location and the availability of abundant parking spaces, it symbolizes the latest shopping trend for the new generation of Taiwanese consumers. It also represents Toys "R" Us's business strategy in Taiwan which opts for locations in first-class shopping malls popular among shoppers with a high propensity to spend, and which offers convenient one-stop shopping for the whole family during the weekend.

Toys "R" Us has four shops in Singapore and five in Malaysia. In 2002, Toys "R" Us in Malaysia rolled out a new business model by cooperating with Metrojaya, a leading department store, to set up a counter specifically for selling toys in the form of "shop within shop." It also created the new brand "Toy Dream." The counter occupies an area of 1,500–2,000 square meters and is located on the same floor as other children product departments. It is designed as a boutique store whose floor is paved with rubber tiles. Having first landed in Malaysia in July 2001 in Johor Bahru, Toys "R" Us now operates four stores in that country, all with a Toy Dream special counter. In February 2000, Toys "R" Us opened its fifth store in Mid Valley Megamall, the largest shopping mall in Malaysia.

Currently, Toys "R" Us total turnover generated from Asia is approximately HK$1 billion and its gross profit amounts to 33–34% of turnover. Its net profit, however, is still quite thin. Victor Fung considers that opportunities still abound for the further development of existing markets. He is also considering the idea of bringing Toys "R" Us to the Chinese mainland. But in view of the complex issue of import tariffs which could translate into much higher retail prices in China's domestic market, he feels that much examination is probably needed before any step is taken.

The Listing of CRA on GEM

The Circle K business, brand, and trademarks were subject to the licensee agreement signed between Circle K (Hong Kong) under Convenience Retail Asia and Circle K (U.S.A.) on March 20, 1985. That agreement was later amended to grant Convenience Retail Asia the exclusive rights to use the brand and trademarks of Circle K in Hong Kong, Macau, and Southern China till the end of 2025. Thereafter, the agreement will be automatically renewed on an annual basis unless one party gives notice of termination to the other. As Circle K had been making steady progress since 1998 and with China's accession to WTO, which set the scene for the opening up of the Chinese domestic market, the management of Convenience Retail Asia thought that it was the right time for its Circle K business to spin-off and go public. In October 2000, Convenience Retail Asia Limited (CRA) was set up as Circle K's holding company. CRA proceeded immediately to renegotiate its Circle K licensee agreement with Circle K (U.S.A.). Subsequently, the agreement was further amended to extend CRA's geographical coverage to Eastern and Northern China, but on the condition that by the end of 2005, CRA should have set up no less than 100 and fifty Circle K stores in Eastern and Northern China, respectively. The two parties to the agreement also agreed that CRA's convenience store business can be expanded to the Philippines, Thailand, Malaysia, and Singapore at a later stage, but no legally-binding undertaking had been reached.[4] The Circle K brand being owned by Circle K (U.S.A.), Circle K (Hong Kong) could only go public under the name of its holding company, CRA.

In January 2001, CRA made an offer of its share on the Growth Enterprises Market (GEM), Hong Kong's second board, at an offer price of HK$1.05–1.15 a share. Of the 163.9 million shares on offer, 131.12 million shares (80%) are to be allotted to professional and institutional investors and the remaining 32.78 million (20%) should be made available to retail investors. After the allotment and public sale, Li & Fung Retailing held 71.25% of CRA's share. CRA predicted that its annual net profit would not be less than HK$45 million.

CRA was seeking to achieve three objectives through public listing. First, the listing will provide the necessary funds for entry into the Chinese market. Second, it will enhance Circle K's brand awareness, reputation, and market position. Third, it can boost the staff's morale and their sense of belonging by allowing them a share in the company's profits through share ownership.

---

[4] *Convenience Retail Asia Limited IPO Prospectus, 2001.*

CRA promised that upon becoming a public company, it will continue to follow a customer-oriented business strategy with the vision of becoming "the fastest-growing and preferred convenience store chain in Hong Kong" and "customers' preferred brand," as well as "the fastest-growing and preferred convenience store chain in China." To achieve that, CRA implemented a five-pronged strategy covering a marketing and branding plan, an expansion plan, a service enhancement plan, a quality categorization plan, as well as a supply chain management and logistics plan.

At a road show for his company's IPO, Richard Yeung, CEO of CRA, said: "Our IPO is mainly motivated by the prospects of the China market. Through this IPO, we wish to raise the capital we need for creating Circle K's presence in the Pearl River Delta and expanding our network in China, Hong Kong, and Southeast Asia." He added that the funds raised from the IPO will be mainly used to expand Circle K's retail network in the Chinese mainland, including the southern, eastern, and northern parts of China. CRA was committed to increase the numbers of stores in both Hong Kong and China to 650 and 390, respectively, within the next ten years. CRA also envisaged that its China business will breakeven after three years. According to Bruno Li, the chief financial officer, CRA would team up with companies like China Resources Enterprise, Limited, to develop in the Chinese mainland. Given China Resources Enterprise's extensive retail network in the Chinese mainland, he believed that the forging of cooperation with it would enliven CRA's prospects in China.

Institutional investors in Europe and the U.S. in general responded positively to the allotment of CRA's shares because they had much confidence in Li & Fung Retailing Group—CRA's largest shareholder, CRA's management, and the Group's determination to enter the Greater China market. The market's response to both the allotment and public offer was extremely good, which were oversubscribed by fifteen and ten times, respectively. Because of this enthusiastic response, Li & Fung Retailing eventually decided to price the 163 million CRA shares at HK$1.15 a share, which represented a P/E ratio of 14, which meant that the IPO helped to raise nearly HK$188 million for CRA. Net proceeds for the company amounted to approximately HK$167 million. CRA intended to spend about HK$94 million on setting up hundred Circle K stores in the Pearl River Delta, about HK$52 million on establishing a distribution center and an administrative office in Guangzhou, about

HK$42 million on installing a computer system to develop the company's business in China, and about HK$56 million to build up Circle K's network in the eastern and northern parts of China.

On January 18, 2001, CRA share was traded for the first time on GEM, closing the day at HK$1.14 or 0.87% lower than its IPO price. Coincidentally, CRA's shares debuted in the year of the September 11 terrorist attacks in the U.S., which plunged the American economy into a state of downturn and shook the world at large. The Hong Kong economy inevitably also suffered as high unemployment persisted, wages fell, both the stock and property markets plummeted, and domestic consumption was seriously affected. In 2002, Hong Kong's retail value and volume were down by 4.1% and 2.6%, respectively, from the previous year.

Despite the difficult operating environment that prevailed after its public listing, CRA forged ahead to reinforce its core competencies and strengthening its brand image, i.e., by renovating its stores in Hong Kong and replacing its original logo with a more eye-catching and modern-looking one. At the same time, it continued to expand its network in Hong Kong, for instance, by opening mini-stores at various MTR stations to take advantage of their passenger traffic and to deepen Circle K's brand awareness. Meanwhile, the company did not overlook the importance of cost management. All these initiatives served to produce satisfactory results. By the end of 2002, the number of Circle K stores grew to 166. On an average day, 400,000 customers visited the stores and over 350,000 transactions have been closed. In 2002, CRA posted a total turnover of HK$1.394 billion and a net profit of HK$72.15 million, up by 7% and 10% respectively, from 2001, and up by 22% and 50% respectively, from 2000 (Exhibit 9.3). However, analysts were still not thrilled by such numbers and considered CRA's prospects to be just mediocre. CRA's biggest challenge, they pointed out, was its concentration in and over-reliance on the Hong Kong market.[5]

In March 2003, the massive outbreak of SARS shriveled Hong Kong's retail sector and tourism all of a sudden. Conditions worsened particularly after the World Health Organization issued its travel warning for Hong Kong.

---

[5] *East Weekly*, January 17, 2001, p. 137.

Exhibit 9.3 Circle K's business performance (HK$ million), 1998–2004

Year	1998	1999	2000	2001	2002	2003	2004
Store expenditure (% of revenue)	26.6%	24.3%	21.9%	22.1%	22.7%	23.3%	24.1%
Revenue (% change)	980.2	972.9 (−1%)	1,139.8 (+17%)	1,305.1 (+15%)	1,393.5 (+7%)	1,526.1 (+10%)	1,757.6 (+15%)
Net profit/loss (% change)	−22.98	6.6	49.12 (+629%)	65.46 (+36%)	72.12 (+10%)	60.71 (−16%)	66.96 (+10%)
No. of stores by year end	107	114	123	146	166	186	205

Source: Convenience Retail Asia Annual Reports 1998–2004.

The value of retail fell by 15.2% and 11.1% in April and May, respectively. The number of visitors to Hong Kong plunged to an all-time low in May, down by 67.8%. CRA recorded a 16% drop in net profit despite an increase of 10% in revenue. The post-SARS recovery of Hong Kong's economy and domestic consumption was long drawn-out. CRA's results in 2004 were still not up to the 2002 levels.

Regardless of the then prevailing hardships, CRA continued to expand in Hong Kong. In 2004, the 200th Circle K store opened at Ocean Shores, a residential estate in Tseung Kwan O, which was considered a milestone for Li & Fung Retailing Group. The opening was officiated by the chairman, Victor Fung, the CEO, Richard Yeung, and the store's manager, Tsang Sau-mui. In 2004, CRA's employees size reached 2,308.

Concurrently, CRA was also preparing itself for entering the Chinese mainland market. At the time when CRA was seeking public listing, there were just about 130 international convenience stores in China. Assuming that each convenience store was to serve 20,000 urban residents, China could potentially accommodate 20,000 such stores. Clearly the mainland's market potential is immense. Yet, as pointed out by William Fung at a seminar on China's first anniversary as a WTO member in end-2001, it would be difficult for China to fulfill her WTO obligations, and it is even more difficult for the provincial and municipal authorities to implement what China has promised. Although after her accession to WTO China would need to open her service sector in five years, and her retail sector in three years, William envisioned that it would take ten to twenty years before the degree of convenience for doing business in China would be comparable to that in other developed countries. In other words, for CRA, the road to the China market is still long and bumpy.

At any rate, CRA has already taken its first step in that direction. In April 2001, CRA formed a joint-venture company—Convenience Retail Southern China Limited (CRSC)—with two Chinese mainland companies to drive Circle K's development in Southern China. The joint venture is 62.5%-owned by CRA, 35%-owned by Shanghai Shen Hong Corporation, and 2.5%-owned by China Foreign Trade Development Companies Inc. (CFTDC). Shen Hong is majority-owned by Shanghai Friendship Group, which is engaged mainly in the operation of Shanghai Lian Hua Supermarket and Shanghai Friendship Department Store. CFTDC is a state-owned enterprise in Guangdong. It is a multifunction business promotion organization that facilitates export-trade and provides logistics and trade-related services.

Regarding the joint venture, Richard Yeung said, "We feel very privileged to have Shen Hong and CFTDC as our partners in the Chinese mainland. CRA will certainly benefit from the solid business experience of Shen Hong and its parent company, Shanghai Friendship Group, and also from CFTDC's extensive knowledge in business development."

The newly formed CRSC immediately proceeded to apply to the Central Government, the Guangdong Provincial Government, and the Guangzhou Municipal Government for license to operate convenience stores. At the same time, it commissioned a number of market studies regarding the operating models of convenience stores in China so that it could develop the most competitive model that would match the characteristics and requirements of the retail market in Guangzhou. CRSC also asked a survey firm to conduct a study on pedestrian flow and pedestrian traffic analysis in 160 different locations at the city center of Guangzhou. The purpose was to select locations that could ensure high turnover.

On August 5, 2002, CRA's joint-venture project in Guangzhou was given the green light by the State Economic and Trade Commission. The Guangzhou joint venture will now be 65%-owned by CRA, 25%-owned by Guangzhou Grain Group Limited, and 10%-owned by Shanghai Shen Hong Corporation. The total capital expenditure for the joint venture would be in the region of 100 million yuan. Richard was excited by this development which he regarded as a major step forward for CRA in penetrating the China retail market. On November 22, 2003, the first Circle K store in

Guangzhou was officially opened at 48 Zhong Shan Ba Lu. By the end of 2004, there were twenty Circle K stores in Guangzhou.

Li & Fung Retailing is determined to establish itself as the leading retail chain group in Guangzhou. With its foothold firmly established in Guangzhou, it can now move on to build up its network in other cities in the region. At present, Circle K has already set up 232 stores in Hong Kong, twelve in Macau, forty in Guangzhou, five in Zhuhai, and six in Dongguan.

Chapter 10

The Li & Fung's Global Supply Chain Management Model

"We were no longer looking for a particular country that could churn out a complete product with good quality. Instead, we were dissecting the whole value chain of production processes and improving each process along the way and making the product in the global sphere. By so doing, we not only offset the costs of logistics and transportation but could also charge higher fees for our higher value-added services. We were able to produce and deliver more sophisticated products more efficiently. If you look carefully at the world's largest trading firms, you will find that all of them are heading toward becoming the best player in the global arena."

—Victor Fung

The Rise of Supply Chain Management in Response to Economic Globalization

Since the 1980s, with the advancement in science and technology, the globalization of the world economy has become increasingly a reality. According to the International Monetary Fund (IMF), globalization is referred to as the growing economic interdependence of countries worldwide through the increasing volume and variety of cross-border transactions in goods and services, free international capital flows, and more rapid and widespread diffusion of technology. In general, globalization is understood as the integration of all national and regional economies of the world as a holistic entity. It is a historical process that ensures the free movement and rational allocation of factors of production in accordance with market demand. This is manifested in the massive flow of factors of production and the allocation of resources worldwide, which will gradually do away with all kinds of barriers and obstacles. Economic globalization is witnessed in major areas, such as production, technology, trade, market competition, and consumption.

Prior to the 1980s, the management model of enterprises across the world had basically been one of vertical integration, which means that because of the need for possessing production resources and controlling production processes, the enterprise would expand its scale of operation or acquire partial ownership of its supplier firms. With the advent of economic globalization, advancement in information technology, intensifying market competition and fast-changing market demand, the vertical integration model has also revealed some intrinsic weaknesses, such as the enterprise's increasingly heavy investment burden and exposure to both market and industry risks. In addition, a larger number of firms have been forced to engage in businesses they are not good at.

In the later part of 1980s, given the shortcomings of the vertical integration model, more and more enterprises have subscribed to the concept of horizontal integration. This means an enterprise can use external resources to respond quickly to market demand, while focusing only on its core pursuits, such as product and market development. Insofar as production is concerned, it would produce only the crucial parts and components, or even outsource everything to other firms. According to a survey conducted in 1996, the U.S. manufacturing industry outsourced a production volume worth US$100 billion. When asked why they were keen in outsourcing, 64% of the firms replied that they did it to control and reduce operating costs; 48% said they wanted to improve their core businesses, and 43% said they had to build up the capacity for becoming a world-class company. Horizontal integration has thus created a supply chain that link up all the enterprises involved—from the supplier to the manufacturer, and from the manufacturer to the distributor. This has thus given birth to supply chain management (SCM).

In the early 1990s, to ensure the leading position of the U.S. industries in the global economy, the U.S. House of Representative commissioned Iacocca Institute of Lehigh University to conduct a study on business management strategies. The institute invited representatives of the Ministry of Defense, the industrial sector, and the academia to form a study group with thirteen large companies as core members and the participation of over a hundred firms. The study group published a report entitled *21st Century Manufacturing Enterprise Strategy* after analyzing some 400 research reports produced in recent years on the U.S. manufacturing industry. The report concluded that global competition has expedited market changes to such an extent that the individual enterprise is unable to keep pace with these changes by relying solely on its resources. To tackle this threat that affects the survival and development of enterprises worldwide, the report suggested—as the answer to the buyer's market that prevails amid intense global competition—the adoption of Agile Manufacturing (AM) which is based on the "virtual enterprise" or dynamic coalition model. Under AM, enterprises will use a flat organizational structure that can quickly bring together different factors of production and replace the pyramid-like management structure with a sufficiently autonomous and dispersed model, thereby transforming the relationship between enterprises from one of competition into one that encompasses both competition and cooperation simultaneously, thus leading to a "win-win" situation. AM is made possible by the open availability, use, and integration of information via the Internet.

At that time, "virtual enterprise" was still very much just an idea. How it can be put into actual practice had yet to be figured out. The emergence of SCM has paved way for AM to become a reality. AM and SCM share the common concept of allowing an enterprise to have access to resources not only available internally, but also from the whole economy through the formation of strategic alliances among enterprises for mutual gain. With the use of AM since the 1990s, SCM has been sought after by enterprises worldwide as the most important business model.

In 1997, PRTM (Pittiglio Rabin Todd & McGraith), a U.S. management consulting firm, conducted a survey regarding SCM on 165 enterprises from six different industries: chemicals, computer equipment, telecommunications, services, manufacturing, and semiconductors. The survey found that through implementing SCM, enterprises have been able to reap a multitude of benefits:

- Total SCM cost (as a percentage of revenue) reduced by 10%;
- The rate of timely delivery for medium-sized firms increased by 15%;
- The order-placement to production cycle was shortened by 25–35%;
- The productivity of medium-sized eterprises has increased by over 10%;
- The financial results of blue-chip enterprises have improved by 15–20%;
- The inventory for medium-sized enterprises has decreased by 3%, whereas their blue-chip counterparts has decreased by 15%; and
- The cash-flow cycle of blue-chip enterprises has become shorter than that of other enterprises by 40–65 days.[1]

As Martin Christopher, a logistics expert, has put it, competition in the 21st century is likely to be between supply chains, not individual firms. Small and medium-sized firms with unique advantages in making parts and components will be keenly sought after by large assembling firms and sourcing agents. A Japanese scholar has also compared this to a midfield combat in a football match. Anyone who can have control over suppliers will have a definite advantage over the rest. This advantage boils down to the supply chain's capability to integrate.

---

[1] Ma, et al. (2000), p. 52.

Li & Fung—From Intermediary to Global Supply Chain Manager

In the 100 years since its founding in 1906, particularly since the dawn of economic globalization in 1980s, Li & Fung has undergone fundamental changes in the role it plays, evolving from a simple intermediary to a global supply chain manager, in four stages of major transformation, as encapsulated below.

Stage 1: Intermediary

When Li & Fung was founded in Guangzhou by Fung Pak-liu and Li To-ming in the early 20th century, the world economy was experiencing the Steamboat Era, while in China the Qing Dynasty was just a breath away from its demise. Because he had a good mastery of the English language, Fung Pak-liu became an intermediary between Chinese suppliers and U.S. buyers. For its role as the key communication link between sellers and buyers, Li & Fung was earning a commission of about 15%.

During the time of Fung Hon-chu, Li & Fung was still basically an intermediary earning commissions from both sides of the trading table. After World War II, the nature of the trading business conducted by Li & Fung changed from reexporting from China to exporting from Hong Kong. However, in the course of time, Li & Fung found that its role as intermediary was diminishing with the maturity of buyers and suppliers.

Stage 2: Regional Sourcing Company

In the early 1970s, Victor and William Fung returned to Hong Kong from the U.S. after graduating from college. Hong Kong's manufacturing sector was already well-developed. Confronted with the rise of trade protectionism and the imposition of textile quotas by Western countries, Hong Kong manufacturers resorted to relocating their labor-intensive production lines offshore. As a sourcing agent for the U.S. and European clients, Li & Fung also started expanding its sourcing network from Hong Kong to Taiwan, Korea, Singapore, and the Chinese mainland; gradually growing into a regional sourcing company and extending its supply chain upstream and downstream.

In an interview with Joan Magretta of *Harvard Business Review*, Victor described Li & Fung's transformation in detail, "Most big companies can manage their own sourcing if they just need to deal with Hong Kong—they'd know which ten factories to deal with and wouldn't need any help," he said.

"But dealing with the whole region was more complex. In textiles, quotas govern world trade. Knowing which quotas have been used up in Hong Kong, for example, tells you when you have to start buying from Taiwan. Understanding products was also more complex. We knew that in Taiwan synthetics were better, but that Hong Kong was the place to go for cottons. We can provide a package from the whole region rather than a single product from Hong Kong."

"By working with a larger number of countries, we were able to assemble components. We call this 'assortment packaging.' For example, I sell a tool kit to a major discount chain. I can buy the spanners from one country and the screwdrivers from another and put together a product package. That has some value in it—not great value, but some value."

During this stage, Li & Fung's role changed from that of a sourcing agent to that of "a manager and deliverer of manufacturing programs."

"In the old model," Victor explained, "The customer would say, 'This is the item I want. Please go out and find the best place to buy it for me.' The new model works this way. The Limited, one of our big customers, comes to us and says, 'For the next season, this is what we're thinking of—this type of look, these colors, and these quantities. Can you come up with a production program?"

"Starting with their designers' sketches, we research the market to find the right type of yarn and dye swatches to match the colors. We take product concepts and realize them in prototypes. Buyers can then look at the samples and say, 'No, I don't really like that, I like this. Can you do more of this?' We then create an entire program for the season, specifying the product mix and the schedule. We contract for all the resources. We work with factories to plan and monitor production so we can ensure quality and on-time delivery."[2]

---

[2] Magretta (1998), pp. 102–114.

Stage 3: Manager of "Dispersed Manufacturing"

The global economic downturn in the early 1980s added fuel to protectionist sentiments among industrial powers in the West. At the same time, neighboring economies like Taiwan, Korea, and Singapore are becoming more competitive. All these presented a harsher operating environment for Hong Kong's manufacturing exports. Between 1982 and 1985, the Hong Kong economy experienced a slump it had never witnessed since the start of its industrialization. Its average real GDP growth fell to 4.7% during this period. In 1985, it even saw zero GDP growth. When Hong Kong manufacturers were struggling for survival in the face of both internal and external hardships, a new development gave new impetus to the colony's economy. In 1979, the Chinese mainland rolled out her open-door economic policy. This policy not only enabled Hong Kong to become once again an entrepôt for China's external trade, but also allowed Hong Kong manufacturers to invest in or outsource their production to special economic zones in Southern China, thus solving their most serious problems stemming from the shortage of land and labor.

In the mid-1980s, Hong Kong's labor-intensive industries and production lines began migrating on a massive scale to the Pearl River Delta in Southern China. This migration was more or less complete toward the end of the 1990s. According to a survey conducted by the Hong Kong Trade Development Council, in 1998, Hong Kong companies were operating some 400,000 factories in Southern China and employing a workforce of over 5 million.[3] Apart from China, some Hong Kong manufacturers were also opening factories in Southeast Asia and other parts of the world like Brazil, the Czech Republic, Honduras, Mauritius, Mexico, Poland, South Africa, and Zimbabwe, thus creating a dynamic production network headquartered in Hong Kong. The integration of this network with the global market network has given birth to an even more powerful global economic network.

As pointed out by a 1997 study by MIT (Massachusetts Institute of Technology) entitled "Made by Hong Kong," the consequence entailed by the large-scale migration of manufacturing activities was that the scale of Hong

---

[3] Hong Kong Trade Development Council (1998), p. 13.

Kong's manufacturing has greatly expanded, even as production within Hong Kong itself has shrunk. "Made *by* Hong Kong" has grown, even as "Made *in* Hong Kong" has declined."[4] According to the MIT study, under the concept of "Made by Hong Kong," supply chains for Hong Kong products has extended from Hong Kong to overseas, covering areas like the Pearl River Delta in Guangdong, other inland provinces in China, Indonesia, the Philippines, Myanmar, South Africa, and even South America. The manufacturing network of "Made by Hong Kong" is supported by products or services "Made in Hong Kong," including management, design, R&D, marketing, backup services, telecommunications, quality control, product inspection and certification, financing, as well as parts and components that are still made in Hong Kong. As a result, while traditional manufacturing has virtually demised, services like finance, trading, transportation, and others have prospered. Hong Kong's supply chain management has also extended to other parts of the world.

Following the dispersion of Hong Kong's industries and production processes all over the world, Li & Fung has also evolved into a manager of "dispersed manufacturing." Under "dispersed manufacturing," Li & Fung would engage in high value-added activities in Hong Kong, such as product design and quality control, while outsourcing other low value-added processes to the best possible locations, thus attaining the goal of supplying "global" products in every sense of the word.

In its 2003 publication, *Supply Chain Management: The Li & Fung Experience*, the Li & Fung Research Center cited the example of a stuffed doll to illustrate how that is done in practice. Taking into account factors like price and quality, Li & Fung would buy the fabric from Korea and the stuffing material from the Chinese mainland. Having sourced all the raw materials needed, the making of the final product would be outsourced to, for instance, Qingdao in China.

"Managing dispersed production was a real breakthrough," Victor observed. "It forced us to get smart about not only in logistics and transportation, but also dissecting the value chain."[5]

---

[4] Berger and Lester (eds.) (1997), p. xii.
[5] Magretta (1998), pp. 102–114.

"Managing dispersed manufacturing, where not everything is done under one roof, takes a real change of mind-set," he continued. "But once we figured out how to do it, it became clear that our reach should extend beyond Southern China. Our thinking was, for example, if wages are lower farther inland, let's go there. And so we began what has turned into a constant search for new and better sources of supply." Prompted by this new way of thinking, Li & Fung actively expanded its sourcing network worldwide through a spate of acquisitions, including companies like Inchcape Buying Services (Dodwell), Swire & Maclaine, Camberley, and Colby.

"We were no longer looking for a particular country that could churn out a complete product with good quality," said Victor. "Instead we were dissecting the whole value chain of production processes, improving each process along the way, and making the product in the global sphere. By doing so, we not only offset the costs of logistics and transportation, but could also charge higher fees for our higher value-added services. We were able to produce and deliver more sophisticated products more efficiently. If you look carefully at the world's largest trading firms, you will find that all of them are heading toward the direction of becoming the best player in the global arena." And Li & Fung was obviously one of them.

Li & Fung's dispersed manufacturing management model is also known as "borderless manufacturing." This Hong Kong model of borderless manufacturing has become a new paradigm for the region," said Victor. "Today, Asia consists of multiple networks of dispersed manufacturing–high-cost hubs that do the sophisticated planning for regional manufacturing. Bangkok works with the Indonesian peninsula, Taiwan with the Philippines, and Seoul with Northern China. Dispersed manufacturing is what's behind the boom in Asia's trade and investment statistics in the 1990s—companies moving raw materials and semi-finished parts around Asia. But the region still depends on the ultimate sources of demand, which are in North America and Western Europe. They start the whole cycle going."[6] (Exhibit 10.1)

---

[6] Magretta (1998), pp. 102–114.

Exhibit 10.1 Evolution of Li & Fung's business model

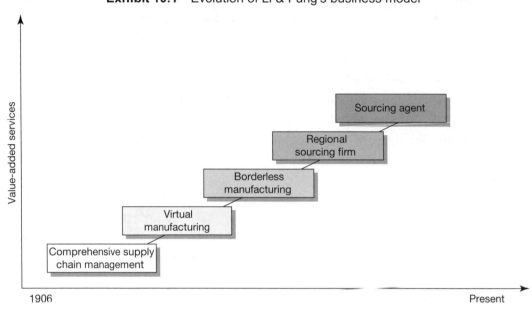

Source: Li & Fung Research Center (2003). *Supply Chain Management—The Practical Experience of the Li & Fung Group*, p. 85.

Stage 4: Global Supply Chain Manager

After the mid-1990s, Li & Fung started developing "virtual manufacturing" on the basis of its dispersed manufacturing model upon acquiring Camberley. Under the new model, Li & Fung would supply goods to customers on a contractual basis, which means that Li & Fung now assumed the role of a direct supplier to customers. Of course, Li & Fung still did not own any factory, but would rather outsource all production to various manufacturers. It would play the prominent role of coordinating and monitoring the entire production process by providing all the crucial support, ranging from product design, raw material sourcing and production management, to quality control, logistics, shipping, and other important aspects (Exhibit 10.2).

At this stage, Li & Fung has essentially become a global supply chain manager. For every single order coming from its clientele in the U.S. and Europe, Li & Fung will come up with the best possible supply chain to bring about the most cost-competitive products and widest profit margin. The scope of Li & Fung's service covers market research, product design

Exhibit 10.2   Coverage of Li & Fung's supply chain management services

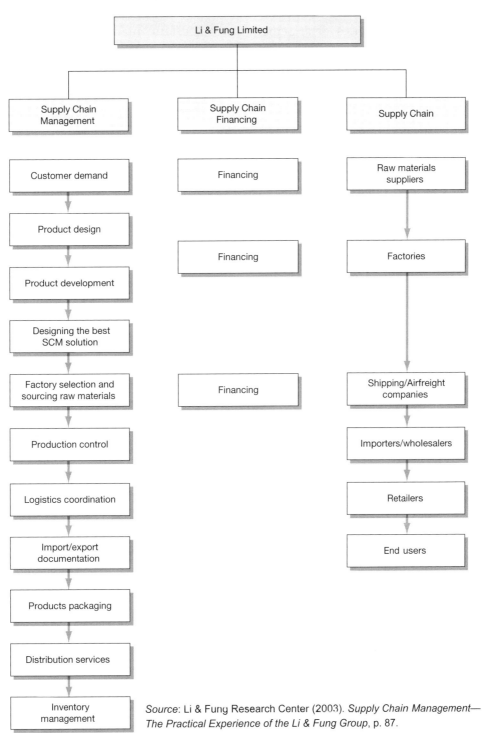

Source: Li & Fung Research Center (2003). *Supply Chain Management—
The Practical Experience of the Li & Fung Group*, p. 87.

and development, raw material sourcing, selecting manufacturers and production supervision. In addition, Li & Fung also takes care of customs clearance and logistics arrangement. It also offers financing arrangements to enterprises that have a crucial part to play in the supply chain and possess good potential, including raw material suppliers, manufacturers, import wholesalers, and retailers. The purpose is to ensure that enterprises on both the supply and demand sides of the supply chain can operate in their best conditions.

Li & Fung's Global Supply Chain Management Model

Till now, no definition of the term "supply chain" or "supply chain management" has been universally adopted in the academic world. At first, supply chain was considered as an internal process within the manufacturing enterprise. Subsequently, having consider the environment outside the supply chain as well, it was defined as "the product transformation process through which a product is put together by the manufacturing, assemblage, distribution, and retail processes of different enterprises to the chain before it reaches the consumer."

In *Supply Chain Management: The Li & Fung Experience*, Li & Fung Research Center proffered the following insight: "Based on various discussions and practices, we can draw the following conclusions:

(1) A supply chain starts from the customer's or consumer's demand and links up various business activities from processes like product design, raw material supply, production, wholesaling, and retailing (possibly involving transportation and warehousing in the interim), to delivery to the end user.

(2) Participants in a supply chain include enterprises and departmental units within an enterprise. The supply chain requires these units to interact and build relations with each other, and inter-enterprise and intra-enterprise cooperation is equally important.

(3) The analysis of a supply chain's process and operation can be conducted on four aspects: work flow, physical flow, information flow, and funds flow. Information flow drives work flow, which determines physical

flow, which in turn translates into funds flow."[7] This passage fairly reflects what Li & Fung understands by supply chain.

Li & Fung considers that the purpose of supply chain management is to optimize the supply chain by spending the lowest amount of money to ensure the efficient operation of all the processes within the chain, from sourcing to delivery to the end user, including the work flow, physical flow, information flow, and funds flow mentioned above."[8]

Since the 1990s, an increasing number of enterprises have made SCM an integral part of their strategic agenda. Renowned multinational enterprises like Hewlett-Packard, IBM, and Dell have achieved tremendous success in SCM. Based in Hong Kong and operating globally, Li & Fung also stands out as a shining example, so much so that the Harvard Business School has conducted several case studies on its SCM. *Harvard Business Review* has described Li & Fung's model as "supply chain management, Hong Kong style" which translates as "fast, global, and entrepreneurial." The author believes that the Li & Fung's SCM model is endowed with inter alia, and has the following characteristics. First, to strive for the so-called "soft $3" in the retail price, Li & Fung has been actively enhancing the management of product supply chains in its global network and ensuring closer cooperation among enterprises in the supply chains. After relisting in 1992, Li & Fung Limited (Li & Fung Trading) has been actively expanding its global sourcing network to cope with economic globalization and the rising trend of "dispersed manufacturing." Apart from more new offices being opened in different parts of the world, it also embarked on a series of mergers and acquisitions, such as Inchcape Buying Services (Dodwell), Swire & Maclaine, Camberley, Colby, and Janco Overseas Limited (a buying agent based in Hong Kong). In addition, it formed strategic alliances with major partners in Europe and Asia, including Nichimen Corporation of Japan. Today, Li & Fung Trading's global sourcing network covers some forty countries with over seventy offices.

---

[7] Li & Fung Research Center (2003), pp. 6–7.
[8] Li & Fung Research Center (2003), p. 11.

A large and efficient global sourcing network facilitates Li & Fung's various product groups in optimizing the product supply chains for individual clients. It is also important for ensuring that the best services are offered to clients at the lowest cost. For clients, cost control is crucial for ensuring competitiveness. For Li & Fung, therefore, the key challenge is to look for the most productive and cost-effective production arrangement for its clients worldwide.

Victor Fung once gave a very pertinent example to illustrate how Li & Fung's global supply chain is managed. "Say, we get an order from a European retailer to produce 10,000 garments," he said. "It's not a simple matter of our Korean office sourcing Korean products or our Indonesian office sourcing Indonesian products. For this customer, we might decide to buy yarn from a Korean producer, but have it woven and dyed in Taiwan. So we pick the yarn and ship it to Taiwan. The Japanese have the best zippers and buttons, but they manufacture them mostly in China. Okay, we then go to YKK, a big Japanese zipper manufacturer, and we order the right zippers from their Chinese plants. Next, we determine that because of quotas and labor conditions, the best place to make the garments is Thailand. So we ship everything there. And because the customer needs quick delivery, we may divide the order across five factories in Thailand. Effectively, we are customizing the value chain to best meet the customer's needs."

"Five weeks after we have received the order, 10,000 garments arrive on the shelves in Europe, all looking like they came from one factory, with colors, for example, perfectly matched. Just think about the logistics and the coordination."

"This is a new type of value added, a truly global product that has never been seen before. The label may say 'Made in Thailand,' but it's not a Thai product. We dissect the manufacturing process and look for the best solution at each step. We're not asking which country can do the best overall job. Instead, we're pulling apart the value chain and optimizing each step—and we're doing it globally. Not only do the benefits outweigh the costs of logistics and transportation, but the higher added value also enables us to charge more for our services. We deliver a sophisticated product and we deliver it fast."[9]

---

[9] Magretta (1998), pp. 102–114.

For developing the best supply chains for its customers across the globe, Li & Fung places particular emphasis on close cooperation among enterprises in each supply chain. Through its global sourcing network, it maintains long-term and intimate relationships with various types of manufacturers, thereby fostering mutual trust with them. Li & Fung gave each manufacturer a certain quantity of production orders at reasonable prices. In return, the manufacturers meet Li & Fung's requirements on production capacity, speed, and other production-related details. They will also offer the highest flexibility that enables Li & Fung to optimize the supply chains for clients.

As competition intensifies in the international market, Li & Fung becomes more focused on the so-called "soft $3" in the retail price. The thinking goes like this. Say a product sells at $4 in the U.S. It takes only $1 to make but it will be extremely difficult to cut down on the manufacturing cost any further. The other $3 constitute the total value of all the other components in the supply chain, including product design, raw material sourcing, logistics and transportation, wholesaling and retailing, information, management, and so on. If a company wants to save, it should do so on these components. As long as the retail price remains constant, savings from the supply chain will translate directly into higher profits. This is essentially the Fung brothers' business philosophy. To earn the "soft $3," Li & Fung keeps on improving its SCM, which also explains why its profit margin always remains at the high industry level.

Second, Li & Fung focuses on building the management structure for a complete supply chain that extends from sourcing to distribution and retailing. It also persists in reinforcing its core businesses and core competitiveness. In the mid-1980s, the scope of Li & Fung's SCM grew from sourcing to cover retailing. Upon acquiring Inchcape's marketing and related businesses in the 1990s, Li & Fung expanded to distribution as well, thus attaining a complete supply chain that encompasses sourcing, distribution and retailing, and becoming a real global supply chain manager (Exhibit 10.3).

Studies have shown that, depending on the market player's core businesses and competencies, the key emphasis of SCM is to play a professional and irreplaceable role in the supply chain, so that it can maintain its competitive edge in the global environment. For this reason, Li & Fung considers its professionalism to be of paramount importance. The Li & Fung Group's SCM consists of three main components: Li & Fung Limited (Trading), Integrated Distribution Services (IDS) Group, and Li & Fung Retailing Group, which includes Convenience Retail Asia Limited (CRA). These three components

Exhibit 10.3 Li & Fung Group's organizational structure

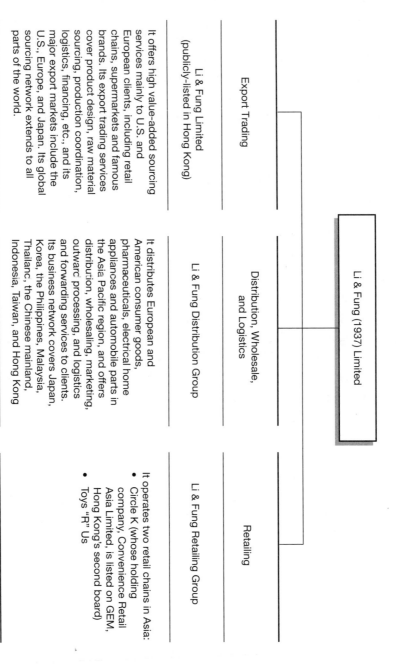

Li & Fung (1937) Limited

Export Trading

Li & Fung Limited
(publicly-listed in Hong Kong)

It offers high value-added sourcing services mainly to U.S. and European clients, including retail chains, supermarkets and famous brands. Its export trading services cover product design, raw material sourcing, production coordination, logistics, financing, etc., and its major export markets include the U.S., Europe, and Japan. Its global sourcing network extends to all parts of the world.

Distribution, Wholesale, and Logistics

Li & Fung Distribution Group

It distributes European and American consumer goods, pharmaceuticals, electrical home appliances and automobile parts in the Asia Pacific region, and offers distribution, wholesaling, marketing, outward processing, and logistics and forwarding services to clients. Its business network covers Japan, Korea, the Philippines, Malaysia, Thailand, the Chinese mainland, Indonesia, Taiwan, and Hong Kong.

Retailing

Li & Fung Retailing Group

It operates two retail chains in Asia:
- Circle K (whose holding company, Convenience Retail Asia Limited, is listed on GEM, Hong Kong's second board)
- Toys "R" Us

The staff's dining hall which can also be transformed into a workplace.

Blue color hues are exclusively used for the office of Li & Fung Trading's Group 8 (LF8).

A training room modeled on Harvard University's lecture room.

Each department has designated dining and resting areas.

Teleconferencing, an indispensable communication means for
Li & Fung to stay in touch with over 70 offices worldwide.

A place of relaxation for customers during meeting breaks.

occupy the upstream, midstream, and downstream positions respectively of the supply chain, offering competitive services to customers through their core businesses, while outsourcing other non-core service segments.

Li & Fung Limited, a listed company at the upstream position, is engaged mainly in sourcing products (mostly apparel and hard goods) from its Asian network on behalf of European and U.S. clients. For decades, the company has been focusing exclusively on its core business—sourcing, which includes order taking, product design, raw material sourcing, production control, quality management, while outsourcing non-core areas, such as manufacturing and transportation to competent manufacturers and forwarders (Exhibit 10.4).

Exhibit 10.4   Li & Fung Limited's upstream position in the supply chain

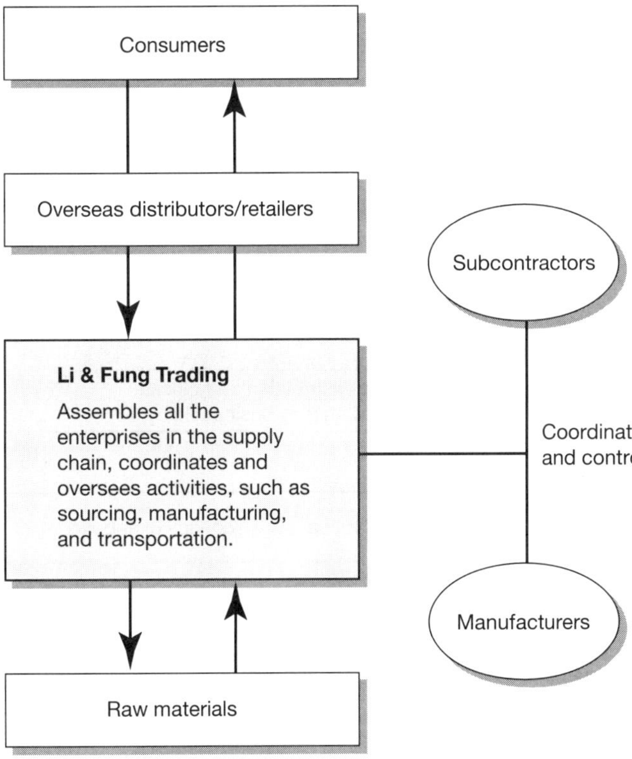

Source: Li & Fung Research Center (2003). *Supply Chain Management—The Practical Experience of the Li & Fung Group*, p. 28.

By cooperating with Li & Fung, manufacturers can also enhance their professionalism by upgrading their core strengths in manufacturing, including production technology, process innovation, and production management. The close cooperation between Li & Fung and manufacturers engenders a highly cost-effective and efficient supply chain that provides the most competitive products and services to clients.

Situated at the midstream position of the supply chain, IDS's core businesses are distribution and wholesaling which consists of marketing, brand building, category management, logistics, and sales-channel development and management. Unlike Li & Fung Trading that sources for overseas buyers, IDS mainly promotes manufacturers' and brand-owners' products, such as foodstuff, household goods, and pharmaceuticals. Its market base is largely located in the Asia Pacific region (Exhibit 10.5), and its client network encompasses hypermarkets, supermarkets, convenience stores, grocery stores, hospitals, clinics, dispensaries, traditional drugstores, and dentists. Given this business nature, IDS has been actively developing its distribution network and playing a bridging role between suppliers (manufacturers) and local wholesalers and retailers, as well as opening new sales channels for products.

Exhibit 10.5 Li & Fung Distribution's midstream position in the supply chain

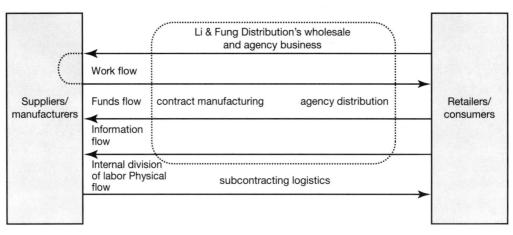

Source: Li & Fung Research Center (2003). *Supply Chain Management—The Practical Experience of the Li & Fung Group*, p. 40.

In the downstream the supply chain, Li & Fung Retailing operates two retail chains—Circle K and Toys "R" Us. Its core business is—by keeping abreast of the market trend—to build up the two retail chains' brand image and enhance after-sales service, as well as improve the work flow, physical flow, funds flow, and information flow, with the aim to minimize inventory stock and improve efficiency (Exhibit 10.6).

The third characteristic of Li & Fung's SCM is the offering of one-stop value-added services to customers through a "pull" supply chain that is constructed with the client as the focal point, and with market demand as the driving force. Currently there are two different supply chain operating models—the "push" and the "pull" types. The "push" type centers on the manufacturer, who will buy raw materials from suppliers to make products, which will then go through different layers of distributors before reaching the end users or consumers. Under this model, distributors and retailers are in a passive position and there is a low degree of integration among the participants in the supply chain. And, to play safe, everyone is inclined to keep a higher level of inventory in case there is a change in the market demand. In contrast, the "pull" model is driven by the end users or consumers. It is the end users' demand that drives the production activities upstream and, pulls or sets in motion the whole supply chain. Under this model, there is a

Exhibit 10.6 Li & Fung Retailing's downstream position in the supply chain

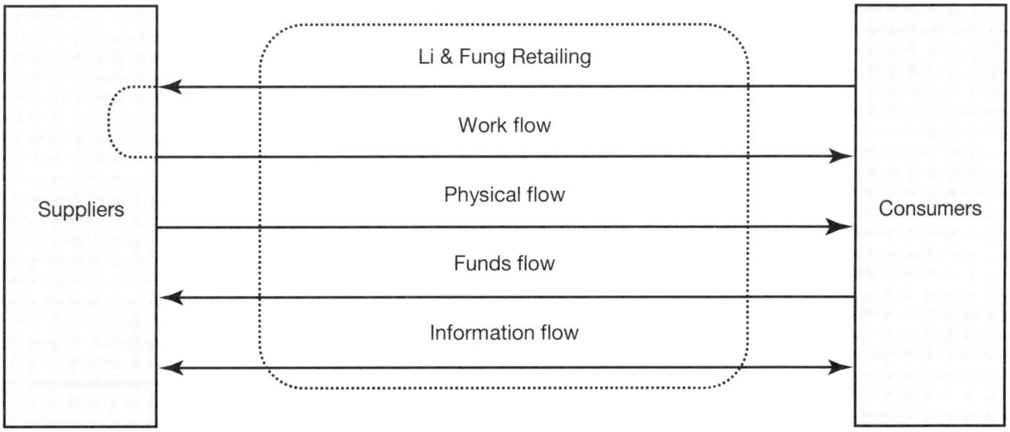

Source: Li & Fung Research Center (2003). *Supply Chain Management—The Practical Experience of the Li & Fung Group*, p. 40.

higher degree of integration, faster information exchange, lower inventory, and quicker response to market demand among the participants.

Li & Fung's SCM belongs to the "pull" type; that is, centered on the client and is market-driven. Also, Li & Fung's clients are mostly retailers in Europe and the U.S. who are highly conversant with the needs of the consumer market and are good at selling products and serving customers. But they are also aware that it is not economical for them to manage production directly. They have, therefore, chosen to appoint Li & Fung as their agent to select manufacturers and suppliers, devise the whole production plan and work flow, and take care of everything from quality management to production schedule until their products are packed and shipped. Based on clients' needs, Li & Fung has expanded the scope of its business from sourcing to include a whole range of value-added services by playing the multiple roles of sourcing agent, trade supplier, and even direct supplier (Exhibit 10.7).[10]

Exhibit 10.7 Li & Fung Limited's four business models

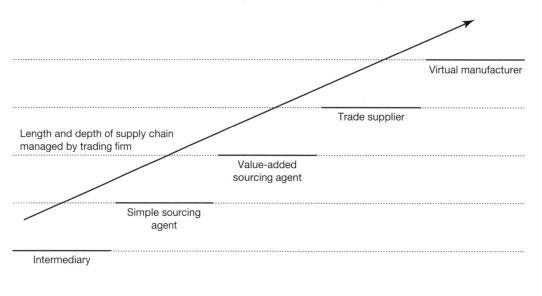

Source: Li & Fung Research Center (2003). *Supply Chain Management—The Practical Experience of the Li & Fung Group*, p. 37.

---

[10] O'Connell in his *Harvard Business Case Studies*, "Li & Fung (Trading) Limited."

Sourcing Agent

As a sourcing agent, Li & Fung will, considering the client's needs and requirements, choose the appropriate supplier(s), provide product designs, and carry out all the sourcing plans. The actual sale-and-purchase agreement will be signed directly between the client and the supplier(s) while Li & Fung will charge a commission for its labor.

Value-added Sourcing Agent

As a sourcing agent, Li & Fung will provide other value-added services in addition to sourcing. These services include:

- Conducting all kinds of market studies to understand consumers' needs and furnishing clients with information on the latest trends in major markets;
- Studying and developing raw materials and components (such as fabrics, laces, and other garment accessories), with a view to providing clients with the latest information;
- Designing and developing products on the latest market trends;
- Matching the needs of clients regarding raw materials with the supplying capabilities of different regions, selecting together with clients the best countries and regions for sourcing, carrying out borderless manufacturing, and realizing higher value-added through product globalization;
- Overseeing the sourcing, shipping, and allocation of raw materials and parts and components to various factories;
- Offering technical support during the production process to ensure that the product quality and each aspect of the production complies with clients' requirements;
- Delivering quick-response production by not only monitoring the supply of major raw materials, but also managing inventory strategically and replenishing for clients at the right time and quantity;
- Planning for consolidated transportation and offering shipping and delivery services; and
- Applying information technology in product development and identifying new suppliers, as well as designing Web pages for overseas clients.

Direct Trade Supplier

As a trade supplier, Li & Fung enters into contract directly with the client to supply end products so that the client does not need to deal with suppliers. In this role, Li & Fung earns not commissions for its service but profit on making the product itself. Typical examples of the trade suppliers under the Li & Fung banner are Camberley and Lloyd Textile Trading that are in the virtual manufacturing business.

Using Flow Management and Information System to Optimize the Operation of Supply Chains

Supply chain management is a kind of flow management that covers work flow (business flow), physical flow, funds flow, and information flow, of which work flow is the most crucial part, although it cannot do without the support of the other three. The level of flow management affects the degree to which the manager can supply clients with products at the most competitive prices and with the best services and, hence, the extent to which the manager can earn the "soft $3." For this reason, Li & Fung's supply chain management lays great emphasis on the design, implementation, review, and constant improvement of flow management.

Take the Circle K convenience stores under Li & Fung Retailing Group as an example. In 1998, facing an increasingly competitive operating environment, the Group revamped its SCM model and under the leadership of CEO Richard Yeung, embarked on a series of drastic reforms. Based on target customers' needs, it rebuilt the Circle K store's image, clearly defined its product mix, and started offering quality service to customers. To enhance the store chain's logistics and delivery system management, the Group invested HK$20 million in setting up an integrated supply chain network that allows speedy and low-cost suppliers to make use of both a direct delivery system and a warehouse delivery system. In respect of information flow management, Circle K has set up an electronic data interchange (EDI) system, a warehouse management system (WMS), and an electronic point-of-sale (e-POS) system to obtain accurate and timely information that is used for improving its sales plan. By optimizing the operation of its supply chain through the improvement of its flow management and information system, Circle K succeeded in reducing its total operating expenses from 26% of sales in 1998 to 21% in 2000, thereby reversing its deficit position.

Establishing a Flexible and Entrepreneurial Management Structure and Mechanism

To cater to clients' needs effectively, Li & Fung has developed a unique management structure and mechanism, including a customer-centric organizational structure, a flexible and merit-based salary system, and a strong top management and backup system, which provides indelible support to the Group's supply chain management. This is elaborated in the following section.

Li & Fung's e-Business

Since the 1990s, with the rise of electronic exchange, more and more companies have begun to conduct transactions on the Internet. Some people could not help asking the question: Would this new trading model eventually lead to the demise of intermediaries like Li & Fung? The Fung brothers did some examination on their own. "Do we still have a useful role to play?…Are we being replaced as an intermediary?" Questions like these would be the starting point for Li & Fung's three-year plans.

At an interview with *Harvard Business Review* in 2000, William Fung talked about the challenges faced by Li & Fung: "About three or four ago, Victor and I discussed the Internet and its impact on us. Our starting point was a defensive posture: Would the Internet disintermediate us? Would we get Amazoned by someone who will put together all of the information about buyers and factories online? After a lot of research we realized that the Internet facilitates supply chain management and we weren't going to be disintermediated. The key is to have the old economy know-how and yet be open to new economy ideas."[11]

---

[11] Li & Fung Research Center (2003), p. 143.

On another occasion, William said: "Way back in 1996, we found that the Internet was having a powerful impact on the world. We were always asking ourselves whether Li & Fung would succumb to this impact and be wiped out in due course. But until now, we have not been adversely affected at all. On the contrary, we have benefited greatly from the Internet because we can now interact with and offer customized services to small and medium-sized enterprises (SMEs) at low costs. In the past, it was hardly profitable for us to deal with a company that gave us less than HK$100 million worth of business. We have no problem with that nowadays, thanks to the Internet." In William's view, online trading cannot possibly take the place of market players like Li & Fung because doing business is more than bringing buyers and sellers together, which is an archaic notion and low-value activity.

"If it is purely a matter of matchmaking," William said, "we don't have to do it on the Internet. Even a backward country can have an organization like the Hong Kong Trade Development Council to bring buyers and sellers together. If Li & Fung could be replaced so easily, it would have vanished long before the invention of the Internet."

Victor also pointed out: "The Internet is a revolutionary technology but a new technology is still nothing but a technology. We take a very progressive approach with regard to the application of technology. My grandfather was shocked by the first appearance of the telephone. The invention of the facsimile machine shortened our response time to just a few days. Now with the Internet, we expect an answer in a few hours, if not less. With the application of broadband and WAP technology, time lag is shortened even further."

The Fung brothers believed that there was no need to worry about the rise of the Internet but Li & Fung should respond with the right measures. One of these measures is the development of its own online capabilities. The Fung brothers were also convinced that Li & Fung's e-business should start from within rather than from outside. Victor has said that he could be certain that the Internet technology would infiltrate the whole Li & Fung Group if and only if a solution came from within. For this reason, Li & Fung was not interested in setting up an independent subsidiary to take charge of its e-business. "Setting up an Internet department is tantamount to setting up a facsimile department which uses only the fax machine and nothing else," said Victor. "E-commerce cannot possibly foster intimate relations between clients and suppliers. What it can foster is just molecule-thick and a mile apart." To Victor and William, through the "close and deep" relations built up with clients and its wealth of SCM experience, Li & Fung would continue to play the role of a value-added intermediary. As William said, "The reason why Li & Fung has not been displaced by its offline competitors is exactly the same as that for online ones."

In the latter half of the 1990s, Li & Fung stepped up its investment in the e-business and gradually constructed an information system supported by the Internet and an Intranet. The aim was to coordinate both internal and external information flow, as well as maintain close contact with business partners, including clients, suppliers, manufacturers, distributors, logistics operators, and the government. By doing so, it hoped to do away with obstacles due to different time zones and locations and thereby upgrade its SCM (Exhibit 10.8). Through this information system, Li & Fung can achieve three kinds of interconnection. First, the Group's eighty-eight offices and hundreds of clients spread out in forty countries would be lined up to create a global business model. Second, the Group's capital, human resources, products, and business opportunities would be pooled. As soon as a business opportunity arose, the Group can quickly transmit the product information in its possession and arrange for sourcing, production, delivery, and financing, while deploying the manpower required for doing all these. Third, its clients and suppliers' business flow, physical flow, and information flow would be interlinked so that it can offer one-stop services to clients.

In 1995, Li & Fung launched a sophisticated and sprawling Intranet that linked up sixty-eight offices and thousands of manufacturing units located

Exhibit 10.8 Li & Fung's information system structure

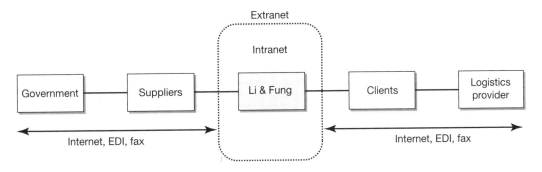

Source: Li & Fung Research Center (2003). *Supply Chain Management—The Practical Experience of the Li & Fung Group*, p. 177.

in forty countries, with the objective of simplifying and expediting internal communications. The Intranet not only has created a platform of information flow for internal communication and communication with suppliers, but has also given rise to new opportunities for Li & Fung to develop and fine-tune its business model. The Intranet has enabled the staff to get around departmental, organizational, regional, and time-zone restrictions to build up expeditiously and effectively the most economical sales network and maximize profit margins. In 1997, Li & Fung established its first Extranet with a major client to facilitate cost-effective exchange of trade-related information, order tracking, product development, and so on. By the end of 2000, Li & Fung had established ten such Extranets to enhance communication with major clients and is able to undertake online product development and order tracking, as well as simplify the communication process on the movement of orders with the supply chain.

In March 2003, Li & Fung announced its Internet-based e-business development strategy. Through its capital investment company in San Francisco, it partnered with Castling Group, an Internet venture capital company in the U.S. to form an e-business subsidiary, lifung.com. The idea was to develop the B2B market through e-business, targeting the 20,000 U.S. retailers with annual turnover of under US$100 million each and the 2,800 U.S. wholesalers with cash flow below US$50 million each. The total production of these potential clients amounted to approximately US$54 billion. Li & Fung intended to leverage its extensive experience and sales network to provide these SMEs with wholesale service with functions like logistics, sourcing, and auto ordering.

Market research indicated that owing to the size of their orders and the lack of economies of scale, these SMEs were forced to pay more to wholesalers in return for inferior services. They would have very little say, for instance, in product specifications, and were often neglected by suppliers whose attention was naturally devoted to the bigger customers. Moreover, they would have difficulty accessing the latest market information and capturing the market trend. There was, therefore, demand among these SMEs for low-cost and good-quality services enjoyed by the large firms. For Li & Fung, under the old economy, the order size by the SMEs would often fall short of manufacturers' minimum requirements. However, through its e-business platform, many smaller orders can be combined to achieve economies of scale. At the same time, it can offer a multitude of product selections and, to a certain extent, customizing services so that the SMEs can also have their unique products. Because there was no minimum quantity to the order size, the SMEs can reduce their inventory and make use of Li & Fung's e-business platform for replenishment, thus responding quicker to market changes. Given all these considerations, William Fung expected the revenue generated from lifung.com would be in the region of US$2 billion. In other words, the new e-business venture would be the main driver for profit growth in Li & Fung Trading's next three-year (2002–2004) plan.

In this connection, Li & Fung (1937), the parent company of Li & Fung Limited, announced the placing of existing and new Li & Fung Limited shares though Goldman Sachs and Cazenove. Initially, 48 million existing shares were to be placed at HK$32.50 a share to raise US$200 million. Subsequently, in view of enthusiastic market response, Goldman Sachs and Cazenove exercised their rights due to the oversubscription to buy in an additional 12 million shares, making a total placement of 60 million shares and raising funds totaling US$250 million. William Fung indicated that about US$200 million would be earmarked as capital for developing e-business.

In September 2000, Li & Fung announced that it had embarked on two new e-commerce projects, a joint venture and a wholly-owned enterprise. YetiMo.com, a 50/50 joint venture between Li & Fung and Lion Nathan Limited of Australia, was to be formed with an investment of approximately US$2.25 million to supply corporate promotional merchandise through a Web-enabled interface. Lion Nathan Limited is an internationally renowned brewer with principal facilities in Australia, New Zealand, and China brewing for leading beer brands. YetiMo.com would profit from Lion Nathan's strategic relationships in the beverage industry and open up a totally new market segment for Li & Fung's sourcing and merchandising services. At the same time, Li & Fung would launch an online initiative, Electronic Stock Offer (eSO), to offer the excessive inventories of its 6,000-strong suppliers to several large discount retailers. Involving an investment of US$2–3 million, eSO would provide a much needed service and assistance to Li & Fung's existing suppliers with excessive inventories due to overproduction or order cancellations. William Fung predicted that the two new e-commerce projects should be able to generate profit by the end of 2001 or early 2002.

A study conducted by Morgan Stanley of the U.S. forecast that by the end of 2000, Internet users in the Asia Pacific region (outside Japan) would reach 68 million, rising to 176 million in 2004 at an average growth rate of 27% a year and outdoing Europe and America. Within the region, the Chinese mainland, Australia, India, and Korea that accounted for 85% of the region's Internet population would have the biggest income potential for online advertising and B2B e-commerce. The report went so far as to indicate that by 2004, the total revenue for the B2B e-commerce market would reach US$30 billion. Thus, Li & Fung's two e-commerce projects were considered as extremely good strategic investments that could generate higher revenues in the coming four to five years.

In February 2001, lifung.com was officially launched under the new name of StudioDirect.com. It was meant to offer customized services to SMEs in the U.S. market by helping them to establish their own brands without the need to place sizeable orders. StudioDirect.com's focus was on combining smaller orders from U.S. buyers and allowing these buyers to order from an array of 200 different designs of products at wholesale prices. The products included male and female apparels, golfing wear, home furnishings, etc. The selling point of this website was its standardized approach and efficiency so that buyers only had to decide on details such as the color of buttons or the texture of a garment. Li & Fung predicted that the revenue to be derived from this portal would be in the region of HK$15.6 billion in three years.

In April 2000, the burst of the U.S. dotcom bubble dealt a fatal blow to virtually all e-businesses worldwide. Li & Fung's e-commerce projects also could not escape from it. In 2000, StudioDirect.com registered a loss of HK$23 million, forcing the Group to make a provision of HK$169 million. In view of the change in market conditions, Li & Fung also restructured StudioDirect's business from a one-stop e-commerce portal into an interface with suppliers of golfing brands. Its share in StudioDirect was also reduced from 57% to 15%. Owing to persistent losses, StudioDirect was closed in end 2003. While maintaining that it was not an incorrect move for Li & Fung to venture into e-commerce, William also realized that the timing was probably not right, and it would perhaps be better to wait at least ten more years.

Chapter 11

The Fung Brothers' Business Management Philosophy

"Just about every company I know says it is customer-focused. What, in fact, does that mean? Usually it means that they design key systems that fit their customers, they hope, most of the time. Here we say—and do—something different: We organize for the customer. Almost all the large trading companies with extensive networks of supplies are organized geographically, with the country units as their profit centers. As a result, it is hard for them to optimize the value chain. Their country units are competing against one another for business."

—Victor Fung

"The Brainiest Businessmen of Asia"

Mr Fung Hon-chu obviously had high hopes for his two sons and he was not disappointed. In July 1999, Victor and William appeared on the cover of *Far Eastern Economic Review* and were described as "the brainiest businessmen of Asia." This should speak volumes about the extent to which the Hong Kong and international business community would go in extolling the Fung brothers' success in running Li & Fung.

Victor Fung was born in Hong Kong in 1945. He attended King George V School in his early years. He went on to complete his education in the U.S., graduating from Massachusetts Institute of Technology (MIT) in 1966 with a bachelor's and a master's degree in electrical engineering. In 1970, he obtained his Ph.D. degree in business economics at Harvard University. Upon graduating from Harvard, he joined Citibank in the U.S. for a brief period before becoming an assistant professor of the M.B.A. and corporate finance programs at Harvard Business School. Victor married his Shanghainese girlfriend, Julia Shen, in the U.S. in 1969.

In 1976, Victor returned to Hong Kong and joined the Li & Fung Group, which was still very much a traditional family firm, as a manager. Together with his brother William, Victor initiated various corporate reforms to revamp Li & Fung's management structure and succeeded in turning it into a public company. In 1977, Victor became the managing director of Li & Fung (Trading) Limited and in 1980, was promoted as the managing director of Li & Fung Limited. After privatizing Li & Fung Limited in 1986, Victor and William were its two largest shareholders, with Victor becoming board chairman.

Highly versatile in modern business management, Victor has succeeded not only in growing the family business but also in transforming Li & Fung into Hong Kong's leading trading group and building for himself the reputation as an expert in venture capital investment. In 1986, with three other partners, Victor set up Prudential Asia Capital Fund, an investment and merchant bank in Asia whose U.S. parent was Prudential Insurance Company. Victor was the chairman of this Asian subsidiary. He then immersed himself in the venture capital sector and in 1988 became the chairman of the Hong Kong Venture Capital Funds Association. He was also appointed as a board director by several prestigious corporations in Hong Kong, including Hong Kong Telecom, Kerry Properties, and Oriental Overseas (International). In 1995,

Victor was named Businessman of the Year by *Forbes Asia*. In 1996, he was elected one of the Top 25 Managers by *Business Week* and placed among the world's 600 most influential persons in the financial sector by *Global Finance*.

Toward the end of the 1980s, Victor began to take up more public service in Hong Kong by accepting appointments to several government advisory committees and semigovernmental bodies, including the Hong Kong Governor's Business Council, Public Service Commission, Judicial Officers Recommendation Commission, Securities and Futures Commission, Trade and Industry Advisory Board, Central Policy Unit, Hong Kong Export Credit Insurance Corporation, Hong Kong Community Chest, and World Wildlife Fund.

Victor's turning point in Hong Kong's political scene was his appointment by Governor Sir. David Wilson, as Chairman of Hong Kong Trade Development Council (HKTDC). HKTDC is one of Hong Kong's most high-powered semigovernmental organizations. Its former chairmen included political heavyweights such as Sir. Chow Sik-nin, Sir. Kan Yuet-keung, T.K. An, and the Baroness Dunn. Baroness Dunn was an executive director of the Swire Group and had been a senior member of both the Executive and Legislative Councils of Hong Kong. She was said to have recommended Victor to the governor. A former legislative councillor once said: "Victor Fung was then a member of the Central Policy Unit. He had a lot of ideas on Hong Kong's economic policies. He and Dunn were on good terms and he often participated in economic promotion missions headed by her to countries like the U.S. and Japan. Victor was intelligent but he was still quite new for the job of HKTDC chairman."[1]

Victor broke HKTDC's decade-old tradition by becoming the first chairman who was not also simultaneously an Executive Councillor or Legislative Councillor of Hong Kong. "I could not figure out at the time why the Hong Kong government had picked me," Victor recalled. "With hindsight, it was a wise thing to do because during the transitional period prior to the handover of Hong Kong's sovereignty to China, HKTDC's chairman should ideally be outside the sphere of politics and the political interactions between China and Britain. I think it was really fortunate for HKTDC that I do not have

---

[1] *Next Magazine*, Hong Kong, September 18, 2003, p. 44.

a political background and was immune to the dispute between Governor Chris Patten and the Chinese side after 1992."

The HKTDC chairmanship was a milestone in Victor's personal career. HKTDC was a large organization with a staff of 750 worldwide. Its nineteen board members were either senior government officials or representatives of major trade associations. Victor was highly committed to the job and initiated a host of reforms. Having regard to Hong Kong's economic restructuring, he actively promoted trade in services in addition to the diversification of trade in commodities. Prior to 1991, HKTDC's income was derived mainly from a levy imposed on exports but by the time Victor stepped down as chairman, the export levy made up only a third of the Council's total income.

During his tenure as HKTDC Chairman, Victor was also a member of advisory bodies such as the Hong Kong-U.S. Business Council in 1989 and the Hong Kong-Japan Business Cooperation Committee in 1991. In 1993, he became the chairman of the Hong Kong-Korea Business Roundtable. All these are high-powered committees for Hong Kong to keep in close touch with its major trade partners. Victor once sat on the Eminent Persons Group of Asia-Pacific Economic Cooperation (APEC) that was responsible for formulating an economic vision for APEC's eighteen-member states. In 1996, Victor was appointed as Hong Kong's representative on APEC's Business Advisory Council and co-chairman of the Committee's Finance and Investment Group. The Council was the spokesperson for business affairs in Asia Pacific.

Spearheaded by HKTDC, the Hong Kong/European Union and European Union/Hong Kong Business Cooperation Committees were set up in July 1997, with Victor as chairman of the former; and Peter Sutherland, chairman of Goldman Sachs International and former director-general of GATT, as chairman of the latter. Secretarial support for the two committees was provided by HKTDC. The European Union (E.U.) has been Hong Kong's third-largest trading partner after the Chinese mainland and the U.S. Approximately 250 companies from the E.U. in various industries have set up regional headquarters in Hong Kong. There are about 50,000 E.U. expatriates in Hong Kong, who form the largest E.U. community in all Asian cities. The formation of the two bilateral committees was meant to create an even better environment for trade growth between the E.U. and Hong Kong. At the inaugural meeting of the Hong Kong/European Union Business Cooperation Committee, Victor pointed out that upon becoming a Special Administrative Region of China, Hong Kong would need to foster more extensive relationships with its trading partners. The bilateral committee, which arrived after Hong Kong/U.S. Economic Cooperation Committee and the Hong Kong/Japan and Business Cooperation Committee, was expected to bring the Hong Kong/E.U. partnership to new levels. Hong Kong would play a bigger role as the springboard for European firms seeking to expand their markets in the Asia Pacific region.

During his nine-year tenure as HKTDC's chairman and hence Hong Kong's *de facto* trade ambassador, Victor spared no effort in opening up new markets for Hong Kong. Given his rich international connections, global vision, and business experience, the results were phenomenal. During those nine years, HKTDC's overseas offices increased from twenty-six to fifty-six, and were active in promoting Hong Kong in various markets. Prior to Hong Kong's reunification with China, the project to build an extension to the Hong Kong Convention and Exhibition Center commenced. Under Victor's leadership, the whole project was completed within budget and on schedule. The outward appearance of the extension resembles a flying seabird which symbolizes Hong Kong and imparts a new image to HKTDC.

In May 1999, Victor succeeded Mr. Wong Po-yan as the chairman of Airport Authority Hong Kong (AA). Before that, the fiasco surrounding the opening of the new Hong Kong International Airport (HKIA) at Chek Lap Kok, Lantau Island, had drawn lashing condemnations from the public. Upon his ascension to the hot seat, Victor clearly defined HKIA's mission as to be the leading aviation hub in the Asia Pacific region. Discarding AA's former indecisive style, he set out to enhance HKIA's competitive position by slashing fees and studying how to make the best use of land resources in Lantau Island, including the development of a logistics center and an airport city (SkyCity), and how to match the long-term development of Hong Kong Disneyland. On his agenda was also the plan to turn AA into a public company. To reinforce Hong Kong's position as an international aviation hub, he found it necessary to link up port facilities at the new HKIA with fourteen ports situated in various parts of the Pearl River Delta so that HKIA could benefit from having the whole Delta as its hinterland. These farsighted and practical plans once again demonstrated Victor's strength of mind and capabilities and won public acclaim.

In September 2001, Victor was appointed to succeed Sir. T.L. Yang as council chairman of Hong Kong University (HKU). At that juncture, HKU was going through a crisis—the widely reported "Robert Chung Incident"—that sparked off public uproar on academic freedom at the university, leading eventually to the departure of vice-chancellor Cheng Yiu-chung and pro-vice-chancellor Wong Siu-lun. Sir. Yang, who had served as council chairman for sixteen years, also stepped down. HKU is the oldest university in Hong Kong and its council chairman has considerable influence in the formulation of policies for education and other sectors of the economy. The fact that after the AA chairmanship Victor was asked to take another hot seat was a reflection of Hong Kong government's recognition of his capabilities.

Victor Fung taught at Harvard University as a young man and was honored with the Harvard Medal for his contribution. After returning to Hong Kong, he never really gave up his interest in teaching. He was in charge of certain courses at the Faculty of Business Administration of Chinese University of Hong Kong. Prior to his appointment as council chairman, he had been a Professor Emeritus of HKU since 1996. He became a member of HKU Council in 1997. He was also director of MIT Alumni Association in Hong Kong, chairman of Harvard University Alumni Association in Hong Kong, as well as director and trustee of Harvard Hong Kong Alumni Trust Fund.

Victor believes in academic and policy research. In 2001, he initiated a research project entitled "Project 2022" by bringing together a group of academics and business elites. The research report discussed the part played by the Hong Kong/Pearl River Delta cooperation in Hong Kong's economic restructuring, which generated a great deal of interest within the Hong Kong community. "I like organizing forums more than anything else," he said. "To me, it is more meaningful than making money because nothing gives me more intellectual stimulation than participating in a discussion or even debate with a group of people on a specific subject from different perspectives."

Owing to his background and experience, Victor was welcomed as a good candidate for the position of HKU's council chairman by both staff and students in general. The staff cherished the hope that he could lift HKU out of its quagmire as effectively as he did with the new HKIA's disastrous debut. Council Member, the Hon. James To, also thought that with his global vision, Victor should be able to play a positive role in moving HKU forward.

Upon assuming the chairmanship of HKU, Victor openly lauded HKU as a highly reputable tertiary institute in the region. He thought that it should aspire to be one of the world's top twenty-five universities and this long-term objective should be the new challenge of the university's next vice-chancellor. He stressed that HKU should measure itself against global, rather than regional standards and outperform itself in the pursuit of academic excellence. "In a survey conducted by *Asiaweek* in 2000," he said, "HKU was ranked No. 3 among all universities in the region. This is a good indicator that we are already up to certain standards."

In 2001, prior to the appointment of Anthony Leung Kam-chung to the position of Financial Secretary, which was vacated by Donald Tsang Yam-kuen who became the Chief Secretary, rumor had it that Victor Fung was the frontrunner for it. However, more people tended to think that Victor would be a major candidate for the next Chief Executive of HKSAR. Amidst endless speculations that Victor would be the rising star on Hong Kong's political stage, Victor gave an interview to *Asiaweek* in February 2004, denying that a new goal had appeared in his life to replace that of being a successful entre-preneur, given his training in business management. "I am not running for the position of HKSAR's Chief Executive," he stated emphatically. "Politics is not my best love. What I'm still passionately striving for is the perfection and implementation of Li & Fung's supply chain management and the creation of a trading platform unique to Hong Kong."[2]

In 2003, Victor Fung was honored with the Gold Bauhinia Star by the HKSAR government for his distinguished services to Hong Kong. On February 24, 2004, he was appointed as chairman of the newly-established Pearl River Delta Business Council, the members of which are business leaders and professionals, including representatives of trade associations and sectors like banking, shipping, textiles, accounting, legal services, logistics, science and technology, real estate, construction, environmental protection and education, as well as SMEs and think-tanks. An HKSAR government spokesman said that "this private sector-led business council will complement the govern-ment-to-government framework of the Hong Kong-Guangdong Cooperation Joint Conference" and "foster closer economic cooperation within the Greater Pearl River Delta region."

Compared to his elder brother, William Fung has a lower profile. Born in Hong Kong in 1949, William also attended King George V School. He con-tinued his education in the U.S., graduating from Princeton University with

---

[2] *Yazhou Zhoukan*, Hong Kong, February 8, 2004, p. 29.

a B.Sc. in engineering and computer studies, and an M.B.A. from Harvard University. When he returned to Hong Kong to join Li & Fung in 1972 and took part in its IPO, he was only twenty-three. William's wife, Sylvia, is the daughter of Chou Wen-hsien, the chairman of Windsor Industrial Corporation. His foster father was the late T.K. An, a former political heavy-weight in Hong Kong.

Li & Fung's success today owes much to the intimate relations between the two Fung brothers. At an interview many years ago, William said not half-jokingly, "Should I be crippled, I have no doubt in my mind that he (Victor) will take care of me for the rest of my life." Admitting that it would be hard to attribute any particular reason for this fraternal love, he said, "This is probably a family tradition. Our grandfather was a Catholic and had only one wife. He could have had many more, given his wealth." Because relationships within the Fung family are not complicated, everybody gets along superbly with everybody else.

As regards the management of Li & Fung, there was a clear division of labor between the two brothers. William once described this division as something like this: the "V" in "Victor" stands for "Vision" while the "W" in "William" stands for "Work." "He does the strategy while I do the administration," he said. On another occasion, William was even more explicit. "Victor does the planning by looking at long-term prospects," he said. "He is resourceful and well-connected. Furthermore, he has a vision and keeps abreast of the global trend. I work hard like an administrator should. Doing business is not as complicated as making air-jets and tankers, but if you don't administer and execute it well, you won't succeed. There is much tacit understanding between us and we know our respective roles well. In general, Victor focuses on the main direction and long-term stuff while I focus on the finer details on a day-to-day basis."

Joan Magretta of *Harvard Business Review* who did an intensive interview with Victor in 1998 said: "Victor is a business leader who is clear-minded and always has his eyes on the long term. Above all, he can detach himself from his heavy daily workload and look at the entire Li & Fung's operations and market direction from a macro perspective." William remarked, "We are a perfect team, not only in running Li & Fung, but also in investment. Whenever we invest in anything, we always do it on a fifty-fifty basis. In this regard, we are quite old-fashioned Chinese."

William's outstanding achievements have also been highly acclaimed in the international business community. In 1996, he and Victor were both elected among the Top 25 Managers by *Business Week* and were named Businessman of the Year 2005 by *Forbes Asia*.

In fact, William made his debut in Hong Kong's political scene even earlier than his elder brother. He was appointed a member of the Basic Law Consultative Community in 1985 in his capacity as council member of HKTDC. In the early 1990s, he was appointed as a member of the HKSAR Selection Committee and the National People's Congress Preparatory Committee for HKSAR. He was later made a member of Chinese Peoples' Political Consultative Conference (1998–2003). In 1993, William was appointed by the Hong Kong government as chairman of Pacific Economic Cooperation Council (PECC). The objective of PECC is to promote regional economic cooperation. Hong Kong members of PECC representing the business sector, academia, and the government are appointed by the Financial Secretary.

As a prominent businessman in Hong Kong, William has served various positions in the Hong Kong General Chamber of Commerce, including General Committee Member (1984–1996), Chairman of Industrial Affairs Committee (1989–1993), Second Vice-Chairman (1992–1993), First Vice-Chairman (1993–1994), and Chairman (1994–1996). He was also Chairman of Hong Kong Exporters' Association and Member of HKSAR Financial Secretary's Economic Advisory Council. He is a non-executive director of HSBC Holdings, vice-chairman of Hong Kong and Shanghai Banking Corporation, and independent non-executive director of China Light & Power, Bank of Communications, Tech Holdings and chinadotcom Corporation. William has also made significant contribution to education. From 1992 to 1997, he was a council member of Lingnan College (now Lingnan University). From 1988 to 1990, he was a member of the Advisory Committee of Business Administration Faculty of City Polytechnic (now City University). In 1995, he was made a founding member of the Advisory Council of Hong Kong Polytechnic University and a council member of Chinese University. In the same year, he was made an Officer of the British Empire (OBE).

In 1999, the Hong Kong University of Science and Technology conferred the degree of Doctor of Business Administration *honoris causa* on William. In 2000, he was among the fifty "Stars of Asia" selected by *Business Week*. Out of the fifty, seven came from Hong Kong, including Li Ka-shing, the chairman of Cheung Kong Holdings; and George Shen, the chairman of Securities and Futures Commission. As prominent business leaders in Hong Kong, William and his brother, Victor's business philosophies are highly regarded.

Three-Year Plans to Drive Constant Improvement

In comparison with other Hong Kong companies, Li & Fung became unique after its buyout by Victor and William in that its development follows three-year plans with clearly defined goals and targets. According to William, Li & Fung's three-year plans have been inspired by the Five-Year Plans of Communist China. While the three-year plans are forward-looking, they are not for the too distant future. The Fung brothers are convinced that a plan for a fixed number of years is useful for achieving midterm targets and moving the company forward progressively. Under such plans, the company can establish specific business goals and set out to achieve them step by step and systematically. It can also pursue corporate transformation and improvement on a continuous basis.

There are basically two main schools of thought insofar as planning theory is concerned, namely, the "rollover" and the "zero-based" types. Li & Fung adopts the latter. As pointed out by William, Li & Fung feels deeply about the mutability of the market environment after a series of transformations and, therefore, always starts making a new three-year plan by asking the same question: "Is it worthwhile to continue doing this business?" While doing a zero-based plan is obviously more complicated and time-consuming, the flip side of the coin is that the management is free from any historical burden and is, therefore, more clear-minded they can evaluate and make projections on the future by taking into account the latest market environment and the company's current condition.

Li & Fung's top management considers five-year plans to be too long for keeping up with the quick changes in the market. Conversely, yearly or two-year plans would be a little too short for setting and implementing any meaningful corporate goals. To strike a balance, they settled for the three-year plan under which the first year is for planning and commencing, the second year is for implementing at full steam to achieve the goals, and the third year is for achieving and reviewing the goals. The three-year plan allows the various departments sufficient turnaround time to cope with changes in the external environment and to seize the best opportunity to achieve the goals.

To William, the three-year plan is crucially important. "Our three-year plan is zero-based,' he said. "We review it every three years to see whether we still have a good reason to survive in the latest macroeconomic environment. Our plan encompasses self reflection. We ask ourselves whether we are still playing a useful role and or are we going to be dumped as an intermediary."

William recalled a story he had heard while doing his M.B.A. degree in the U.S. It goes like this: A factory specializing in horse-whips devoted itself to do nothing else but perfect their skills and make their only product, oblivious to what was happening outside. Horse-whips went out of demand and the company also went out of business. "This story demonstrates all too well,' said William, "the paramount importance of being attuned to the market."

The Fung brothers believe that only second- or third-rate enterprises will wait for changes to arrive before finding ways to adapt. The first-rate enterprise will be able to anticipate changes and adjust or initiate reforms ahead of the others. For this reason, Li & Fung conducts a comprehensive review of itself every three years to decide whether any adjustment or reform is necessary.

"To us, China operates a marvelous system," William explained at an interview. "Her five-year plans are fixed and well-prepared. Our three-year plans are also fixed. The idea is to have fixed goals and not to waver. When we start planning, we will first look at the fundamentals of the company's business. We will then work backward by deciding what we want to achieve in the next three years and then how far away we are from our goals. After that, we will figure out what we have to do to achieve these goals."[3]

According to Victor and William, the making of Li & Fung's three-year plans takes four steps. First, by analyzing the business environment, they will make a forecast of the scenario for the next three years. Because the operating environment holds sway over the prospects of any enterprise, Li & Fung starts with an in-depth analysis of aspects such as export markets,

---

[3] Li & Fung Research Center (2003), p. 199.

sourcing markets, exchange rates, product technology, information technology, clients, and consumers' demand, to anticipate the scenario in three years (Exhibit 11.1).

Exhibit 11.1 Scenario analysis of Li & Fung's three-year (1999–2001) plan

Item	Scenario Analysis
Export markets	• Slowdown in U.S, and U.K. markets • Europe in between slowdown and revival. • Japan in recession.
Sourcing markets	• Southeast Asia still unstable. • Chinese mainland stable.
Foreign exchange	• Euro circulation has impact on markets. • Chinese yuan and HK dollars not to be devalued. • Uncertainties over Thai Baht, Malaysian Dollar, and Japanese Yen.
Product technology	• No major technology breakthrough is expected from major labor-intensive products.
Information technology (IT)	• IT application to gain momentum and become the major driving force for all business areas. • Clients to have higher demand for IT.
Clients	• Continue to demand value, quick response, and ethics compliance. • Focus on supply chain management. • U.S. clients continue to downsize and outsource; Europe consolidating.
Globalization	• Clients and production processes increasingly globalize.
Consumers	• Markets increasingly segmented or more market zones. • Massive diversification. • Higher demand on value. • Gradual acceptances of new retail channels, e.g., direct sales and on-line shopping.
Competition	• Trading firms and manufacturers facing competition from an increasing number of companies dealing in small variety of products. • Some clients may wish to manage their own supply chains.
Conclusions	• A sophisticated scenario—pressure to change. • Yesterday's model of success may not work tomorrow. • A customer-driven business model is needed. • An understanding of supply chain management is needed.

Source: Li & Fung (Trading) Limited.

Second, based on the company's vision and the projected scenario, they will come up with a development goal that is challenging. A company's vision is its long-term objective that defines the direction and goal toward which it should move. Li & Fung's vision is "to be the premier trading firm that delivers the right product at the right price at the right time to companies and consumers across the world." Guided by this vision, Li & Fung formulates its business goal once every three years after taking into consideration changes in the environment. This goal must be achievable and challenging. Li & Fung believes that a challenging goal will force both the management and the staff to leave behind their former models of success and sense of complacency and, through painstaking efforts in seeking new markets and ways of operation, achieve higher goals.

Third, they will look back at the company's status quo from the vantage point of the new goal, determine the distance in between, and figure out the strategy to beat that distance. According to William, a new school of thought regarding business management has arisen recently in the U.S. The enterprise will first and foremost jump to the future and consider the future scenario of the global economy before defining its own development model and goal and planning for the future. Li & Fung's three-year plan integrated this "working backward" approach to determine how far it will have to go before achieving its goal. It will then make use of the SWOT analysis to evaluate its strengths, weaknesses, opportunities, and threats to come up with a development strategy.

As William stressed, a new mindset is indispensable for using the reverse thinking method to develop a strategy for beating the distance between now and then. He illustrated with this lively example: "If we are given three hours to go from here (LiFung Tower, Cheung Sha Wan) to Tsim Sha Tsui, we may consider jogging. However, if we have only fifteen minutes to cover the same distance, there is simply no way we can do it on foot. We must think of something else, such as by taking a taxi." William believes that the "working backward" approach is conducive to promoting the use of new methods and new channels in achieving goals. For example, in implementing the 1996–1998 three-year plan, Li & Fung made a breakthrough from its previous organic-growth model by acquiring and integrating Dodwell, thus accomplishing the goal of doubling turnover and profit.

Fourth, they will formulate an implementation plan for the strategy, which will be modified with the circumstances. The implementation plan takes into account the resources and required manpower, the actual timetable, and how different departments of the company should adjust themselves to meet the requirement of the plan (Exhibit 11.2). Of course, Li & Fung's three-year plan is not immutable. Instead it can be adjusted and fine-tuned as and when necessary in accordance with the external environment. For instance, in 2001, Li & Fung was presented with the unforeseen opportunity to acquire Colby. This opportunity was not only beyond its anticipation but would cause it to fall short of some of its original targets. Li & Fung went ahead to acquire Colby regardless on the belief that, as in the case of Dodwell, this acquisition would bring in immense benefits in the long term.

Exhibit 11.2   Li & Fung's formulation of the three-year plan

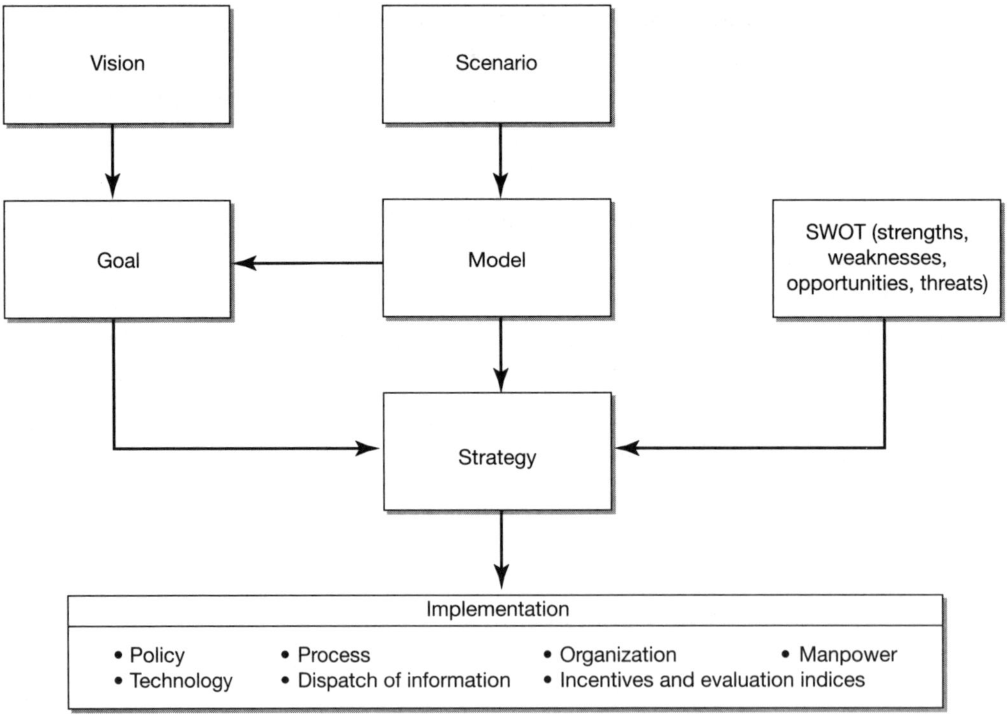

Source: Li & Fung Research Center (2003), p. 204.

In fact Li & Fung started implementing three-year plans since its privatization in 1989. After a restructuring exercise in the ensuing three years, Li & Fung Group's trading business went public again. In 1993, Li & Fung formally launched its first three-year plan with the goal of achieving a total turnover of US$1 billion and replacing Inchcape Buying Services (IBS) as Hong Kong's leading trading firm. In implementing this plan, Li & Fung focused on plugging the loopholes, so to speak, within its sourcing network in order to cover new sourcing markets. In 1995, it acquired Dodwell and completed its first three-year plan ahead of schedule. Li & Fung's second three-year (1996–1998) plan focused on widening Dodwell's profit margin. By integrating Dodwell into its corporate structure, Li & Fung succeeded in doubling profit and raising its profit margin back to the 3% level. In the third three-year (1999–2001) plan, Li & Fung's goal was to grow its total turnover and profit margin by 50% and 1%, respectively, and to double its gross profit. However, because of the unanticipated acquisition of Colby as well as the provisioning for its investment in e-commerce, it failed to double its gross profit, but it still grow its total turnover by 50%.

Overall, Li & Fung's three-year plans have been a shinning success. In 2000, Li & Fung Limited's share price outdid the Hang Seng Index by 75%, making Li & Fung one of the top twenty listed companies in Hong Kong.

Li & Fung's fourth three-year plan commenced from 2002. It focused more on increasing profit margin than M&A in order to achieve the goal of doubling its profit, from HK$905 million in 2001 to a targeted HK$1.8 billion in 2004. The implementation strategy centered on cost control, the development of high-margin new business segments and, where appropriate, the acquisition of chiefly non-U.S. and non-garment firms to achieve market diversification. William made it clear that Li & Fung would actively pursue the development of high-margin businesses such as virtual manufacturing, with a view to boosting their contribution to the Group's turnover to 30%. The remaining 70% was still to come from traditional businesses, the profit margin of which would be raised to 3.5%, so that the overall profit margin could reach 4.25%. Unfortunately, owing to the 911 terrorist attacks on U.S. and the SARS outbreak, Li & Fung was unable to achieve all its 2002–2004 three-year plan targets. While its turnover and net profit still grew by 43% and 61%, respectively, it was only able to increase its profit margin to 3.24% (Exhibit 11.3).

Exhibit 11.3 The outcome of Li & Fung's three-year plans (HK$ million)

Year	1992	1995	1998	2001	2004
Turnover	3,980	9,213	14,313	32,941	47,171
(growth %)	–	(131%)	(55%)	(130%)	(43%)
Operating profit	149	242	470	905	1,595
(growth %)		(73%)	(94%)	(93%)	(76%)
Net profit	160	225	455	951	1,530
(growth %)		(36%)	(102%)	(109%)	(61%)
Turnover	3,980	9,213	14,313	14,313	47,171
(growth %)	–	(131%)	(55%)	(130%)	(43%)
Profit margin	–	2.6%	3.3%	2.7%	3.24%

Source: Li & Fung Limited Annual Reports, 1992–2004.

Li & Fung's Unique Management Structure and Operational System

In running Li & Fung, Victor and William are guided by an unshakable belief that the customer-oriented approach and the entrepreneurial spirit are both crucially important. This conviction underscores the whole Li & Fung Group's unique management structure and operational system.

First, Li & Fung's organizational and operational structure is flexible and customer-oriented. Having gone public in 1973, Li & Fung has gradually set up an organizational and operational structure that is client-based, rather than region-based. Currently, Li & Fung has more than a hundred units or divisions that are charged with servicing the needs of specific clients. Each of them operates like a separate enterprise. The division manager is fully empowered to make decisions to meet the fast-changing needs of clients. At the interview he gave to *Harvard Business Review* in 1998, Victor explained clearly the true meaning of "customer-oriented."

"Just about every company I know says they are customer-oriented," he said. "What, in fact, does that mean? Usually it means that they design key systems that fit most of their customers, they hope, most of the time. Here we say—and do—something different: We organize for the customer. Almost all the large trading companies with extensive networks of suppliers are organized geographically, with the country units as their profit centers. As a result, it is hard for them to optimize the value chain. Their country units are competing against one another for business."

"Our basic operating unit is the division. Whenever possible, we will focus an entire division on serving one customer. We may serve smaller customers through a division structured around a group of customers with similar needs. We have, for example, a theme-store division serving a handful of customers, such as the Warner Brothers stores and Rainforest Café. This structuring of the organization around customers is very important—remember that what we do is close to creating a customized value chain for every customer's order."

"Hence, customer-oriented divisions are the building blocks of our organization. Consider our Gymboree division, one of our largest. The division manager, Ada Liu, and her team in the headquarters have their own separate office space within the Li & Fung building in Hong Kong. When you walk through their doors, every one of the forty or so people you see is focused solely on meeting Gymboree's needs. On every desk is a computer with direct software links to Gymboree. The staff is organized into specialized teams in areas such as technical support, merchandizing, raw material purchasing, quality assurance, and shipping. And because Gymboree buys in volume from China, the Philippines, and Indonesia, Ada has dedicated sourcing teams in the branch offices in all these countries. In maybe five of our twenty-six countries, she has her own team, people she hired herself. When she wants to source from, say, India, the branch office helps her get the job done."[4]

Victor also talked about the Li & Fung way of ironing out differences with suppliers in a certain country or region. "In most multinational companies, fights between the geographical side of the organization, and the product or customer sides are legendary—and predictable. From the product side, it is 'How can I get better service for my customers? It may be small for you in Bangladesh, but it's important for my product line globally.' And from the country side, it's 'Look, I can't let this product group take unfair advantage

---

[4] Magretta (1998), pp. 102–114.

of this particular factory because it produces for three product groups, and I'm responsible for our relationships in this country overall.'

"Here's our solution to this classic problem: Our primary alignment is around customers and their needs. But to balance the matrix, every product-group executive also has responsibility for one country. It makes them more sensitive to the problems facing a country director and less likely to make unreasonable demands." (Exhibit 11.4)

Second, Li & Fung has established an operating system that is conducive to entrepreneurship. As a large-scale trading firm with the characteristics of a small enterprise, Li & Fung's rapid development is attributed to two major factors. One is its ability to remain flexible in a market environment that is fast changing. The other is its ability to attract and retain the professionals it needs, thus allowing them to actualize their entrepreneurial aspirations. Li & Fung's organizational structure is made up of an array of small product groups or divisions and it encourages entrepreneurship. Each division has a business portfolio of US$20–50 million and is headed by a capable entrepreneur who runs the division as if it is his or her own company.

"We like to call these division managers 'Little John Waynes' after the Hollywood icon who often played the righteous and patriotic cowboy of the West shooting at the bad guys," said Victor. "In other words, they are always on the move and are never complacent with just sitting in the office signing documents. Moreover, they are not just executives; they are also equipped with sales and marketing experience."[5]

"If they are not working for Li & Fung," said Victor, "They will most likely set up their own firms." As pointed out in *Harvard Business Case Studies*, the majority of Li & Fung's top-notch trading staff, including sales managers, product group managers and executive directors, are all capable of starting their own trading firms and competing with their employer. For this reason, Li & Fung must necessarily have an effective operating system to retain them and allow them to become entrepreneurs.

On another occasion, William said: "My brother and I went to college in the U.S., but we still feel deeply that business organizations as a whole are

---

[5] *Hong Kong Economic Times*, January 25, 1996, p 17.

Exhibit 11.4 Li & Fung Limited's organizational structure in 1998

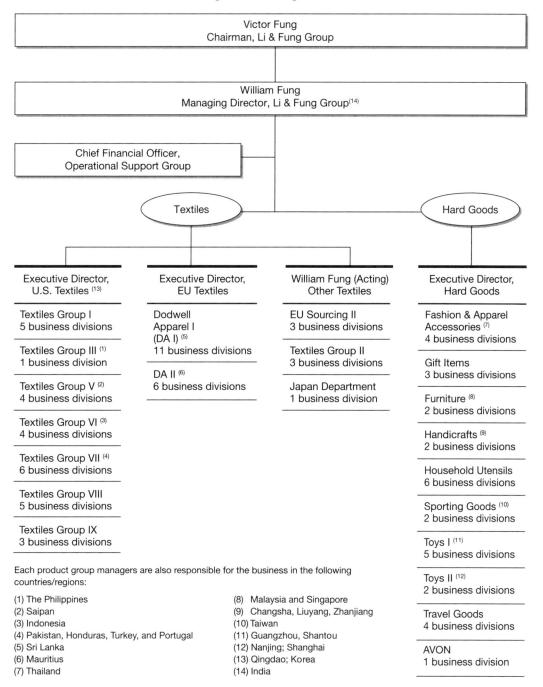

Victor Fung
Chairman, Li & Fung Group

William Fung
Managing Director, Li & Fung Group[14]

Chief Financial Officer,
Operational Support Group

Textiles

Hard Goods

Executive Director, U.S. Textiles [13]

Textiles Group I
5 business divisions

Textiles Group III [1]
1 business division

Textiles Group V [2]
4 business divisions

Textiles Group VI [3]
4 business divisions

Textiles Group VII [4]
6 business divisions

Textiles Group VIII
5 business divisions

Textiles Group IX
3 business divisions

Executive Director, EU Textiles

Dodwell
Apparel I
(DA I) [5]
11 business divisions

DA II [6]
6 business divisions

William Fung (Acting) Other Textiles

EU Sourcing II
3 business divisions

Textiles Group II
3 business divisions

Japan Department
1 business division

Executive Director, Hard Goods

Fashion & Apparel
Accessories [7]
4 business divisions

Gift Items
3 business divisions

Furniture [8]
2 business divisions

Handicrafts [9]
2 business divisions

Household Utensils
6 business divisions

Sporting Goods [10]
2 business divisions

Toys I [11]
5 business divisions

Toys II [12]
2 business divisions

Travel Goods
4 business divisions

AVON
1 business division

Each product group managers are also responsible for the business in the following countries/regions:

(1) The Philippines
(2) Saipan
(3) Indonesia
(4) Pakistan, Honduras, Turkey, and Portugal
(5) Sri Lanka
(6) Mauritius
(7) Thailand
(8) Malaysia and Singapore
(9) Changsha, Liuyang, Zhanjiang
(10) Taiwan
(11) Guangzhou, Shantou
(12) Nanjing; Shanghai
(13) Qingdao; Korea
(14) India

Source: Li & Fung Research Center (2003), p. 204.

an integral part of society and by virtue, they cannot detach themselves from social ethics and human relations. After returning to Hong Kong, we discovered that Hong Kong and the U.S. are different in many ways; for instance, the Chinese in general are more entrepreneurial. Many want to be their own boss and compete with others in every aspect." Given this awareness, the Fung brothers treat each operating unit of Li & Fung as a small enterprise that can compete with other companies in the world outside. Of course, Li & Fung will give the greatest possible support to each of these units.

"This is just like what we Chinese mean by 'endowing a tiger with a pair of wings,'" William continued. "The employees feel that they are their own bosses and will, therefore, do their very best. For our part, we give them all the financial support they need. They are, therefore, convinced that it is better to work for Li & Fung than to set up their own business."

Consequently, Li & Fung sees it fit to allow division managers to have a certain degree of autonomy in management and operation. Division heads are empowered to make their own decisions in all practical aspects regarding clients' production plans, such as the choice of factories or whether to continue with delivery or not. To most of the managers, this independence above all else is the most appealing thing about working at Li & Fung, because it makes them feel as though they are running their own business. From the management perspective, Li & Fung has a flat organizational structure with a high degree of flexibility and competitiveness. As described by Victor Fung, this is a "plug-and-play" structure where a team can be created or collapsed overnight.[6]

Third, Li & Fung considers an incentive scheme as an indispensable and integral part of its system of management, and implements a flexible and effective pay and perks system. While allowing division managers to run their business independently, Li & Fung has also set up a remuneration system that links staff promotion and pay to the company's business performance. All the staff, regardless of their rank and job nature, are rewarded by taking into account their annual performance appraisal and division's results. There is basically no upper limit to the income of managers. According to informa-

---

[6] *Asiainc*, May 2001, pp. 34–35.

Li & Fung's third-generation helmsmen, the Fung brothers William and Victor, in 1994.

Victor Fung (seated, center) as Chairman of the Hong Kong Trade Development Council in 1991.

William Fung, a member of the Hong Kong Basic Law Consultative Committee,
with the members in Beijing, May 1985.

Seated first row, fourth from left:
William Fung, Chairman of the Hong Kong General Chamber of Commerce (1994–1996),
at the Chamber's Christmas Dinner in 1995.

Premier Zhu Rongji (right), accompanied by Victor Fung (left), Chairman of Airport Authority Hong Kong, on a tour of Hong Kong International Airport on November 20, 2002.

tion dated 1994, bonuses constitute 269%, 99%, 31%, and 4–9% of the remunerations of executive directors, product group managers, business division managers, and other staff, respectively (Exhibit 11.5). William Fung made it clear that high pay is a must for retaining senior staff, and Li & Fung practices this belief to the letter in designing its remuneration system. Given its extensive supplier network, administrative support, and performance-based reward system, Li & Fung actually enables its top-notch trading staff to earn more as its employees than as owners of small firms.

Under this system, Li & Fung's staff turnover rate is relatively low. Its records indicate that in 1994, the turnover rate of staff above product group managers (Grade 1) was 0%, that of business division managers (Grade 2) was 9.1%, and those of division managers (Grade 3) and product managers (Grade 4) were 29.7% and 29.9%, respectively. According to Henry Chan, the executive director, the company focuses particularly on retaining Grade 1 and Grade 2 staff, i.e., product group managers and business division managers, because they form the crucial links between Li & Fung and customers, as well as suppliers.

The fourth main feature of the Li & Fung management system is that the top management maintains very rigorous supervision over the system itself

Exhibit 11.5 Composition of Li & Fung (Trading) Limited's staff remuneration in 1994

Staff Grade	Designation	Bonuses as a Percentage of Salary (%)
S	Executive director	269
1	Product group manager	99
2	Business division manager	31
3	Division manager	8
4	Product manager	8
5A	Senior sourcing officer	7
5B	Sourcing officer	7
6A	Assistant sourcing officer	5
6B	Sourcing clerk	4
7	7	5
8	8	9

Note: Salaries and bonuses vary with individual employees. The percentages are the averages for respective grades of trading staff.
Source: Li & Fung Research Center (2003), p. 72.

while delegating sufficient power to the divisions. The Li & Fung system is in fact one that amalgamates strict central control with considerable delegation of power. All the product groups are empowered to run their own business but two areas—financial management and information management—are strictly controlled by the headquarters.

Li & Fung's headquarters is responsible for finance, information technology, and administration so that the hundred or so product groups at the frontline can enjoy the strongest and most effective support they need. To facilitate interdepartmental communication and coordination among various regions across the world, Li & Fung's Policy Committee holds regular meetings for division managers to discuss important courses of action. The Committee also disseminates the latest information on the group's operation. Li & Fung's central database has records of all the manufacturers that have contact with the company. Through its seventy branch offices in forty countries or regions, the company can identify for its clients the best producers of parts and components and the best ways to produce them. It can also offer the best supply chain solution to clients.

In a nutshell, Li & Fung's management system encompasses both the flexibility of the small firm and the strong financial backing and reputation enjoyed only by large-scale business conglomerates.

Expansion to Contiguous Areas by Capitalizing on Core Strengths

Founded in Guangdong in 1906, Li & Fung was the forerunner in exporting Chinese products, including those made of porcelain, silk, jade and ivory, as well as firecrackers and fireworks. After moving to Hong Kong in 1937, its product range expanded to consumer items like electrical and textile products. In the 1970s when Victor and William took over the company's management from their father, Li & Fung was facing much hardship because manufacturers in Asia were beginning to deal directly with customers in the West and trade intermediaries found their commissions drastically reduced. The Fung brothers realized that it was no longer viable to engage exclusively in trading end products.

In those days, Li & Fung's major products were garments and textiles. Their customers did not want to manufacture these products themselves because it was not easy to adapt to the fast-changing Asian market. Seizing this opportunity, Victor and William approached Levi Straus and The Gap, offering to help them identify outlets and manage their business in Asia. After a while Li & Fung turned their attention to other contiguous areas and engaged in the more complicated business of supply chain management—from selecting and sourcing raw materials, to arranging delivery with distributors in the West. In considering Li & Fung's value chain and expansion plan, Victor would stress the importance of focusing on customers. In fact, some of its departments have been set up specifically to serve individual customers. This corporate structure is meant to ensure a high degree of reliability for customers and it can be duplicated to serve more major accounts. In 1995, Li & Fung acquired Dodwell, paving the way for venture into other products and neighboring regions, such as India.

Victor and William also realized that an enterprise endowed with immense core competitive strengths would be in a superior position to develop new products or new markets. To better utilize these strengths, it should diversify and venture into these new areas. Its business should be professional but broad-based and geared toward achieving economies of scale and the highest possible profitability. For these purposes, Li & Fung extended the reach of its supply chain downstream to retailing in the 1980s. It then proceeded to expand to distribution which occupies a midstream position in the supply chain in the late 1990s. From then on, Li & Fung has been enjoying the advantage of an operation that covers the upper, middle, and lower streams of a global supply chain.

Li & Fung's success in expanding into contiguous business areas could be attributed to the following three main factors:

(1) The choice of the most suitable business areas for development;
(2) The development of new areas into ones that entail strong cash flow, thus resulting in significant profitability; and
(3) The well-defined objective to be the industry leader, thus fending off competitors.

The experience of Li & Fung illustrates how a company can successfully diversify and expand to connected business areas. It also demonstrates how, under adverse circumstances, a company can create its own opportunities for sustainable growth and high-speed development in the future.

People—Li & Fung's Most Valuable Asset

In 1996, Victor Fung was named both Businessman of the Year by DHL and *South China Morning Post* of Hong Kong, as well as the World's Top Manager by *BusinessWeek*. Both awards were meant to give recognition to Victor's achievements in managing the Li & Fung Group, turning it from a traditional Chinese trading house into a modern Asian multinational. At an interview, Victor described himself as a businessman straddling East and West with a high regard for traditional Chinese concepts and adept in Western management. For this reason, under his and his bother William's leadership, Li & Fung has become a company with a management model that is full of Asian characteristics, i.e., embracing both "systems" and "humaneness."[7]

As a trading group with little hard assets, Li & Fung's rapid development obviously owes much to the quality and quantity of its human resources. Through a well-designed and competitive human resources management system, Victor and William aim to attract and retain the talents they need. As aforementioned, Li & Fung delegates a certain degree of operational autonomy to the divisional managers so that they can feel as though they are running their own business. There is also a flexible and comprehensive pay and perks system that pegs the staff's remuneration and career prospects to the company's business performance. Unlike many other Chinese family firms, Li & Fung allows those capable—rather than those with close blood relations with the family—to be promoted to senior positions. The composition of Li & Fung Limited's board is such that the executive directors, other than the managing director William Fung, include many who have been with the company for years and have earned their current positions, such as Henry Chan, Danny Lau, Annabella Leung (who was previously with Dodwell), and Frank Leung, the chief financial officer. A sound human resources system ensures that Li & Fung has the best talents in the industry.

Naturally to a family business like Li & Fung, not all Western experiences are applicable. William Fung has pointed out that while the Western business

---

[7] *Next Magazine*, Hong Kong, September 18, 2003, p. 44.

management model has its merits, it cannot be borrowed in its entirety or else it will clash with Hong Kong's homegrown culture. For example, the Western personnel management system is hardly suitable for Hong Kong. William has admitted that in the 1970s, Li & Fung was still very much an old-style Chinese firm with a lot of "dead wood" but unlike in the U.S. where employees are expected to do well at all times or "face the axe," he knew he simply could not follow suit and do the same in Hong Kong. He said, "In the U.S., efficiency overrides everything else. The so-called human factor is never a consideration. When I first returned to Hong Kong in the 1970s, I was full of Western ideas about business management. But my father said to me in so many words: 'If you treat the staff well, they will treat you well in return, and vice versa. If you don't treat them humanely, then don't expect them to have a sense of belonging to the company. Moreover, human beings are not machines. They have emotional ups and downs that can be caused by the human factor in, say, dealing with a new customer and that can affect their productivity.' I don't subscribe to the so-called "business is business" approach in the U.S.-style personnel management. We incorporate Chinese thinking in our management system where appropriate. We treasure talents. Even though some of our employees have reached retirement age, we still retain them if they are valuable to us. The export business is badly in need of professional talents. Having said that, we believe that when it comes to areas like training, marketing, finance, and so forth, the American management model is the best choice. No doubt about that."

By merging Western management skills with traditional Chinese values, Li & Fung has become more efficient while retaining the characteristics of a Chinese firm, particularly where the human dimension is concerned. On this point, both Victor and William have stressed that they owe it to their father. Victor has admitted that he does not run Li & Fung by relying on what he has learned about business economics, but on what he has learned from his father instead.

Li & Fung also attaches a high degree of importance to training as a crucial tool for enhancing the quality of managers on a constant basis. The Fung brothers believe that to sustain growth, a company's managers must be inculcated with the idea of lifelong learning and self-improvement so that they can adapt to the fast-changing market environment. Li & Fung, therefore, has a standing policy of training for both the management and staff.

Regular training courses and seminars are organized on the latest business management theories and practical experiences. The headquarters of Li & Fung Trading in Cheung Sha Wan has a lecture hall and training rooms. The lecture hall is designed modeled on the Harvard lecture room with advanced audio-visual equipment and is fit for holding multimedia conferences and training. The training rooms are used for general staff training purposes.

Li & Fung regularly organizes various types of training classes and seminars in accordance with the needs of the economic environment. For example, in March 1999, Li & Fung Retailing Group organized an annual seminar on the subject of how to make use of adversity quotient (AQ) to attain the goals for the next two years. At the seminar, Group Chairman Victor Fung personally delivered a speech and a management consultant was invited as a keynote speaker.

Since the mid-1990s, Li & Fung's management model that merges both the East and West and its practical results have won international acclaim. In *Asiamoney*'s 100 Best-Managed Companies in the Asia Pacific, Li & Fung was ranked seventh among the thirty-two Hong Kong companies selected (Hutchison Whampoa and HSBC were first and second, respectively). The list was selected by 178 international fund managers after taking into consideration eight main factors such as corporate strategy, management capability, investor relations, and accountability to minority shareholders. On investor relations, Li & Fung was ranked third along with both HSBC and PCCW. On corporate strategy, it was ranked third along with Sun Hung Kai Properties. On overall strategy and overall investor relations, it was ranked seventh and tenth, respectively. In 2000, Li & Fung was ranked second in the Hong Kong category of *Asiamoney*'s 100 Best-Managed Companies list, outperforming Hutchison Whampoa and HSBC in several aspects.

Chapter 12

Taking up the Challenges of the New Century

"Li & Fung's experience demonstrates how entrepreneurship can successfully drive economic prosperity. I am really very proud of it. Economic globalization and China's accession to WTO are expected to give rise to both new challenges and opportunities. Given Hong Kong's solid strengths in traditional trading and the gradual opening of China's import market to the outside world, Hong Kong is set to benefit, particularly from facilitating the integrated development of the mainland's economy and adding value to China's export business led by the Pearl River Delta."

—Victor Fung

Becoming a Top Ten Public Conglomerate

In 1992 when Li & Fung Limited was relisted on Hong Kong's stock exchange, its annual turnover was HK$3.98 billion. After acquiring companies like Inchcape Buying Services (Dodwell), Swire & Maclaine, Camberley, and Colby since the mid-1990s, its turnover surged at a breakneck speed, reaching HK$47.17 billion in 2004—up more than 10 folds. Led by this upsurge in business turnover, Li & Fung Trading's net profit also soared from HK$133 million to HK$1,529 million in this twelve-year period, representing a 10.5-fold growth (Exhibit 12.1). Consequently, Li & Fung has not only emerged as the largest sourcing group, but also a leading public-listed business conglomerate in Hong Kong.

At first, Li & Fung Limited's relisting did not attract much attention in the Hong Kong stock market. By the end of 1992, its share price was HK$2.25 and market cap was merely HK$1,125 million. However, its market cap kept rising steadily in the ensuing years. By 1998, Li & Fung Limited's share price climbed to HK$16.05, making it the sixth best-performing stock in Hong Kong. By the end of 1998, Li & Fung Limited's market cap had risen above the HK$10-billion mark, reaching HK$10.182 billion, or up by

Exhibit 12.1　Li & Fung Limited's business performance (HK$ million), 1992–2004

Year	Revenue (Growth rate)	After-tax Profit (Growth rate)
1992	3,980 (+39%)	133 (+53%)
1993	5,382 (+35%)	196 (+47%)
1994	6,125 (+14%)	553 (+182%)
1995	9,213 (+50%)	225 (−59%)
1996	12,514 (+36%)	300 (+33%)
1997	13,346 (+7%)	375 (+25%)
1998	14,313 (+7%)	455 (+21%)
1999	16,298 (+14%)	575 (+26%)
2000	24,992 (+53%)	893 (+55%)
2001	32,941 (+32%)	951 (+6%)
2002	37,281 (+13%)	1,080 (+14%)
2003	42,631 (+14%)	1,211 (+12%)
2004	47,171 (+11%)	1,529 (+26%)

Source: Li & Fung Limited Annual Reports.

50%. By virtue of this glaring growth, the Fung brothers' business group became the seventeenth on the list of top twenty public-listed conglomerates in Hong Kong. In 1999, Li & Fung Limited's share price and market cap rose further to HK$19.50 and HK$25.23 billion, respectively, lifting it to the sixteenth position. Throughout 2000, Li & Fung Limited's share continued to perform strongly, rising to the top position among the best-performing blue-chip stocks. The Fung brothers' business empire frog-leaped to the twelfth position among the largest public conglomerates in Hong Kong. In the same year, Li & Fung Limited was made a constituent stock of MSCI Index Series, Hang Seng Index, and FTSE Global Index, respectively.

Under the impact of the U.S. economic recession after September 11, 2001, Li & Fung Limited's market cap slipped to HK$25.187 billion. However, the Fung brothers still maintained their twelfth position because of the listing of Convenience Retail Asia (CRA). In 2002, Li & Fung Limited's share price continued to fall but still outperformed the market, lifting the Fung brothers up one position. The next year, Li & Fung Limited's share price experienced a phenomenal growth of 81% and the company's market cap soared to HK$38.606 billion. That, coupled with CRA's HK$1.505 billion, meant that the Li & Fung Group's total market cap had already passed the HK$40.1-billion mark. In the same year, the Fung brothers' business empire became the ninth largest public-listed conglomerate in Hong Kong (Exhibit 12.2).

Concurrently, Li & Fung Trading also emerged as a major player in the international arena. In the Asian weekly *Yazhou Zhoukan's* 1997 annual ranking of the world's top 500 Chinese enterprises, Li & Fung occupied only the 221st position. But it moved up steadily thereafter to the sixteenth in 2000. Owing to the ramifications of the September 11 incidents on the world economy, it slipped to twenty-ninth in 2004, but moved up to twenty-sixth in 2005. The company's total market cap and pretax profit exceeded US$6 billion and US$200 million, respectively (Exhibit 12.3). Into the 21st century, Li & Fung Trading has become a world-renowned Chinese multinational enterprise.

Exhibit 12.2 Ranking of Li & Fung Limited and the Fung family, and its major shareholders, in the Hong Kong stock market

Year	Closing Share Price at Year-end (HK$)	Total Market Cap at Year-end (HK$ million)	Family's Dividend Income (HK$ million)[1]	Ranking as a Public Company
1992	2.25	1,125	—	—
1993	6.10	3,050 (+171%)	—	—
1994	5.05	2,778 (−9%)	—	—
1995	6.90	3,858 (+39%)	—	—
1996	6.85	4,255 (+10%)	—	—
1997	10.85	6,779 (+59%)	—	—
1998	16.05	10,063 (+48%)	147 (10th)	17th
1999	19.05 (9.75 after subdivision)	25,229 (+151%)	182 (9th)	16th
2000	14.20	40,620 (+61%)	218 (8th)	12th
2001	8.75	25,187 (−38%)	295 (7th)	12th
2002	7.40	21,386 (−15%)	313 (8th)	11th
2003	13.30	38,606 (+81%)[2]	359 (8th)	9th
2004	13.10	38,205 (−1%)[3]	425 (7th)[4]	13th

Notes:

1. Number in bracket is the ranking among Hong Kong families.
2. Taking into account CRA's market cap of HK$1,505 million, Li & Fung Group's market cap was HK$40,111 million.
3. Taking into account CRA's market cap of HK$1,913 million and IDS's market cap of HK$1,560 million, Li & Fung Group's total market cap was HK$41,478 million.
4. Including HK$42 million from CRA.

Source: Hong Kong Economic Journal.

Exhibit 12.3 Li & Fung Limited's ranking among the world's top 500 Chinese firms

Year	Rank	Market Cap (US$ million)	P/E Ratio	Turnover (US$ million)	Pretax Profit (US$ million)	Net Profit (US$ million)	Total Assets (US$ million)
1997	221	701	17.3	1,618	41	–	374
1998	81	1,018	20.8	1,722	53	–	411
1999	85	1,536	25.8	1,848	61	–	448
2000	16	6,818	87.2	2,097	79	–	542
2001	19	4,711	69.8	3,204	119	–	936
2002	24	3,889	38.5	4,234	99	100	901
2003	25	3,724	26.9	4,780	151	139	496
2004	29	4,255	27.0	5,465	169	157	1,185
2005	26	6,060	30.5	6,048	213	196	1,458

Source: *Yazhou Zhoukan*, various issues.

The Challenges—Li & Fung's Base in Hong Kong, the China Market, and International Network

With the arrival of the 21st century, Li & Fung faces three major challenges as a Chinese multinational firm that is based in Hong Kong; the first of which concerns whether Hong Kong will continue to prosper and play a strategic role in the Asia Pacific economy, particularly the Chinese economy.

During the transitional period of Hong Kong's reunification with China, many traditional British firms—notably the Jardine Matheson group—were actively becoming internationalized by re-domiciling in other parts of the world, restructuring, increasing their overseas investment, or even changing their place of primary share listing. All these were intended to minimize the risk of investing in Hong Kong after 1997. Some Chinese enterprises also followed suit by investing overseas in places like Canada, the U.S., Australia, Europe, and Southeast Asia. These strategic moves were prompted more or less by the worry over Hong Kong's economic future after 1997.

For Li & Fung, Hong Kong has been for a long time the place of growth and base. It has always taken a bullish view on Hong Kong's economic prospects. Even during the transitional period, it did not stop planning ahead for its development in Hong Kong. In a seminar held in Beijing in March 1997, Victor Fung said openly, "As a Special Administrative Region under the 'one country, two systems' principle, Hong Kong will continue to benefit from what has made it tick in the past, including most notably the rule of law, a clean and capable civil service, fair competition in the market, freedom of information, an economic system that adheres to the principles under the Basic Law, the Hong Kong government's economic policy of positive non-interventionism, low tax rates, and a truly free market with minimal restrictions."[1]

"A look at history will tell us," he pointed out at the same occasion, "that all economic powers will have at least one city that can potentially become internationalized. These cities will usually be found where trading routes converge and where people from different cultures and backgrounds come

---

[1] Speech by Victor Fung at a seminar in Beijing, March 28, 1997.

together. They will prosper by conducting trade in accordance with international standards and practices."

At an interview given to *Yazhou Zhoukan* in July 1997, Victor further remarked that the most important cornerstone that had to be jealously guarded by Hong Kong was the rule of law. To him, everything depends on the rule of law, be it the protection of individual freedom, the handling of business disputes or the maintenance of social order. In the external sphere, the key thing is of course to ensure that international trade is free from obstacles.

"The worst that could happen is that the lifeblood of international trade and market access is severed from Hong Kong," he said. "Should this happen, we must reassess the chance of Hong Kong's continual success. The mere thought that this could happen gives me nightmares that keep me awake all night. Trade prospects affect our economic well-being, which is in turn the foundation of confidence. The maintenance of the rule of law and free international trade is a must for Hong Kong's future."[2]

To Li & Fung's management, Hong Kong will continue to play three major roles in the 21st century—a regional supply chain management hub, a logistics hub, and an offshore financing center. Victor believes that after adding pre-production and post-production values to manufacturing in the Chinese mainland in the past twenty years, it is imperative for Hong Kong to meet the needs of buyers across the world in the 21st century with speed, innovation, dexterity, and customization while remaining a global supply chain manager. He thinks that Hong Kong should make the best use of its advantages to reinforce its position as a supply chain management center and logistics hub in Asia.

As a regional supply chain management hub, Hong Kong will maintain its status as a regional logistics hub and particularly as a logistics center for air cargo. Victor said at an interview, "To solidify Hong Kong's position as a business and trade center, we must strive to become an air-logistics hub. Should we lose out to others on this front, there are no way we can remain a business and trade center."[3] As he also pointed out, Hong Kong is situated at

---

[2] *Yazhou Zhoukan*, July 13, 1997, p. 46.
[3] *Ming Pao*, Hong Kong, September 4, 2001, p. A5.

a privileged geographical position that enables it to reach half of the world's population within five hours by air. This is highly cost-effective for airfreight forwarders and shippers. Hong Kong must, therefore, make haste to develop high value-added logistics to become a regional fulfillment center by taking advantage of the competitive strengths of Hong Kong International Airport and the hinterland that exists in the Pearl River Delta.

To Li & Fung, Hong Kong also serves the important function as an offshore financing center for the region. First, it acts as a venture capital center by being a matchmaker between overseas venture capital entities and emerging Mainland companies. Hong Kong is the regional headquarters for venture capital investors in the China market and also the capital management center for all sorts of investment funds and conglomerates. Equipped with thorough knowledge of the operations of both the mainland and international firms, Hong Kong's venture capital investors can aptly offer superior services to mainland clients on financing, design, marketing and backroom support, and introduce them to overseas financing sources, technology, management, and potential business partners. Second, Hong Kong is an ideal place for raising funds through public listing. Victor believes that because investors based in Hong Kong have a deeper understanding of mainland enterprises than their overseas counterparts, the shares of mainland companies, especially hi-tech companies, listed in Hong Kong are likely to enjoy higher circulation. This will be a plus for them should the need to raise more funds at a later stage arise.

Unfortunately, after the reunification with China in 1997, Hong Kong entered a long period of economic slump as a result of the Asian financial turmoil. Unemployment was high. Deflation persisted. Everyone in Hong Kong was adversely affected in one way or another. The wealth of businessmen diminished, and a substantial percentage of the middle class had their property downgraded to "negative equity." Some residents were living below the poverty line. The economic hardships that persisted lead to more grievances in society. Questions were raised as to whether the free economic system that Hong Kong had adhered to for decades was still working, and whether the people could benefit from the fruit of Hong Kong's past economic success. This uncertainty resulted in an antagonistic attitude toward capitalists on the one hand and the wish that the government could become more "interventionist" in the economy on the other. Labor disputes were running rampant.

Dissatisfaction with the government was fueled by a series of administrative blunders. There were frequent demonstrations initiated by politicians who were hungry for votes.

From the business perspective, Hong Kong's operating environment was showing signs of deterioration. Eden Woon, CEO of Hong Kong General Chamber of Commerce, said publicly that Hong Kong seemed to be on the verge of becoming a welfare economy. "There seems to be a voice in our society clamoring that as a businessman, you have to share every dollar you make with the rest," he said at an interview, "But it does not work that way in a capitalist society. If you make money, you should reinvest somewhere so that more people can benefit."[4] In 1998, Li Ka-shing said openly that because political harmony was absent in Hong Kong, he would put on hold his billion-dollar investment plans. Hong Kong's economic ailment and social conflicts came to a head-on during the Severe Acute Respiratory Syndrome (SARS) outbreak in 2003.

Another challenge faced by Hong Kong at that juncture was its weakening position in the Chinese mainland, especially in the Pearl River Delta. After China's accession to WTO and the gradual opening of the mainland's market, Hong Kong's role as a bridge between China and the rest of the world diminished. Most strikingly, with the rise of the Yangzi River Delta and the emergence of Shanghai as the center of the Chinese economy, and the growing economic strength of Guangdong, particularly Guangzhou, grave doubts were cast on the positioning of Hong Kong as the leading city in Southern China. These doubts were not unfounded. For example, because of the high cost of transportation in Hong Kong, freight traffic in the Pearl River Delta was gravitating northward to Yantian Port in Shenzhen instead. Besides, the fast development of Nansha Port in Guangzhou was also formidable. For a company like Li & Fung which is based in Hong Kong, its long-term development necessarily depend on Hong Kong's economic stability and importance to the Chinese mainland.

The second major challenge to Li & Fung is how to develop the Chinese mainland's market with unlimited potential. Apart from historical reasons,

---

[4] *Capital*, Hong Kong, February 1999, p. 15.

the Li & Fung Group is headquartered in Hong Kong because of the latter's position in China and the immensely rich potential of the China market. In 1993, a major report produced by the Business and Professionals Federation of Hong Kong called *Hong Kong 21—A Ten-year Vision and Agenda for Hong Kong's Economy* pointed out that the reunification with China would be Hong Kong's greatest challenge and also an excellent opportunity for it to prosper further. Once it enter the vast consumer market and invest in the manufacturing sector of the Chinese mainland, the influence of the Hong Kong's economy would be felt more extensively, and it was likely that southern China would rise as the "Fifth Little Dragon" after Hong Kong, Taiwan, Korea, and Singapore. The report pointed out that the fast-growing wealth of the region would be conducive to the development of China as a whole, and the integration of resources between Hong Kong and southern China would certainly give rise to an economic powerhouse.[5]

In March 1997, just months before Hong Kong's reunification with China, Victor delivered a speech in his capacity as the chairman of Hong Kong Trade Development Council at a seminar in Beijing. He said, "The mainland and Hong Kong are excellent economic partners. The mainland is endowed with an enormous pool of human resources, knowledge, and natural resources. It is facing the future with tremendous confidence, determination, and economic strengths. Hong Kong, on the other hand, is rich in business sense and in technological and management knowledge. It is also a regional business center. The integration of these respective advantages will create an unprecedented economic force in the world."[6]

On October 24, 2000, Victor made a speech at the Chinese Central Party School in Beijing entitled "Globalization and the New Trend of Economic Cooperation between Hong Kong and the Mainland." In this speech, he pointed out even more explicitly that "for Hong Kong, the biggest business opportunity to arise from China's becoming a full WTO member is the opening of a consumer market with the greatest potential. Foreign-invested enterprises in China, including those from Hong Kong, would soon be able to enter

---

[5] Business and Professionals Federation of Hong Kong (1993), pp. 5–6.
[6] Speech by Victor Fung at a seminar in Beijing on March 28, 1997.

the Chinese domestic market and establish distribution networks in various locations for selling products made by Hong Kong companies in China. To manufacture and sell products in China will be the next critical development for Hong Kong's manufacturing sector...With the opening of China's domestic market, the prospects of Hong Kong enterprises will be spectacular, given their advantages in both marketing and manufacturing."[7]

In fact, Li & Fung has always attached a great deal of importance to its development in China. In the early days, it was mainly engaged in exporting products made in China. Today, China remains its most important sourcing base. Li & Fung's buying offices in China are located in all major cities along the Chinese coast: Dalian, Beijing, Qingdao, Shanghai, Nanjing, Liuyang, Guangzhou, Shenzhen, Dongguan, Weizhou, Shantou, Zhongshan, and Zhanjiang. The exports handled through these buying offices generate some US$500 million worth of foreign earnings for China. In April 2004, IDS, under the Li & Fung Group, became one of the first distribution companies allowed to set up a wholly-owned subsidiary under the Closer Economic Partnership Agreement (CEPA). This subsidiary enables IDS to conduct distribution and import/export of consumer products on a nationwide basis. In its IPO prospectus, IDS proudly declared that it was well-prepared to capture the opportunities arising from the Chinese mainland's economic growth.[8]

However, Li & Fung's development in China has not been without a hitch. The company started increasing its investment in China in the early 1990s. In 1993, it invested in a logistics project in Panyu and the Food Town project in Heshan, respectively. The former was forced to be suspended due to the Central Government's restrictions imposed on foreign investors and the HK$1,000 million that was invested could by no means be recovered. The latter did not meet with success because of the impact of China's macroeconomic adjustments and the Asian financial turmoil. These two unsuccessful attempts in a way reflected Li & Fung's lack of deep understanding of the

---

[7] Speech by Victor Fung at Chinese Central Party School in Beijing on October 24, 2000.
[8] *IDS Group Limited Global IPO Prospectus*, November 24, 2004.

Chinese mainland's macroeconomic cycles and hence inadequate assessment of the investment risks that could exist in China.

At the start of the 21st century, Li & Fung resumed its investment in China through CRA, the operator of Circle K convenience stores in Hong Kong. However, for various reasons, the progress made by Circle K was slow after setting foot initially in Guangzhou. When it went public in 2001, CRA stated in its IPO prospectus that Circle K would open its first store in Guangzhou in the third-quarter of 2001, with a view to having a network of hundred stores in that provincial capital and other parts of the Pearl River Delta by the end of 2003. Li & Fung Retailing also came up with a new operating model—"the new generation of convenience stores"—for the Circle K stores in Guangzhou. Yet, by the end of 2004, the total number of Circle K stores was only twenty, whereas its major competitor, 7-Eleven, already had nearly 200.

Starting from 2005, CRA's wholly-owned subsidiary in China, Convenience Retail Southern China Limited, had begun a two-pronged approach of development in Southern China. While continuing to open "5-star convenience stores" in the prosperous commercial districts and high-end residential districts in Guangzhou, it will also open small-scale Chinese-style stores. By the end of 2005, the number of Circle K stores in Guangzhou had already increased to thirty-five. Concurrently, with its base in Guangzhou, Circle K has also been extending its reach to the western and eastern parts of Guangdong Province. Through a joint venture with Coca-Cola in Macau, Circle K's franchised stores have been opened in Macau and Zhuhai. In Eastern Guangdong, while continuing to open wholly-owned stores, it has also, through a 40%-owned joint venture with a chain store group in Dongguan, opened mostly (60%) franchised stores that cater to the wider public. Through this two-pronged approach, CRA aims to expand its Circle K network in Southern China to 800 stores in three years. Of course, it remains to be seen whether this target can be achieved. The opening of China's domestic market takes time; as well as getting to know the China market also takes time.

The third challenge is how to forestall "system failure" in its global expansion. A key advantage that Li & Fung possesses for its future development is its global network established in the last two decades. As a trans-regional and trans-industry supply chain manager, Li & Fung has been providing a vertical range of one-stop value-added services to customers, covering areas such as product design and development, sourcing of raw materials, selection of manufacturers, arrangement and management of production, quality control, as well as export documentation and shipment. This peculiar business nature has enabled Li & Fung to grow its scale of operation and enlarge its global network. Li & Fung Limited, for instance, has already established some seventy offices in forty countries and regions to coordinate the whole production process of products. At the same time, its sales network has extended beyond the U.S., its traditional major market, to other countries and regions, including Europe, Canada, Australia, Central America, and Latin America. IDS, another public company under the Li & Fung Group, operates in nine different economies across Asia with over forty distribution centers and warehouse systems that provide services to more than 220 multinational companies all over the world.

As pointed out by Nobel Prize laureate Ronald Coase in his classic article, "The Nature of the Firm" (1937) that introduces the concept of transaction costs into economic theory, the market and the firm are two interchangeable systems for the allocation of resources. While the allocation of resources in the market is determined by price, the allocation of resources by a firm is decided by its man-in-charge, i.e., the entrepreneur. An obvious characteristic of the firm is its ability to replace the pricing mechanism. By arranging to produce what it needs internally, a firm can save transaction costs, including those involved in seeking contractors, bargaining, enforcing a deal, overseeing, and penalizing any breach of contract.

The firm's wish to save transaction costs, as well as factors such as imperfect competition and uneven information, can lead to "market failure," which usually forces the firm to become bigger, especially through vertical integration. Under this circumstance, activities formerly regulated by the market are carried out internally within the firm through the setting up of various departments or units, the undertaking of various economic functions, and the establishment of a sizeable hierarchy. However, the allocation of resources by a firm also entails management costs, including those needed for running the organization and coordinating production.[9]

---

[9] *Academic Research*, Issue 2, 2003, pp. 37–38.

Through continuous expansion and the globalization of its corporate network, Li & Fung has drastically reduced transaction costs but also raised management costs. How to strike a balance between the two, particularly how to prevent "organization failure" that could result from expansion, will be another challenge it must face.

Corporate Governance and its Future Development

"Family business" has been defined as one that is owned or managed directly by two family members or more, or one whose leadership is hereditary within the family. Under this definition, an overwhelming majority of the world's companies (90% in the U.S., and 85% in the E.U.) are family businesses.

In the case of Hong Kong, the proportion of family firms is also extremely high—at least 90% according to some estimates. Many of these firms have a long history. The oldest British firm, Jardine Matheson, is over 170 years old. Founded in 1906, Li & Fung is now aged hundred. Despite the success still enjoyed by many existing family firms, it is commonly believed locally and overseas that the wealth of a family can rarely be sustained beyond the third generation, so much so that some people would go so far to say that the first, second, and third generations are responsible for the founding, preservation, and downfall of a family business, in that order. According to a U.S. study, approximately 70% of the family businesses have failed to be passed down to the second generation, and 88% the third generation. Only 3% of such firms would still be in existence in and beyond the fourth generation. Another study conducted in the U.S. has given more or less similar findings. Of all the family firms, only 15% could continue to the third generation or beyond.

On the contrary, the story of Li & Fung has debunked the myth that a family's wealth could never last beyond the third generation. Following the success of their grandfather Fung Pak-liu and their father Fung Hon-chu, Victor and William have been spearheading the family's business to ever higher levels of success and breaking new grounds. The Fung brothers' achievements can be attributed to several factors, a key one of which is effective corporate governance.

Corporate governance can be broadly understood as the interrelationship among the company's stakeholders, including shareholders, the board of directors, the management, and other relevant parties such as creditors, employees, customers, regulators, auditors, and the general public. Good corporate governance depends largely on the separation of ownership and management. Under a good governance structure, the responsibilities of different units in a company are clearly delineated. Hong Kong's level of corporate governance has always been considered below par by overseas investors. According to a survey conducted in 1998 by Professor Ho Shun-man of the Accountancy Department of the Chinese University of Hong Kong, among over 600 finance directors and over 500 financial analysts in Hong Kong, the positions of board chairman and CEO of only 40% of listed companies were held by different individuals; the majority of 34% of the boards was controlled by family members who were not shareholders; 28% of the companies was implementing a remuneration system that was pegged to business performance; 24% of the companies did not have an audit committee; and only 15% of the companies had a directors' remuneration committee. Furthermore, most of the companies adopted a conservative, passive, and unilateral policy with regard to disclosure.[10]

In terms of corporate governance, Li & Fung can be considered exemplary among listed companies in Hong Kong, particularly the family-controlled ones. This has been achieved in a number of ways. First, through privatization, Li & Fung has achieved a more effective shareholding arrangement by bringing together shares that used to be dispersed among various family members. There are basically two types of shareholding arrangements among family firms: the dispersed type and the centralized type. The development of a family firm usually results in dispersed shareholding. After one or two generations, a family firm's shares would generally end up in the coffers of a considerable number of family members. Such a family firm can choose either to engage outside professionals to take charge of management or to leave it for the family members to do it themselves. Most Chinese family firms would opt for the latter. The main drawback of this option is that it may damage the firm or reduce its operational efficiency because of inadequate supervision or the members' focus only on self-interest. It may also

---

[10] *Hong Kong Economic Journal*, January 22, 1999.

end up undermining the family's control should some of the members decide to sell their shares.

The centralized arrangement is the only safe way of maintaining the family's control of the firm. It has two problems, though. The first problem is that in reality only very few members of the family are in control of the firm. Secondly, the controlling members must have considerable financial resources to initiate a buyout or compensate other family shareholders for surrendering their interests.

However, this arrangement also carries substantial benefits. First, because shareholders' interests are linked up with the management's, the decision-making process will be fast and is thus conducive to administrative efficiency. Second, because the family members in control have to fight for their shareholding and management rights, the entrepreneurial spirit within the firm is likely to be maintained. Last, because only very few family members have a say in the firm, it is relatively easy to bring in outside professional managers.

In 1989, the Fung brothers initiated a privatization project to centralize Li & Fung's shares that were dispersed among the family members. By doing so, they succeeded in maintaining Li & Fung's vitality, efficiency, and entrepreneurship. That also became a turning point for Li & Fung to grow rapidly from an ordinary family business into a multinational conglomerate.

Secondly, Li & Fung's corporate governance framework includes an effective oversight mechanism made possible by its board composition. Good corporate governance demands that the board performs an effective major role in overseeing the firm. At a speech given to the Hong Kong Institute of Directors in June 2001, Victor Fung said, "Of course we can't talk about corporate governance without looking at how the board is supposed to function as the governing body of the corporation…As you all know, the board is primarily responsible for doing two things: (1) to oversee the long-term development strategy and business plan of the company (but not to run the company on a day-to-day basis); and (2) to take care of the selection, evaluation and remuneration of the top management. These, it would seem, are just elementary as far as the board's functions are concerned. Yet, how the board can perform these functions effectively and satisfactorily is a far more complex issue."

Studies have shown that when a family's control over a firm remains unchallenged and not subject to effective oversight, the family members concerned would usually lack the incentive to strive for the biggest benefit for the firm, and would indulged in seeking self-interests. In a survey on the connection between business results and family influence on the board among Hong Kong's top 200 companies before 1997, it was found that companies controlled by families in general performed worse than those that were not. Statistics collected by the survey show that with the exception of a few that had a board that functioned effectively, most family-controlled companies in Hong Kong and Southeast Asia did not perform as satisfactorily as their counterparts.[11]

For obvious reasons, the board's oversight is of great importance to a company's performance. Whether the board can play its role effectively depends to a large extent on its composition and operation. Studies have revealed that among Chinese family enterprises, those that lack effective oversight by the board have the following common characteristics. One, the roles of the board chairman and CEO are mixed up, and power is highly concentrated in a single family member who doubles as both the board chairman and CEO. Two, members of the controlling family usually occupy a significant number of seats on the board. According to Professor Ho Shun-man's study, among family-controlled companies, nearly 40% would have more family members on the board and such companies would appoint considerable number of family members as executive directors, thus ensuring genuine "family control." The third common characteristic is that the independent directors tend to have a low degree of independence. Some so-called independent directors are in fact relatives and friends of the founding family. Should a conflict of interests arise between the family shareholders and the company or small shareholders, the so-called independent directors would seldom try to balance the two sides' interests or protect the interests of minority shareholders.

The restructured and relisted Li & Fung Limited makes it a top priority to ensure that the board's oversight is effective. The separate positions of board chairman and CEO are taken up by Victor and William, respectively. Victor

---

[11] *Hong Kong Economic Journal Monthly*, August 2000, p. 61.

has said explicitly, "I am of the view that the roles of board chairman and CEO should be separated. If they are one and the same person, other directors would shy away from criticizing the management or raising any objection at board meetings to avoid embarrassment." On the other hand, members of the Fung family make up a very small proportion of Li & Fung's board membership. In 2004, among the thirteen board members, only Victor and William were from the family, constituting only 15%, whereas there were four independent directors, all of whom were highly credible and well-respected business leaders in their own rights. Its composition and operation ensure that Li & Fung's board can perform its oversight role effectively, which is also one main reason why the company can boast good corporate governance.

Thirdly, Li & Fung is an efficient organization by virtue of its separation of ownership and operation. In advanced economies like the U.S., Europe, and Japan, the ownership and operation of companies are generally separated. U.S. companies are run by professional managers while in Japan, the managing director or management committee has the final say. There is also an emerging trend in these countries where senior professional managers are becoming the owners. The situation is quite different in Hong Kong. Ownership and operation are still closely intertwined. The board chairman still holds sway over important matters and participates directly in operation and management. Or, the board will be composed of executive directors, who will lead or manage the company directly, and the managers will remain just employees taking orders from above. In other words, genuine professional management is sill uncommon among companies in Hong Kong.

For Li & Fung, although there are executive directors on its board, in reality it has already separated ownership from operation through the separation of roles between the board chairman and CEO and, more significantly, through the implementation of an operation system that encourages entrepreneurship and a flexible and efficient remuneration system. With such an operating system that empowers the divisional managers to run their respective divisions, Li & Fung Trading has in fact fostered a professional management team that is richly experienced in the industry. Outstanding representatives of this team include non-executive director Lau Butt-farn and executive directors Henry Chan, Danny Lau, and Annabella Leung.

Under its third-generation helmsmen, Victor and William, Li & Fung has established an effective and superior corporate governance framework, which not only shatters the myth that a family business never survives beyond the third generation but also earns it a place among the top listed companies in Hong Kong. One of the main challenges that the Fung brothers must face is how to perpetuate this system of good corporate governance. Although they have not yet reached retirement age, Li & Fung, just like all family businesses, will invariably have to face the issue of succession, which is a key determining factor for the company's future. The fourth generation of the Fung family are joining the firm one-by-one and undergoing the painstaking process of on-the-job training. The question has been raised as to whether Victor will follow the Harvard style of management by entrusting the Li & Fung business empire to capable professional hands, or simply pass it on to his and William's offsprings. One way or the other, it is probably the biggest challenge to the two brothers. At the global level, it may also be the biggest challenge to Chinese family businesses all over the world.

Appendix A

Chronology of Events

Date	Event
June 1840	First Opium War initiated by Britain.
January 26, 1941	Occupation of Hong Kong Island by the British navy led by Captain Charles Elliot.
1841	Founding of Gilman & Co. in Canton (Guangzhou).
June 7, 1841	Captain Elliot declares Hong Kong as a free port on behalf of the colonial authorities.
1856	Anglo-French Allies attack Guangzhou and furious citizens burned down the offices of the Thirteen Hongs.
September 1862	Shamian taken as concession by Britain and France after the signing of the Shamian Concession Agreement with Governor Lu Songguang.
1877	Founding of Hutchison & Co. in Hong Kong.
1880	Birth of Fung Pak-liu in Heshan, Guangdong.
1891	Founding of Dodwell & Co. in Shanghai.
1895	Fung Pak-liu enters Queen's College, Hong Kong.
June 9, 1898	The Qing government is forced to lease New Territories in Hong Kong to Britain.
1902	Fung Pak-liu graduates from Queen's College.
November 28, 1906	Founding of Li & Fung in Guangzhou by Fung Pak-liu and Li To-ming.
October 1911	Kowloon-Canton Railway commences operation.
1911	Birth of Fung Hon-chu in Guangzhou.
1915	Fung Pak-liu joined the Panama-Pacific International Exposition in the U.S. as a delegate from the Chinese government.
1916	Fung Pak-liu gets acquainted with Joseph N. Sipser of Ignaz Strauss & Co. on the trip from the U.S. back to Hong Kong.
1917	Fung Pak-liu opens a Li & Fung office in Hong Kong.

Date	Event
1927	Fung Mo-ying joins Li & Fung upon graduating from Diocesan Boys' School, Hong Kong.
1930	Fung Lai-wah joins Li & Fung upon graduating from Sacred Heart Canossian College, Hong Kong.
1931	Fung Yau-yen establishes Luen Fung & Co.
	Fung Hon-chu graduates from Queen's College, Hong Kong, and joins Li & Fung.
September 18, 1931	Japan invades Northwestern China.
1935	Fung Hon-chu establishes Li & Fung Co. in Hong Kong.
July 7, 1937	Japan launches a full-scale invasion of China on the pretext of the Lugou Bridge Incident.
1937	Li & Fung (1937) Ltd. was set up in Hong Kong.
October 1938	The fall of Guangzhou.
1939	Li & Fung opens Victoria Torch Manufacturing Co. Ltd. in Hong Kong.
December 8, 1941	Japan attacks Pearl Harbor and takes possession of the Shanghai Concessions in China.
	The Pacific War breaks out.
December 25, 1941	Hong Kong falls to the Japanese army.
April 15, 1943	Fung Pak-liu passed away in Guangzhou.
August 15, 1945	Japan surrenders unconditionally.
August 16, 1945	Fung Hon-chu returns to Hong Kong to resume business.
August 30, 1945	British Royal Navy led by Rear Admiral Cecil Harcourt enters Victoria Harbor.
1945	Birth of Victor Fung in Hong Kong.
May 1946	Sir. Mark Young returns to Hong Kong, resumes his governorship, and sets up a civil government.
1946	Li & Fung imports ballpoint pens.
	Fung Mo-ying and Fung Hon-chu become executive directors of Li & Fung.
	Founding of Swire & Maclaine Ltd.
October 1, 1946	Li To-ming sells his 300 Li & Fung shares to the Fung family.
1949	Closure of Li & Fung's office in Guangzhou.
	Birth of William Fung in Hong Kong.
1950	Outbreak of the Korean War.
	The United Nations led by the U.S. imposes trade embargo against China.
1955	Li & Fung redevelops its property at 18–20 Connaught Road Central into the 12-story Fung House.
1959	Hong Kong's domestic exports surpass its reexports in value terms, signifying the start of industrialization.
1960	Fung Hon-chu is appointed as a member of the Urban Council.
1964	Fung Hon-chu is appointed as a Legislative Councillor.
1965	Hong Kong's most serious bank-run since the War.
	Fung Hon-chu is made an O.B.E.
	The most serious riot after the War breaks out in Hong Kong.

Date	Event
1968	Li & Fung sets up President Firecrackers & Fireworks Co. Ltd. in Taiwan.
1969	Li & Fung (Taiwan) Co. Ltd. is established.
December 17, 1969	Far East Stock Exchange is founded by Li Fook-shiu and other financial leaders.
1970	Victor Fung graduates with a Ph.D. in Business Economics from Harvard University.
	Inchcape acquires Dodwell.
	Inchcape Marketing Services Group is established.
1972	William Fung returns to Hong Kong upon graduating from Harvard University.
	Li & Fung (Singapore) Ltd. and Li & Fung (Macau) Ltd. are established.
March 1973	Li & Fung Limited is established after Li & Fung's restructuring.
1973	Li & Fung buys a secondhand freighter, "Kwong Fung."
March 6, 1973	Li & Fung (Retailing) Ltd. is established.
March 27, 1973	Li & Fung issues its prospectus for IPO, which is oversubscribed by 113 times.
April 17, 1973	Public trading of Li & Fung Limited's shares in the Hong Kong stock market.
1974	Victor Fung returns to Hong Kong from Harvard University.
February 4, 1975	Death of Fung Mo-ying.
	Fung Hon-chu becomes Board Chairman of Li & Fung.
1975	Founding of Colby Group.
	William Fung becomes Director of Li & Fung (Trading) Ltd.
1976	The arrest of the "Gang of Four" brings to an end the Cultural Revolution and results in greater political stability in China.
1977	Victor Fung becomes Managing Director of Li & Fung (Trading) Ltd.
	Li & Fung enters into joint venture with a U.S. partner to set up Soabar Systems (Hong Kong) Ltd. to produce labels.
	Li & Fung partners with Leslie Fay in setting up Leslie Fay International Ltd.
1978	Li & Fung sets up a full subsidiary, Lifung Gap Stores Ltd.
	Li & Fung purchases the freighter, "Man Fung."
	The Third Plenary Session of the 11th Central Committee of the Communist Party of China confirms the policy of economic reforms.
1979	Li & Fung partners with Cheung Kong Holdings to redevelop Fung House.
	Li & Fung partners with Peek & Cloppenburg, a Dutch apparel chain, to set up Hillung Enterprises Ltd.
	Lydia Dunn, Executive Director of Swire Group, sets up Camberley Enterprises Ltd.
1981	Victor Fung joins the board of Li & Fung and succeeds Fung Hon-chu as Managing Director.
	Li & Fung partners with Combined English Stores of the U.K. to set up Lifung CES Ltd.
	William Fung becomes Managing Director of Li & Fung (Properties) Ltd.

Date	Event
1982	Li & Fung acquires Minko Consolidators Ltd.
	Li & Fung partners with Groups des Mutuelles Du Mans of France to set up Norman (Hong Kong) Insurance Co. Ltd.
September 1982	British prime minister Margaret Thatcher visits Beijing and raises the question of Hong Kong's future.
1983	Li & Fung Lecture on Commerce and Industry is established at Chinese University of Hong Kong.
December 9, 1984	Signing of the Sino-British Joint Declaration on the future of Hong Kong.
January 1985	Convenience Retail Asia Ltd. is set up as a joint venture between Li & Fung, Circle K Corporation, and UNY.
1986	William Fung succeeds Victor Fung as Managing Director of Li & Fung.
	Li & Fung partners with Toys "R" Us Inc. of the U.S. in opening Toys "R" Us stores in Hong Kong.
	Founding of Prudential Asia Investments Ltd. by Victor Fung.
October 1987	Global stock market comes under the impact of the U.S. market crash.
1988	Victor Fung becomes Founding Chairman of Hong Kong Venture Capital Association.
October 10, 1988	Li & Fung proposes a management buyout to turn itself into a wholly-owned subsidiary of King Lun Co. Ltd.
January 1989	Completion of the privatization of Li & Fung.
November 1989	Hutchison Whampoa Group sells Hutchison Trading to Inchcape.
October 25, 1991	Li & Fung (1937) Ltd., King Lun restructures its export business as Li & Fung Ltd through its full subsidiary.
1991	Victor Fung is appointed Chairman of Hong Kong Trade Development Council.
July 1, 1992	Li & Fung Ltd. is relisted on the Hong Kong Stock Exchange.
January 1993	Li & Fung partners with Heshan Economic Development Company to develop the Heshan Food Town project.
1993	William Fung is appointed Chairman of Pacific Economic Cooperation Council (PECC).
August 1994	Fung Hon-chu passed away in Hong Kong.
January 1995	Li & Fung sets up LF Distribution Centers Ltd. with partners.
July 1, 1995	Li & Fung acquires Inchcape Buying Services Group.
July 21, 1995	Li & Fung Group sets up Lifung (Panyu) Trading Town Co. Ltd. with a Chinese partner through LF Distribution Centers Ltd.
1995	Victor Fung is named Businessman of the Year in the DHL/*South China Morning Post* Business Awards.
	Victor Fung is named Businessman of the Year by *Forbes Asia*.
	Launching of Li & Fung's Intranet.
July 1996	Formation of strategic alliance between Li & Fung and the Agnelli Family of Italy.
1996	Integration of Dodwell into Li & Fung Trading.
	Victor and William Fung are both elected among the Top 25 Managers by *BusinessWeek*.
	Li & Fung sponsors Hong Kong's Chinese New Year fireworks display to celebrate its 90th anniversary.

Date	Event
July 1, 1997	Reunification of Hong Kong with China.
July 1997	Asian financial crisis.
1997	Li & Fung restructures Circle K business.
October 1998	Appointment of Richard Yeung as CEO of Circle K Convenience Stores (Hong Kong) Ltd.
November 1998	Li & Fung (1937) Ltd. partners with four major institutional investors in setting up Li & Fung Distribution Group.
1998	Completion of Phase One of the Lifung (Panyu) Trading Town project.
January 8, 1999	Li & Fung Distribution acquires Inchcape Marketing Services and Inchcape Marketing Asia Pacific from Inchcape Group.
May 1999	Victor Fung is appointed Chairman of Airport Authority Hong Kong.
July 1999	Victor and William Fung appear on the cover of *Far Eastern Economic Review*.
September 1999	Li & Fung and Toys "R" Us, Inc. signs an agreement for the establishment of a new joint venture for developing Toys "R" Us's business in Singapore and Malaysia.
December 29, 1999	Li & Fung comes to an agreement with Swire Group to acquire Swire & Maclaine and Camberley.
1999	William Fung is made Doctor of Business Administration honoris causa by the Hong Kong University of Science and Technology.
	Li & Fung is selected as Best-Managed Company in Hong Kong by *Asiamoney* magazine.
March 2000	Li & Fung announces its e-commerce strategy and sets up a new subsidiary, lifung.com.
October 2000	Founding of Convenience Retail Asia Ltd.
November 8, 2000	Li & Fung acquires Colby Group.
2000	William Fung is selected as one of the 50 "Stars of Asia" by *BusinessWeek*.
December 2000	IDS Logistics establishes a regional logistics and supply chain management center in Singapore.
January 18, 2001	Convenience Retail Asia Ltd. goes public on GEM, Hong Kong's second board.
February 2001	Li & Fung launches StudioDirect.com.
April 2001	CRA forms a joint-venture company, Convenience Retail Southern China Ltd., with two Chinese mainland companies.
September 2001	Victor Fung is appointed Council Chairman of Hong Kong University.
October 31, 2001	Li & Fung enters into a strategic alliance with Nichimen Group of Japan.
2002	Li & Fung Retailing sells Fotomax to China-Hong Kong Photo.
2003	Victor Fung is honored with the Gold Bauhinia Star by the HKSAR government.
	Li & Fung Research Center publishes *Supply Chain Management—The Practical Experience of the Li & Fung Group*.
May 2003	Li & Fung Distribution Group embarks on management restructuring to align core businesses under the IDS Logistics brand.
August 2003	Li & Fung acquires the remaining one-third of the share of U.S. apparel importer, International Sourcing Group, LLC.

Date	Event
November 5, 2003	The brand of IDS Logistics formally used internally by Li & Fung Distribution Group.
December 2003	Li & Fung acquires the sourcing business of Firstworld Garments Ltd. and International Porcelain, Inc.
2004	Li & Fung reaches licensing agreement with Levi Strauss & Co. to design, manufacture, and market men's tops for the U.S. market.
	Li & Fung is licensed by Official Pillowtex LLC to design and manufacture home textiles and home décor items under the Royal Velvet brand.
February 26, 2004	Victor Fung is appointed by the HKSAR government as Chairman of the Greater Pearl River Delta Business Council.
April 2004	IDS (Hong Kong) Ltd. becomes one of the first Hong Kong companies to be granted approval under CEPA to set up a wholly-owned subsidiary in China.
December 7, 2004	IDS Group Ltd. goes public in Hong Kong.

Appendix B

The Fung Family

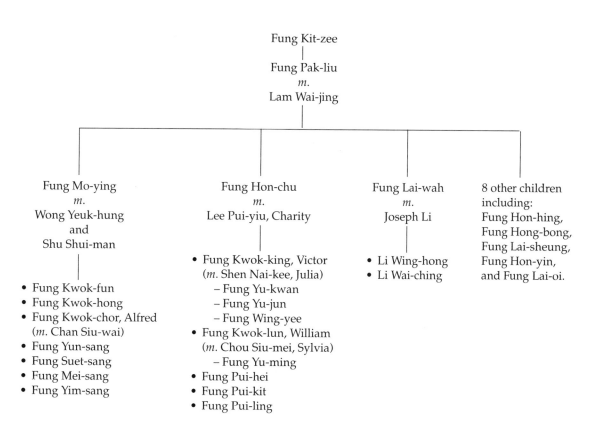

Fung Kit-zee

|

Fung Pak-liu

m.

Lam Wai-jing

Fung Mo-ying
m.
Wong Yeuk-hung
and
Shu Shui-man

- Fung Kwok-fun
- Fung Kwok-hong
- Fung Kwok-chor, Alfred
  (*m.* Chan Siu-wai)
- Fung Yun-sang
- Fung Suet-sang
- Fung Mei-sang
- Fung Yim-sang

Fung Hon-chu
m.
Lee Pui-yiu, Charity

- Fung Kwok-king, Victor
  (*m.* Shen Nai-kee, Julia)
  – Fung Yu-kwan
  – Fung Yu-jun
  – Fung Wing-yee
- Fung Kwok-lun, William
  (*m.* Chou Siu-mei, Sylvia)
  – Fung Yu-ming
- Fung Pui-hei
- Fung Pui-kit
- Fung Pui-ling

Fung Lai-wah
m.
Joseph Li

- Li Wing-hong
- Li Wai-ching

8 other children
including:
Fung Hon-hing,
Fung Hong-bong,
Fung Lai-sheung,
Fung Hon-yin,
and Fung Lai-oi.

Bibliography

Au-yeung, M.Y. (1978). "How the Inchcape Group Captures This Market," *Hong Kong Economic Journal Monthly*, Issue 8, Vol. 2, pp. 52–53.

Berger, Suzanne and Lester, Richard K. (ed.) (1997). *Made by Hong Kong*. New York: Oxford University Press.

Business and Professionals Federation of Hong Kong (1993). *Hong Kong 21—A Ten Year Vision and Agenda for Hong Kong's Economy*.

Chan, M.C. (1996). "Victor Fung—A Businessman Who Merges East and West," *Hong Kong Economic Times*, January 25.

Chan, P.M. (1993). Inchcape—"The Last Hong in Hong Kong," *Capital*, Hong Kong, July issue.

Chen, Z.H. (ed.) (2002). *Guangzhou Stories*. Guangzhou: Guangzhou Press.

Cheng, S.K. (2004). "The Secret to Hong Kong's Core Competitiveness," *Yazhou Zhoukan*, Hong Kong, February 8.

Chiu, Y.N. (1996). "A Thriving Old Tree," *Capital*, Hong Kong, February issue.

Chiu, Y.N. (1996). "Ninety Years, Three Generations," *Capital*, Hong Kong, February issue.

Citibank (1982). "Whether in Canton or Hong Kong, Li & Fung and Citibank Have Been Building Trade Together for 75 Years," *The Asian Wall Street Journal*, June 18, p. 7.

Cotton, Hillary Alexander (1979). "Fashion Marriages Spell Success for Li & Fung," *Hong Kong Trader*, Vol. 5.

Cottrell, Robert (1993). "The End of Hong Kong—The Secret Diplomacy of Imperial Retreat," *Ming Pao Press*, Hong Kong, October.

Economic Information & Agency (1986). *Hong Kong Economy Yearbook*, Hong Kong.

Engardino, Pete (1995). "Asia's New Giants: Many Will Be Global Players—But the Challenges Are Huge," *Business Week*, November 27.

Feng, B.Y. (1996). *British Conglomerates in Hong Kong 1841–1996*. Hong Kong: Joint Publishing (H.K.) Co. Ltd.

Feng, B.Y. (1997). *Chinese Conglomerates in Hong Kong 1841–1997*. Hong Kong: Joint Publishing (H.K.) Co. Ltd.

Feng, Bangyan (1999). *"Classic Cases of Business War in Hong Kong—Mergers and Acquisitions,"* Ming Pao Press, Hong Kong, December.

Fung, Victor (2001). "Corporate Governance," speech at Hong Kong Institute of Directors, June 29.

Fung, Victor K. (1990). "The Role of Hong Kong in Marketing, Distribution and Design," speech at the Guangdong-Hong Kong Economic Cooperation Seminar, July 27.

Fung, Victor K. (1993). "Hong Kong—The Regional Hub for Overseas Chinese." *The Second World Chinese Entrepreneurs Convention Supplement*. Hong Kong: Chinese General Chamber of Commerce.

Fung, Victor K. (1997). "The Importance of the Mainland-Hong Kong Economic Relationship," speech at the seminar on Hong Kong—Linking Up Beijing, Shanghai and Hong Kong and Contributing to Mutual Prosperity," Beijing, March 28.

Fung, Victor K. (2000). "Globalization and the New Trend of Hong Kong-Mainland Cooperation," speech at Chinese Central Party School, Beijing, October 24.

Guangzhou Society for the Research of Historical Cities (ed.) (2001). *A History of the Thirteen Hongs in Guangzhou*. Guangdong: Guangdong Maps Press.

Harvard Business School (2003). Case Studies "Li & Fung: Beyond 'Filling in the Mosaic'" in Li & Fung Research Center, *Supply Chain Management— The Practical Experience of the Li & Fung Group*. Hong Kong: Joint Publishing (H.K.) Ltd., p. 123.

Heung, S.F. (1997). "Victor Fung—A Global Perspective," *Next Magazine*, Hong Kong, September 26.

Ho, M.C. (1992). "The Rise of the Fung Hon-chu Family," *Capital*, Hong Kong, February 1992.

Ho, S.M. (1999). "The Development and Limitations of Corporate Governance," *Hong Kong Economic Journal*, January 22.

Hong Kong Census and Statistics Department. *Hong Kong Monthly Digest of Statistics (1995–1999)*.

Hong Kong Trade Development Council (1998). *Hong Kong's Manufacturing Industries: Current Status and Future Prospects*.

Hu, J. and Zhong, R.P. (2003). "Chinese Family Networks: Nature, Characteristics and Cultural Base," *Academic Research*, Issue 2, pp. 37–38.

Huang, G.C. (1992). Large Hongs in the Past Hundred Years. In *Research Material on Modern History*, Vol. 81. Beijing: Beijing Institute of Modern History, Academy of Social Sciences.

Huang, Q.S. (ed.) (2003). *A History of the Maritime Silk Road in Guangdong*. Guangdong: Guangdong Economy Press.

Hutcheon, Robin (1991). *A Burst of Crackers—The Li & Fung Story*. Hong Kong: Li & Fung Limited.

Jiang, J.Y. (1987). *A Concise History of Guangdong*. Guangdong: Guangdong People's Press.

Jones, Stephanie (1986). *Two Centuries of Overseas Trading: The Origins and Growth of the Inchcape Group*. London: Macmillan Press, Ltd.

Kam, C.K. (1995). *Supermarkets in Hong Kong—The New Retail Trend*. Hong Kong: Commercial Press (H.K.) Ltd.

Kei, S.K. (2004). "The Secret to Hong Kong's Core Competitiveness," *Yazhou Zhoukan*, Hong Kong, February 8.

Lau, S.W. (1998). *A Concise History of Hong Kong*. Hong Kong: Joint Publishing (H.K.) Ltd.

Leong, Elaine (2001). "Eye on CFO: Frank Leong, CFO, Li & Fung, The Best of East and West," *Finance Asia*, February issue.

Leong, Elaine (2001). "The Best of East and West," *Finance Asia*, February issue.

Leung, S.M. and Lee, W.T. (2003). "Billionaires Making Plans for Ten Years—Victor Fung's Goal is CE of HKSAR," *Next Magazine*, Hong Kong, September 18.

Li & Fung Limited (1973). *Li & Fung Limited IPO Prospectus*, March 27.

Li & Fung Limited (1981). *Li & Fung Limited, For 75 Years of Hong Kong's Success*, pp. 16–17.

Li & Fung Limited (1992). *Li & Fung Limited New Issue and Offer for Sale 1992*, pp. 24–25.

Li & Fung Limited (1994). *Li & Fung Limited Annual Report 1994*.

Li & Fung Limited (1999). "An Interview with W.K. Tang, Managing Director, Toys "R" Us, Hong Kong," *Li & Fung Retailing Forum*, Issue No. 7, May 1999, p. 3.

Li & Fung Limited (2001). "Li & Fung Allies with Nichimen for Market Expansion in Japan," October 21.

Li & Fung Limited (2002). *Li & Fung Retailing Group Newsletter*, January 2002.

Li & Fung Limited (2004). *IDS Group Limited Global IPO Prospectus*, November 24.

Li & Fung Limited Annual Reports, 1973–1988.

Li & Fung Limited Annual Reports, 1992–2003.

Li & Fung Limited Press Release (1999). "Li & Fung to acquire Swire & Maclaine and

Camberley," December 29.

Li & Fung Research Center (2003). *Supply Chain Management—The Practical Experience of the Li & Fung Group*. Hong Kong: Joint Publishing (H.K.) Ltd.

Li & Fung Retailing Group Newsletter (1999). "Li & Fung Retailing & Toys "R" Us Expand Joint-Venture Business," July 1999.

Liardet, Andrew (1994), *Dodwell & Company Limited*, March 1994, p. 1.

Lo, H. (1994). *Li & Fung Limited—Company Report*, Sun Hung Kai Research Limited, August 8.

Lynford, Adam. "Hong Kong Stocks Sky-High-Intense Activity on Hong Kong Stock Exchange." *Hong Kong Government Information Services*, Feature Article 6004/2, pp. 19–20.

Ma, S.H. et al. (2000). *Supply Chain Management*. Beijing: Beijing Mechanical Engineering Industry Press.

Magretta, Joan (1998). "Fast, Global, and Entrepreneurial: Supply Chain Management, Hong Kong Style: An Interview with Victor Fung," *Harvard Business Review*, September-October.

Mah, Angela and Lai, Teresa (2000). "Li & Fung Ltd. Two Giants under One Roof," *Morgan Stanley Dean Witter*, November 10.

Ng, S.L. (1937). *A Brief History of Business Celebrities*. Hong Kong: Continental Press.

O'Connell, Jamie (1996). "Li & Fung (Trading) Limited," *Harvard Business Case Studies*, 9-396-075, June 28.

People's Political Consultative Committee (ed.) (1992). *Foreign Firms and Concessions in Guangzhou*. Guangdong: Guangdong People's Publishing House.

Sachs, Goldman (1995). *Hong Kong Research: Li & Fung*, 494, pp. 3–4.

Schroders Asia and Prudential Asia (1988). "Recommendation Regarding Li & Fung Limited's Becoming a Wholly-owned Subsidiary of King Lun Company Limited," November 14.

Shen, J.M. (1988). "Shanghainese Tycoons Dominating Hong Kong's Textiles Industry," *Hong Kong Economic Journal Monthly*, October 1988.

Sin, Y.Y. (1994). *Advancing with Hong Kong—Bank of East Asia*, Bank of East Asia.

So, S.M. (1999). "Hong Kong Business Environment Fast Deteriorating," *Capital*, Hong Kong, February issue.

So, W.K. (ed.) (1933). *A Directory of Business Celebrities in Hong Kong, Shanghai and Guangzhou* (in Chinese). Hong Kong: 香港商務編述公司.

Tam, S.Y. (1997). "Steering China Toward the World Economy—An Interview with Victor Fung, Chairman of HKTDC," *Yazhou Zhoukan*, July 13.

Wang, Gung-wu (ed.) (1997). *Hong Kong History*, Volume 2. Hong Kong: Joint Publishing (H.K.) Co. Ltd.

Wong, H.L., Au, Y.F., and Pang, W.K. (2000). "The Impact of Family Boards and Chain Directors on Corporate Management," *Hong Kong Economic Journal Monthly*, August.

Yue, S.M. and Lau, C.F. (1994). *Hong Kong in the Nineteenth Century*. Hong Kong: 香港麒麟書業有限公司.

Yuen, K.B. (1988). 1988 A Brief History of Hong Kong. Hong Kong: 香港中流出版社.

Zhang, Z.L., Chen, Z.N., and Yao, X.R. (1991). *The Swire Group in Old China*. Shanghai: Shanghai People's Press.

鮑德溫, et al. (2001). *Supply Chain Management—Harvard Business Review*, translated by C.Y. Mo. Hong Kong: Commonwealth Publishing Group.

Index